Pseudo-Cyril of Alexandria

COMMENTARY ON THE APOCALYPSE

Introduction, Translation, and Transcription of a Lecture on Revelation 7–12 from Sixth-Century Egypt

FRANCIS X. GUMERLOCK
WITH FRANCESCA LECCHI & TITO ORLANDI

STONE TOWER PRESS

Pseudo-Cyril of Alexandria
Commentary on the Apocalypse

Stone Tower Press
7 Ellen Rd.
Middletown, RI 02842
stonetowerpress.com

Paperback ISBN: 978-1-7368651-6-3

Formatting and cover design by Amy Cole, JPL Design Solutions

The cover image: Greek Orthodox icon depicting St. Cyril of Alexandria, Thessaloniki, Macedonia, Greece. Alamy image ID: BM2799

Printed in the United States of America

Now come and let us spiritually refresh ourselves in the Apocalypse of the Son of God, even the Apocalypse of the evangelist John, which is precious, gracious, very dear, and wonderful."[1]

Anonymous Syriac commentator

1 Stan Larson, "The Earliest Syriac Commentary on the Apocalypse: Transcription, Translation, and Importance of Brit. Lib. MS. Add. 17,127," Thesis (Birmingham, UK: University of Birmingham, 1984), 141.

Dedications

Francis X. Gumerlock dedicates this book to
Agnes McGarrigle, a friend for forty years

Francesca Lecchi dedicates this book to
Piero Bajetta, my beloved grandfather

Contents

Acknowledgements

Special thanks to Francesca Lecchi of Milan, Italy who provided a first draft of the English translation of the commentary from the Italian translation of Professor Tito Orlandi. Thanks also to Braeden Fallet and Dr. Seth Fabian for their editorial assistance on the translation. Many thanks to Professor Orlandi for comparing our English translation with the Sahidic Coptic text, making very helpful corrections and suggestions, and providing a transcription of the Coptic text. Thanks to Shaneann Fross of the University of Notre Dame for her assistance with sources. Finally, thank you to Dr. T. C. Schmidt of Fairfield University for his proofreading of an early version of this book and for his very helpful suggestions.

PART

Introduction to the Commentary

by Francis X. Gumerlock

This book provides the first published English translation of a lecture on Revelation 7-12 given in an Egyptian monastery by an unknown teacher in the late sixth century. Written in the Sahidic Coptic dialect, the lecture circulated in the name of Cyril of Alexandria (d. 444).

Manuscript and Italian Translation

In the *incipit* the lecture is referred to as an "encomium," or a warm, glowing, and enthusiastic expression of praise. Therefore, throughout the book I shall refer to the text as the *Encomium on Revelation 7-12* or simply the *Encomium*. It is found in a ninth-century Sahidic Coptic manuscript: Pierpont Morgan MS. Copt. 591. According to Christian Askeland, the manuscript has certain markings to suggest that it derived from the scriptorium in the ancient Egyptian city of Touton.[1] It was donated in the year 861 to the monastery of St. Michael the Archangel at Sopehes, which is

1 Christian Askeland, "The Sahidic Apocalypse in early Islamic Egypt," in Marcus Sigismund, Martin Karrer, and Ulrich Schmid, eds., *Studien zum Text der Apokalypse* (Berlin: De Gruyter, 2015), 271-287 at 273, n. 10 & 274, n. 13.

today the Egyptian village of Hamuli in southwestern Fayum.[2] The monastery ceased operations in the early tenth century.

The manuscript was discovered in 1910 and purchased by J. P. Morgan in 1911. Presently it is housed in the Morgan Library and Museum in New York City. It contains seven works by various authors, including a martyrdom account and homilies. Descriptions of the contents of the manuscript are in the writings of Leslie S. B. MacCoull and Leo Depuydt.[3] The *Encomium on Revelation 7-12,* attributed in the manuscript to Cyril of Alexandria, is on folios 12v-34r. Fragments from the *Encomium* are found in manuscripts BnF Copt 131 [3], ff. 58-61 and 131 [7] f. 63, once possessed by the White Monastery. These fragments are presently being edited by Victor Ghica.[4]

In 1981 Tito Orlandi published an Italian translation of the *Encomium,* where it is divided into 52 numbered paragraphs. These paragraph numbers have been retained in brackets in the English translation below.[5] I have added the subtitles.

Setting and Audience

The *Encomium* was most likely delivered in a monastic setting in late-sixth century Egypt.[6] It may have been a homily given during a monastic liturgical service in which the Eucharist followed, since in Paragraph [hereafter Para] 11 the lecturer said: "And we shall receive his body and his blood." But in context, this reception of the body and blood may not

2 Also spelled Faiyum, Fayoum, and Al Fayyum. Folio 32 of the manuscript dates the donation to "Mecheir 20, Diocletian year 577." According to Leslie S. B. MacCoull ("Pierpont Morgan MS.Copt. 591: The Apocalypse Commentary of Pseudo-Cyril of Alexandria," *Studia Patristica* 20 [1989]:33-39 at 33), that equals "14 February A.D. 861."

3 MacCoull, "Pierpont Morgan," 33; Leo Depuydt, *Catalogue of Coptic Manuscripts in the Pierpont Morgan Library,* Vol 1 (Louvain: Peeters, 1993), 301-303.

4 Askeland, "Sahidic Apocalypse," 274, n. 13.

5 Tito Orlandi, ed., *Omelie copte.* Corona Patrum 7 (Turin: Società Editrice Internazionale, 1981), 121-144.

6 Para 1: "In fact the words of God are nourishment of which we cannot be satisfied, especially those whose dwelling is with God, those who have worn the monastic cloth, who made their body a sanctuary of his everlasting glorious name."

be referring to the Eucharist after a homily, but to dining with God in heaven (cf. Matt 26:29). Several times the homilist or lecturer refers to something in the biblical text of Revelation that is not in the lemma, which could be explained if there were a lectionary reading prior to the homily.[7] However, at the end of the "homily," the monks are dismissed to their residence with a benediction (Para 50 & 51), suggesting it was not part of a liturgy, because one would expect Eucharist, not dismissal, after a homily. Paragraphs 50 & 51 strongly suggest that, rather than a homily in a liturgy, the *Encomium* was part of a lecture series on the Apocalypse, most likely by a visiting monk, teacher, or bishop.[8] Also, the text is probably not a copy of the teacher's lecture notes, but more likely a transcription of the lecture by one of the hearers.[9] The one lecturing appears to use a translation of the Book of Revelation into Sahidic Coptic.[10]

Object of the *Encomium*

The praise of the encomium is directed at John, who is described as the apostle, a virgin, a theologian, and the recipient of the mysteries of the Book of Revelation.[11] An example of this praise is shown in the rhetori-

7 For example, in Para 9 the lecturer infers several times that the angels are sealing, but the angels in Rev 7:1-3 are not part of the lemma. In Para10 he mentions the elders of Rev 7:11b, which is not in the lemma. On manuscript evidence that lectionary readings from Rev 3:19-4:6; 7:13-8:3, and 14:6-12 were taking place in Egypt in liturgies in the seventh to ninth century, see Askeland, "Sahidic Apocalypse," 277.

8 MacCoull, "Pierpont Morgan," 37. Para 50 & 51 mention that when the monks get together next, they will learn about the visions of Rev 13-15. Also, in Para 50: "I came among you as a friend or a brother."

9 The lecturer's notes would probably not contain the statement in the conclusion (Para 50): "But I see that the greater part of you criticizes my insufficiency, saying, 'Now the time has come for us [to be dismissed]. Therefore, give us peace so that we might go where we have to go.'" Those sentences seem extemporaneous.

10 Thomas Coffman [T. C.] Schmidt, "The Last Book: Revelation, Commentaries, and the Making of the New Testament," Dissertation (Yale University, 2020), 297-299. For evidence that books of the Bible were translated from Greek into Coptic in the third and fourth centuries, see E. A. Wallis Budge, ed., *Coptic Biblical Texts in the Dialect of Upper Egypt*, Vol 2 (London: Oxford University Press, 1912), lvii, lxxviii-lxxxv.

11 For a discussion of the rhetorical genre of encomia and certain patterns they followed in classical and late antique rhetoric, especially late sixth-century Coptic literature, see Mark Sheridan, "The Encomium in the Coptic Literature of the Late Sixth Century," in Paola Buzi and Alberto Complani, eds., *Christianity in Egypt: Literary Production and Intellectual Trends: Studies in Honor of Tito Orlandi* (Rome: Institutum Patristicum Augustinianum, 2011), 443-464.

cal question, "Which mysteries did you not contemplate, O contemplator of the sacred mysteries?" (Para 4) Throughout the lecture John is referred to by various praiseworthy titles including "great John" (Para 2, 25, 27, & 36), "our father John" (Para 38 & 48), the "theologian" (Para 9 & 37), a "contemplator" (Para 4 & 9), a "mystic" (Para 31), and one "wise in the things of God" (Para 39) who even had the privilege of witnessing the silence before creation and the voice of God which brought about the creation (Para 14). Jesus loved John, the lecturer says, because of his virginal purity (Para 31); and from him hearers can receive light concerning the meaning of the Apocalypse (Para 2). Unlike the reservations that some in the East in late antiquity had concerning the authorship and canonicity of the Book of Revelation, there was no doubt on the part of the lecturer that the apostle John was its author, and that it was a canonical book. According to Askeland, "by the sixth century, the Egyptian church was treating the text of the Apocalypse as an integral part of its biblical canon."[12]

Exegetical Method and Contents of the Commentary

For the lecturer, the biblical Book of Revelation has several levels of meaning, including the literal, typological, and allegorical. Tropology, that is, viewing the biblical passage as a moral lesson for the present audience, is used often as well. This is in keeping with the purpose of the lecture, stated in Para 1, which was to enlighten the hearts of the listeners, rather than to test their thoughts.

On the literal level, the lecturer often sees in the visions of Revelation references to the Hebrew people and their customs, after which he sometimes explains their deeper meanings related to the new covenant. The 144,000 sealed from the twelve tribes in Rev 7 are literally the twelve tribes of Israel, which prefigure the twelve apostles and the church (Para 9 & 28). On Rev 11:1-2 where an angel is to measure the temple, the

12 Askeland, "Sahidic Apocalypse," 272.

lecturer speaks of Levites and sacrifices in the temple of the Lord (Para 32). In Para 28 he mentions the tribes and patriarchs, and in Para 48 the synagogue. Several times he provides a contrast between Judaism and the church (Para 9 & 48). However, the author does not view the Book of Revelation as a prophecy (or history) of the Roman-Judaean conflict of the first century, and he makes no mention of the destruction of Jerusalem and its temple by the Romans in AD 70.

Examples of the lecturer's use of typology, allegory, and tropology will be provided in the following review of its contents.

The *Encomium* starts with a prologue (Para 1-3) and an explanation of Rev 4:2-8 (Para 4-8). The main part of the encomium is an exegetical lecture on Rev 7-12 (Para 9-49), followed by an epilogue (Para 50-52). The prologue introduces the lecture, praises John, and gives a synopsis of what the Holy Spirit showed John in the Revelation. On Rev 4:2-8, the lecturer sees the twenty-four thrones and elders as an allegory for humans, showing their capability for contemplating sacred mysteries and receiving knowledge of heavenly things, John being the prime example.

Revelation Chapter Seven. On the 144,000 sealed in Rev 7:4-8, according to the lecturer, John saw twelve thousand from each of the twelve tribes, literally the twelve tribes of the Jewish people of pre-Christian times. The lecturer says "at the time of the one hundred and forty-four thousand no one had been baptized before, nor had any martyrs shed their blood, nor were there famous virgins, nor had any ascetics practiced any sort of asceticism, nor had any monks dedicated themselves to the monastic life..." (Para 9). However, these 144,000 were a type of what was to come for the Christian people, when *many will come from the east and from the west, and will sit down with Abraham, Isaac, and Jacob in the kingdom* (Matt 8:11), meaning when the entire people of God, Christians and Jews, are united in one body. Viewing the twelve tribes as a type of the "true" or "spiritual" Israel, that is, the church, was typical of patristic exegesis in the East. According to Origen, the camps of the twelve tribes in the book of Numbers "were shadows of the camps related to the mysteries of the true Israel."[13] Origen also interpreted the 144,000 from the twelve tribes in the Book of Revelation as "those who have come to the divine word out of the Gentile world."[14] According to Severus of Antioch, "spiritual Israel" is numbered and established by "the order of the twelve tribes."[15] Later, in Para 28, the lecturer says that the twelve tribes of Israel prefigured the twelve apostles. Therefore, for the lecturer, the 144,000 are the literal tribes of the Jewish people in pre-Christian times, and a type of both the twelve apostles and the entire church.

Some early interpreters of the Book of Revelation saw the 144,000 as Jewish people who would believe in Christ during the future reign of the Antichrist (Victorinus),[16] while others saw them as a symbol of the church (Tyconius, Primasius)[17] or of martyrs or virgins in the church (Cyprian; *Handbook on the Apocalypse of the Apostle John*).[18] But a number of early Christian writers interpreted them as Jews of the first century, whether the first-fruits of those who believed in Christ (Hippolytus),[19] the infants murdered by Herod (*Revelation of Stephen*; Fortunatus of Aquileia),[20] or those who escaped from Jerusalem during its siege by the Romans (Oecumenius).[21] As stated above, the lecturer of the *Encomium*

13 Origen, *On Matthew*, 51. Ronald E. Heine, trans., *The Commentary of Origen on the Gospel of St. Matthew*, Vol. 2 (New York: Oxford University Press, 2018), 630.

14 Origen, *Commentary on the Gospel of John*, I.2. ANF 10:298.

15 Severus of Antioch, *Synodical Letter to Theodosius*. Cited in Pauline Allen and C.T.R. Hayward, *Severus of Antioch* (New York: Routledge, 2004), 166.

16 Victorinus, *Commentary on the Apocalypse*. On Rev 7. William C. Weinrich, trans., *Latin Commentaries on Revelation* (Downers Grove, IL: InterVarsity, 2011), 12.

17 Tyconius, *Exposition of the Apocalypse*. On Rev 7:4-8. FC 124:85; Primasius, *Commentary on the Apocalypse*. On Rev 7:4. CCSL 92:108.

18 Cyprian of Carthage, *To Fortunatus* (ANF 5:505) and *To Quirinus* (ANF 5:538); Anonymous, *Handbook on the Apocalypse of the Apostle John*. On Rev 7:4 in Francis X. Gumerlock, *Early Latin Commentaries on the Apocalypse* (Kalamazoo, MI: Medieval Institute Publications, 2016), 27.

19 Pierre Prigent and R. Stehly, "Les fragments du De Apocalypsi d'Hippolyte," *Theologische Zeitschrift* 29 (1973):313-333 at 320.

20 In Montague Rhodes James, *The Apocryphal New Testament* (Oxford: Clarendon, 1926), 565; Fortunatus of Aquileia, *Commentary on the Gospels*. CSEL, Extra Seriem:20.

21 Oecumenius, *Commentary on the Apocalypse*. On Rev 7:4. In William C. Weinrich, trans., *Greek Commentaries on Revelation* (Downers Grover, IL: InterVarsity, 2011), 105; FC 112:76-78.

first interprets the 144,000 according to the letter as the Jewish tribes in pre-Christian times, although he sees them as also typifying realities of the new covenant. In a later Egyptian Arabic commentary on the Apocalypse, written by Paul of Bush (Bulus al-Busi), that interpretation of the 144,000 as literally pre-Christian Jewish people continued. The thirteenth-century expositor wrote:

> But what we have found in the commentary is that John the Evangelist saw in the spirit all those who died in the Old Testament, the patriarchs and the prophets and the children who were slain by Pharaoh, king of Egypt. It was written in the Torah that because of his disbelief Pharaoh used to throw their sons into the river, so that they would not live. But the children of Israel knew the Lord. There were also those who were put to death by Manasseh, Antiochus, and the rest of the unbelieving kings, and there was also Herod of Bethlehem. Those who were killed were pure, holy, and virtuous. So the total is this number. It is divided by the number of tribes—twelve thousand from each tribe.[22]

The lecturer interprets the *great multitude* in the vision of Rev 7:9-17 as the saints who left this life and are now in heaven with Jesus, that is, the souls of the righteous from every lineage and tribe and language (Para 10). The *great tribulation* out of which the souls came, is not the end-time struggle of the saints with the Antichrist or the universal destruction of the world in the last days, as Oecumenius taught.[23] Rather, it is simply this life, full of preoccupations and upheavals. This interpretation is similar to that of Primasius of Hadrumetum who saw the great tribulation

22 Shawqi Najib Talia, "Bulus al-Busi's Arabic Commentary on the Apocalypse of St. John. An English Translation and a Commentary," Dissertation (Washington, D.C.: The Catholic University of America, 1987), 153-154. In the thirteenth-century West, Alexander of Bremen noted that the 144,000 were exactly half of the 288,000 men mentioned in 1 Chron 27:1-15. Alois Wachtel, ed., *Alexander Minorita. Expositio in Apocalypsim* (Weimar: Böhlau, 1955), 293.

23 Oecumenius, *Commentary on the Apocalypse*. On Rev 7:1-8. In Weinrich, *Greek Commentaries*, 33-34; FC 112:80.

here as simply the "pressures of the faithful," and to that of Andrew of Caesarea who saw it as the "temporary sufferings" of this life.[24]

Revelation Chapters Eight and Nine. In the East, Oecumenius interpreted the *silence in heaven* (Rev 8:1) as that of the astonished angels and supernatural powers at the glory of the Second Coming of Christ.[25] For Andrew of Caesarea, the silence "reveals the good order and piety of the angels as well as the fact that the Second Coming of Christ is unknown, even to angels."[26] Western commentators viewed the silence as either a period of rest in the future time of Enoch and Elijah (*On the Mysteries*),[27] or as the time of the Antichrist (*Handbook on the Apocalypse*),[28] or as a period of short earthly rest for the church after the time of the Antichrist (Bede),[29] or as a silence from the worship of idols (*On the Mysteries*),[30] or as the beginning of eternal rest (Tyconius, Caesarius).[31] For the lecturer of the *Encomium*, the silence is the silence of God before the creation of the world.

The trumpet blasts from the first six of the seven angels (Rev 8-9) are not portrayed as successive judgments occurring upon the earth and its people before the Second Coming, but as symbols of the variety of judgments for different sins at the Last Judgment, when each one is repaid according to his deeds (Para 17). The Last Judgment, which will bring wrath on those who sin, can come at any time (Para 24). The lecturer uses the judgments that come from these trumpet blasts to exhort his hearers to repent from present sins. He asks rhetorically, "What did [the angels] sound [on their trumpets]? They sounded, 'Do good and God will take

24 Primasius of Hadrumetum, *Commentary on the Apocalypse*. On Rev 7:14. CCSL 92:130; Andrew of Caesarea, *Commentary on the Apocalypse*. On Rev 7:14-15. In Weinrich, *Greek Commentaries*, 141.

25 Oecumenius, *Commentary on the Apocalypse*. On Rev 8:1-2. In Weinrich, *Greek Commentaries*, 37.

26 Andrew of Caesarea, *Commentary on the Apocalypse*. On Rev 8:1. In Weinrich, *Greek Commentaries*, 142.

27 *On the Mysteries of the Apocalypse of John*. On Rev 8:1. In Gumerlock, *Early Latin Commentaries*, 58.

28 *Handbook on the Apocalypse of the Apostle John*. On Rev 8:1. In Gumerlock, *Early Latin Commentaries*, 28.

29 Bede, *Exposition of the Apocalypse*. On Rev 8:1. In Weinrich, *Latin Commentaries*, 137.

30 *On the Mysteries of the Apocalypse of John*. On Rev 8:1. In Gumerlock, *Early Latin Commentaries*, 58.

31 Tyconius, *Exposition of the Apocalypse*. On Rev 8:1. FC 134:89; Caesarius of Arles, *Exposition of the Apocalypse*, Homily 6. In Weinrich, *Latin Commentaries*, 75.

away these evils from you.'" (Para 17). The lecturer continues, "For, it is the joy of God when a man contemplates the things that will come upon him and repents and acts righteously before God" (Para 19).

The first angel sent judgment to the earth because of human lust. The second angel sent judgment because of those who deceive in business and practice false swearing (Para 18). The *pit of the abyss* (Rev 9:1) is eternal damnation, "the place where there will be no visit for eternity" (Para 21). By calling hell an "eternal abyss" (Para 34), the lecturer does not seem to hold to an Origenist view, in which the punishment of the wicked in the afterlife is purgative and temporary until the restoration of all things, but rather the lecturer believes in everlasting punishment.[32] In Para 21, the lecturer refers to the abyss as "the place which all the sinners like me will inherit." Rather than a genuine feeling of condemnation on the part of the lecturer, it is more likely an expression of humility fairly common in Eastern patristic literature.[33]

In Para 22, the locusts of Rev 9:3 are homosexual men or transgendered persons, about whom the apostle Paul spoke of in Romans 1. The lecturer pronounces woes on them. In Para 23, the lecturer gives two interpretations, or two levels of meaning, for those who are sealed. First, the sealed are those who experienced martyrdom, "those who received the seal of the blood of martyrdom." But actualizing the passage for his audience, and again using tropology or the passage's moral sense, the lecturer preaches that the sealed are those who walk purely in accordance with their baptism, who live without envy, hatred, lust, murder, or calumny, and who love life and not death. For "he who wishes to sin must know that he is far from the sign of the seal that is in Jesus Christ our Lord." The lecturer also uses the sealing to affirm pro-Nicene, anti-Arian Christology writing, "Blessed, he said, are those who read and understand that the Lamb himself is the consubstantial One of the Father. He is the

32 Severus of Antioch, the earlier champion of non-Chalcedonians who spent years in Egypt in exile, also did not hold to *apokatastasis*. See his *Letter 98* translated in Allen and Hayward, *Severus of Antioch*, 143-146.

33 For example, Severus, *Homily 14*: "But we ourselves—we who are obliged to demonstrate a way of life which is worthy of heaven—do we not even do those things which are fitting for earth, but are suitable for Sheol and the pit of destruction?" Translated in Allen and Hayward, *Severus of Antioch*, 117.

consubstantial One, whom the virgin bore, who marks each on his forehead with the sign of the seal" (Par 23).

Continuing to interpret Rev 9 morally in Para 25 & 26, the lecturer sees in the number of *two times ten thousand* (Rev 9:16) the amount of human sins which the angels will bring to God. The horses point to those whose transgressions spring "in all directions like horses ready for war," while the color of the breastplates of the riders of the horses reveal the different kinds of sins. The fire, smoke, and sulfur coming out of the horses' mouths indicate sins which come out of people's mouths, for which they will give account to God. Although Satan has dragged humans into his net, God is merciful. He loves humankind, wants to free people from the prison of sin, and desires that they repent. While "wrath is ready," one can avoid punishment by not allowing one's sins to become too grievous (Para 25 & 27).

Revelation Chapters Ten and Eleven. The vision of the angel *coming down from heaven* and clothed with a cloud in Rev 10:1-3 represents Jesus "coming down" at his Second Coming. His face shining *as the sun* shows the light of his divinity when he descends from heaven. The *open book in his hand* is his testament (Para 28). Interestingly, the sounding of the seventh angel in Rev 10:7, when the mystery of God is completed, is not interpreted eschatologically. Rather, the mystery is related to the Incarnation, the sacrament of baptism, and the "appearance of the body and blood of Christ" (Para 30). The lecturer interprets the book in Rev 10:8 as the holy Scriptures, which he calls a book of redemption (Para 31).

The Gentiles in Rev 11:2 represent people from every nation who fulfil the will of the Lord and practice righteousness. The outer court of the temple signifies the heavenly mansions they will receive (Para 32). The two witnesses of Rev 11 are literally Enoch and Elijah, which was a common interpretation in both the East and the West.[34] From the two prophetic witnesses, the hearers are encouraged to listen to teachers whose knowledge comes from the Holy Spirit and to seek to please God

34 For the many patristic references, see Thomas W. MacKay, "Early Christian Millenarianist Interpretation of the Two Witnesses in John's Apocalypse 11:3-13," in John M. Lundquist and Stephen D. Ricks, eds., *By Study and Also By Faith*, 2 vols (Salt Lake City: Deseret, 1990), 223-331.

through repentance, which the witnesses' sackcloth signifies (Para 33). The lecturer uses the resurrection of the two witnesses in Rev 11:11 to affirm the doctrine of the resurrection and to cast shame on those who have doubts about it, supplementing his teaching with statements in the Creed about the resurrection of Jesus, his ascension, and Second Coming (Para 36). The section on authorship and date below will discuss whom the lecturer most likely had in mind when speaking about those doubting the resurrection.

On Rev 11:15, which says that the *kingdom of the world has become the kingdom of our Lord,* the lecturer poses a rhetorical question: Did the kingdom of God become God's only on that day? He answers it in the negative, explaining that God has been king before heaven and earth existed (Para 39). Those who call upon the name of the Lord are granted this kingdom, not because of their great virtues, but because of his mercy and love (Para 40).

Revelation Chapter Twelve. The woman in Rev 12:1, *clothed with the sun, having the moon under her feet, and twelve stars as a crown,* who later flies to the desert (cf. Rev 12:5, 14) is the holy Virgin Mary, the *Theotokos* (Paras 41, 43, & 47). Paragraph 41 provides a litany of names for her besides the virgin and *Theotokos,* among which are "city," "appointed time," "security," "stage," "place of rest," and "pure treasure." This interpretation of the woman clothed with sun as Mary differs from Methodius of Olympus's interpretation, adopted by Andrew of Caesarea, that the woman is a symbol of the church.[35] The twelve stars in the crown of the woman represent the twelve apostles (Para 41), an interpretation found in Hippolytus in the early third century and Oecumenius in the early sixth century.[36] When discussing the wilderness into which the woman fled, the lecturer hints that it may be paradise or heaven to where Mary was

35 Methodius of Olympus, *Symposium* 8.5-8 (ACW 27:110-13); Andrew of Caesarea, *Commentary on the Apocalypse,* On Rev 12:1. Weinrich, *Greek Commentaries on Revelation,* 154-155; FC 123:137.

36 Hippolytus, *Treatise on Christ and the Antichrist,* 61. ANF 5:217; Oecumenius, *Commentary on the Apocalypse.* On Rev 12:1-2. Weinrich, *Greek Commentaries on Revelation,* 52; FC 112:108. This interpretation was repeated in the thirteenth-century Arabic commentary of Egyptian provenance by Ibn Katib Qaysar, who attributed the interpretation to Hippolytus. Ibn Katib Qaysar is cited in Talia, "Bulus al-Busi's Arabic Commentary on the Apocalypse of St. John," 189.

assumed after her death, but claims ignorance, teaching that "the place where the virgin went, no man made of flesh knows it up to now" (Para 43). Similarly, Epiphanius in the late fourth century expressed reservation about whether or not this passage teaches Mary's assumption to heaven.[37] Later, in Para 47, the lecturer interpreted the wilderness to which Mary went as "the place where they crucified the Son of God" (Para 47). Also, in Para 48, when the lecturer speaks of the woman being nourished in the wilderness, he portrays the woman as "the holy church" nourished on the sacrifices and offerings of her bishops. This portrayal of the woman as both Mary and the church, and the wilderness as both Golgotha and possibly heaven, illustrates the lecturer's multi-layered interpretive approach to the Book of Revelation.

On the war between Michael and the dragon in Rev 12:7, the lecturer portrays Michael as he is commonly portrayed in early Christian literature. He is an archangel who is a "defender" of humankind and who "always fights for the whole of mankind" (Para 45). The concept of Michael as archangel is present in *1 Enoch* (20.5). His role as protector is described in Dan 10:21 and 12:1 and the *Shepherd of Hermas* (Sim. 8.3.3).[38] According to Christian Askeland, in the Coptic tradition Michael "enjoyed a role perhaps equal to the Virgin Mary."[39]

In Para 46, where the devil is described as *the accuser of the brethren* (Rev 12:10), the lecturer believes that the devil not only accuses humans but also accuses the incorporeal angels. The lecturer then addresses a question related to theodicy about why God allows the evil one to tempt people. He answers that God allows it in order to make the righteous and sinners manifest, and so that rewards and punishments rendered on Judgment Day would be fair. Paragraph 48 offers a glimpse into the liturgical practices of the lecturer and/or of the monastic community

37 Epiphanius of Salamis, *Panarion*, 78.23.9.

38 Darrell D. Hannah, *Michael and Christ: Michael Traditions and Angel Christology in Early Christianity* (Tübingen: Mohr Siebeck, 1999), 34, 98, 165.

39 Christian Askeland, "The Sahidic Apocalypse in Early Islamic Egypt," In Marcus Sigismund, Martin Karrer, and Ulrich Schmid, eds., *Studien zum Text der Apokalypse* (Berlin: De Gruyter, 2015), 271-87 at 281, who mentions the large number of Coptic homilies on Michael. See E. A. W. Budge, *Saint Michael the Archangel: Three Encomiums* (London: British Museum, 1894).

from which the *Encomium* arose, which include the Eucharistic sacrifice and offering, prayer, incense, and hymns.[40] Incense, prayers, and sacrifices offered by priests and the people of God are also mentioned in Para 15 & 16.

Interpretation of Numbers and the Conclusion of the Commentary. One outstanding feature of the lecturer's exegesis is his strange interpretation of numbers, which are difficult to follow. For example, on Rev 7:4 he writes, "...they were going to seal those one hundred and forty-four thousand, each group receiving four thousand in addition to the twelve, and the four thousand dividing into six tribes. Each group is divided under three ancient fathers" (Para 9). On Rev 10:1-3 he mentions seven churches, seven cities, five churches, twelve tribes, and people groups of one thousand, four thousand, five thousand, nine thousand, ten thousand, and twenty thousand (Para 28). In footnotes in the translation, I have tried to make sense of some of these numbers and have listed any Scripture references to which the lecturer may be referring.

On the "forty-two months" of Rev 11:2, the "1260 days" of Rev 12:6, and the "time, times and half a time" of Rev 12:14, the lecturer again puts forward elaborate numerological explanations. For example, "...their number [are] in addition to the seven and a half weeks, which are subtracted from their number, according to the *twelve hundred and sixty days*, plus sixty. These doubled twice, come to six hundred and thirty, which add to their number more than two years and three weeks. And we also add an extra week for Holy Easter" (Para 33); and "...they will defeat the enemy in twenty-eight weeks, and one hundred and three days will pass before he will see the light. And five more weeks will show what they did" (Para 34); and "...the 1260 days will fulfill the number of the fourteen weeks and other three, which remain in the five. These will fulfill the two and three and a half days, coming to the number in the fulfillment of 'times,' which are included in the words spoken by the seven thunders" (Para 48). These statements understandably baffled the Italian translator,

40 On Coptic liturgy in late antiquity and the Middle Ages, see Stephen J. Davis, *Coptic Christology in Practice: Incarnation and Divine Participation in Late Antique and Medieval Egypt* (Oxford, UK: Oxford University Press, 2008), 59-107.

Orlandi, who wrote in a footnote on Para 33 that he did not understand the meaning of the computations.[41] In the section on the authorship and date of the *Encomium*, an attempt will be made to understand some of the numbers in these texts, although not the numbers in Para 33.

Paragraphs 50-52 contain the conclusion of the lecture. In this section, the teacher apologizes for being lengthy, and reveals that he is a visiting friend and brother. He looks forward to the next time they can meet, when they can learn about the contents of Rev 13-15, including the two beasts. He ends the lecture with a Trinitarian benediction.

Theology of the Commentary

God, Christ, and the Holy Spirit. The author believes in God as creator of all things,[42] that he is Triune, and affirms the consubstantiality of the Son and of the Holy Spirit with the Father.[43] The three members of the Trinity reign together (Para 39). The Son is called Jesus, Christ, Jesus Christ, our Lord, the Lord Jesus Christ, our God, Lamb, Son of God, Sun of righteousness, King of kings, Savior, and Only-begotten.[44] Interestingly, although the text comes from a Miaphysite community, I found only one reference to one-nature Christology, where the lecturer in Para 32 says that "only one person" is worshipped. I understand this to be a rejection of the two-nature Christology of Chalcedonians, which Miaphysites saw as logically leading to the worship of two persons. Hence, against that notion, the lecturer claims that "only one person" is worshipped. Surprisingly, there are no *explicit* condemnations of two-nature Christology and Chalcedon, and the Miaphysite Christological formula "one incarnate nature of the Word"[45] is absent. The *Trisagion*

41 Orlandi, *Omelie copte*, 137: *Non comprendiamo il senso di questi computi cabalistici; cf. forse Dan 9,24 ss. Computi simili appaiono nelle lettere di Pacomio.*

42 Para 10, 14, 20, 28, & 45.

43 Para 7, 23, & 52.

44 Para 10, 12-13, 15, 28, 30-31, 41-42, & 47.

45 Aaron Riches, *Ecce Homo: On the Divine Unity of Christ* (Grand Rapids, MI: Eerdmans, 2016), 38.

"Holy, Holy, Holy" hymn, according to the lecturer, is not a hymn directed at Jesus Christ, as some Miaphysites would have it,[46] but is a praise to the holy Trinity (Para 7). There is also no discussion of the energy/energies and will/wills in Christ, which dominated seventh and eighth-century Christological discourse. There may be veiled references to the Council of Chalcedon in 451 in the numerology, as will be shown in the section on authorship and date.

The Holy Spirit is the teacher and Paraclete (Para 13 & 47). Jesus was conceived in Mary by the Holy Spirit's work (Para 10). The Spirit also showed John the visions of the Book of Revelation and guided him in writing them down (Para 2 & 3). He has informed the prophets of old, and still informs prophets and works miracles at the right time (Para 33 & 35).

Mary and the Angels. The lecturer's praise of the Virgin Mary was discussed in the section on the contents of the *Encomium*; but it should be added that the lecturer saw himself and his audience of monks as her children, whom she knows and purifies (Para 41). Besides the lecturer's Mariology, a developed angelology is revealed in the *Encomium*. The angels attend to hymns. They sing and glorify God on behalf of humans, so that God might forgive their sins and crimes (Para 8). Angels are united to humans, and the cherubim and seraphim bless God on behalf of his people (Para 8). They also take the prayers of the people to the altar of the Lamb through the offering of incense by priests (Para 15 & 16). As for their relationship with evildoers, they count their sins and bring this number to God (Para 25). As mentioned above, Michael is portrayed as an archangel who defends and protects humankind.

Scripture and Sacraments. The Scriptures are inspired by God, and the Bible is called a book of redemption and a book of value (Para 31). The sacrament of baptism gives resurrection life, purifies, and through it the Lord's people are marked on the forehead with the sign of the seal (Para 23 & 30). The Eucharist is the "body and blood of Christ" (Para 23).

46 Allen and Hayward, *Severus of Antioch*, 9; V. C. Samuel, *The Council of Chalcedon Re-Examined* (Kent, UK: British Orthodox Press, 2001), 145-146, 154-155, 449; W. H. C. Frend, *The Rise of the Monophysite Movement: Chapters in the History of the Church in the Fifth and Sixth Centuries* (Cambridge, UK: Cambridge University Press, 1972), 168.

Sin and Grace. The lecture is very concerned with sin, divine judgment for sin, the battle between the devil and humans, divine grace, divine mercy, and the need for personal conversion. This is understandable since his audience consists of monks, who by the nature of their vocation are on a continual quest to overcome their sinful passions. The audience is told to put away wicked deeds, to abstain from sin, to not continue in sin, to repent, to purify themselves, and to restrain themselves for God.[47] Positively, they are encouraged to do good, act righteously before God, walk toward the light, love life, put their hope and heart in God, trust in the power of God, and stay firmly attached to Christ by constantly being renewed by the word of truth and by meditating on the words of redemption.[48]

These concerns about sin, the devil, grace, and conversion also correspond to the content of Rev 7-12, which includes a description of a dragon being thrown to earth and its pursuit of a woman and her child. Satan dragged humanity into his nets and kidnapped them (Para 44-45). God, merciful and pitiful, seeing humanity's great misery, wants to take back to himself those who had been made prisoners (Para 21 & 27). The Lamb of God was sacrificed, crucified for the salvation of the human race. (Para 11, 33, 42). God wants people to repent and wants to forgive their sins (Para 19 & 27). These are his "elect," whom God makes faithful, and who are sealed not because of their own virtues, but because of God's great love (Para 39-40).

Eschatology. The lecturer did not see the great tribulation of Rev 7:14 as an eschatological tribulation associated with an end-time Antichrist, nor the trumpet judgments of Rev 8 & 9 as a succession of judgments which will come upon the world in the last days, but rather interpreted them as different portrayals of the Last Judgment itself. In the *Encomium*, the lecturer never mentions an end-time person called "Antichrist" although once he refers to "antichrists" in the plural (Para 35). When he did teach about eschatological events, there is nothing atypical. At the end of the world the dead will be raised and Christ will return to judge,

47 Para 6, 13, 15, 19, 22, 27, 31, & 45.

48 Para 13, 15, 17, 19, 23, 29, 30-31, & 49.

remunerating the good with heaven and rewards, and the evil with punishments in Gehenna (Para 21, 33, & 36). He seems to have believed that the *time, times, and half a time* in Rev 12:14 were already completed by the time of his lecture. These included a time of "false peace" which the lecturer derived from 1 Thess 5:3 (Para 48). Nevertheless, apocalyptic ideas of an imminent end are not explicit and not a major feature in his exegesis of Revelation.

Authorship and Date of the Commentary

Authorship. In the manuscript, the *Encomium* is attributed to Cyril of Alexandria (d. 444) who flourished in the first half of the fifth century. However, MacCoull believed that its tone and style show that it was not written by him. Because of this, and evidence of sixth-century conflicts in the *Encomium*, which occurred much later than Cyril, I have referred to the text as from "pseudo-Cyril of Alexandria." MacCoull attributed the *Encomium* to "a monastic writer of the late sixth or the first half of the seventh century, in an Egypt strongly anti-Chalecedonian in feeling."[49]

The Dating of the Encomium in Previous Literature. Paragraph 34 on Rev 11:7 and Para 39 on Rev 11:15 mentions conflict between the enemies of God and the servants of God. It is common among commentators on the Book of Revelation to identify the enemies of God and conflicts in Revelation with contemporary enemies and conflicts, but MacCoull could not decide if the enemies of this lecturer were the Chalcedonians (adherents of the two-nature Christology of the Council of Chalcedon in 451) or Muslims. Another clue to its date is contained in Para 36 where the author mentions some who had erred concerning the resurrection of the Savior. Here again MacCoull could not decide if these were to be identified as Chalcedonians or Muslims. At the end of the *Encomium*, the lecturer tells his audience that when they get together next, they will learn about the identity of the beasts in Rev 13. Unfortunately, that follow-up

49 MacCoull, "Pierpont Morgan MS. Copt. 591," 39.

lecture, which would likely have provided additional information about the perceived enemies of the author, has not been found.

Tito Orlandi, in the introduction to his Italian translation of the *Encomium*, was more specific in his dating of the text, expressing his belief that it was written after the Arab conquest of Egypt, which took place between the years 639 and 646. He conjectured this from several statements in the *Encomium*, the first of which is the reference to "those who despise the image of God" in Para 29. The Arabs, he said, were against representations of human and divine images. The second reference is in Para 39 on Rev 11:15, where people foolishly said "The kingdom of God has become that of the animal forever." Orlandi claimed that this was a reference to an Arab practice of putting images of animals on their coins.[50] Finally, he interpreted a persecution followed by a time of false peace in Para 48, mentioned in the *Encomium*'s comments on Rev 12:14 , as the persecution of Cyrus (d. 642), the last Melkite patriarch of Alexandria before the Arab invasion, who in the 630s had certain anti-Chalcedonian Coptic Christians massacred, and who made peace with the Muslims.[51] Without giving specific dates, Orlandi concluded that the author wrote during the period of the first Arab persecution of the Copts or the first Coptic rebellion against the Arabs, which took place in the mid-seventh century.[52]

T. C. Schmidt mentions the *Encomium* in his dissertation entitled "The Last Book," which is about standards of canonicity used in the reception and rejection of the Book of Revelation among Christians in the East. He refers to the *Encomium* as a sermon of "an anonymous

50 I have not been able to confirm a *seventh-century* practice of Arabs putting pictures of animals on their coins. The Egyptian *Apocalypse of Pseudo-Athanasius*, IX.9, written about 700 (after the conquest of Egypt by the Arabs), speaks of a nation who will destroy "the gold on which there is the image of the Cross of our Lord, Our God, in order to make all the countries under its rule mint their own gold with the *name* of a beast written on it," whose name has been identified with the caliph Marwan II. See Francisco Javier Martinez, "Eastern Christian Apocalyptic in the Early Muslim Period: Pseudo-Methodius and Pseudo-Athanasius. (Volumes I and II)," Dissertation (Washington, D.C.: The Catholic University of America, 1985), 262, 529, 575-576.

51 Frend, *The Rise of the Monophysite Movement*, 350-351.

52 Orlandi, *Omelie copte*, 125.

Coptic homilist (c. 6th-7th cent. CE)."[53] Although the manuscript in which the *Encomium* is contained is from the ninth-century, no secondary literature dates the delivery of the lecture as late as the eighth or ninth century.[54] One reason for this could be that by the late seventh century Coptic Christians were identifying the beast of Revelation with Mohammed,[55] and in the few comments on the beast in the *Encomium*, there is no such identification. Therefore, the lecture was most likely given before the year 700.

A Fifth-century Terminus a quo. Terminology in the *Encomium* provides a few clues about the earliest possible date for its delivery. Paragraph 7 mentions the *Trisagion*, which is a hymn "Holy God, Holy Mighty, Holy Immortal, have mercy on us," still in use in some Eastern liturgies. According to Sebastian Brock, this hymn "emerged in the fifth century."[56] The author of the Book of Revelation is called John "the theologian" in Para 9 and 37. This appellation for John did not gain widespread use until the mid-fifth century.[57] Mary, the mother of Christ, is called *theotokos*, or God-bearer, in Para 42. Although by the fifth century the term *theotokos* had long been a theological expression of the Alexandrian church, Cyril of Alexandria, at the Council of Ephesus (431) over which he presided, gave the title a certain canonical authority.[58] From these three terms, one

53 Schmidt, "The Last Book," 57.

54 One could argue, however, that the despisers of images in Para 29 refer to Byzantine iconoclasts of the eighth and ninth centuries and that those who had doubts about the resurrection in Para 36 refer to certain eighth and ninth century Byzantines. On the latter, see Ken Parry, "Providence, Resurrection, and Restoration in Byzantine Thought, Eighth to Ninth Centuries," *Studia Patristica* 97 (2017):295-304.

55 For example, John of Nikiu (c. 690), *The Chronicle of John*, 121.10 and pseudo-Athanasius (c.700), *Sahidic Apocalypse of Pseudo-Athansius*, 9.9. See Schmidt, *The Last Book*, 303; Askeland, "Sahidic Apocalypse," 280; Martinez, "Eastern Christian Apocalyptic," 262, 529-530, 576.

56 Sebastian Brock and Brian Fitzgerald, trans., *Two Early Lives of Severos, Patriarch of Antioch*. Translated Texts for Historians 59 (Liverpool, UK: Liverpool University Press, 2013), 10.

57 Panayiotis Tzamalikos, *An Ancient Commentary on the Book of Revelation. A critical edition of the Scholia in Apocalypsin* (New York: Cambridge University Press, 2013), 214-217.

58 On the title *theotokos* for Mary, which Cyril's arch-enemy Nestorius rejected, see Davis, *Coptic Christology*, 33-34; Davis, *The Early Coptic Papacy. The Egyptian Church and Its Leadership in Late Antiquity* (New York: The American University in Cairo Press, 2004), 76-80. On the conflict between Cyril and Nestorius, see Susan Wessel, *Cyril of Alexandria and the Nestorian Controversy: The Making of a Saint and of a Heretic* (Oxford: Oxford University Press, 2004).

can conclude that the *Encomium* was produced after the middle part of the fifth century.

After the Council of Chalcedon (451). Several references to numbers of weeks, and their correspondence with dates of key events for anti-Chalcedonians, suggest that the perceived enemies of the lecturer were the supporters of the Council of Chalcedon. One such clue is in Para 48, where the author comments on the phrase in Rev 12:14: *time, times, and half a time.* He sees the first period, a *time,* as the earliest days of Christianity when the church replaced the Jewish nation as the people of God. He sees a second division of time as the years of the Roman persecutions which resulted in many martyrs, presumably the time spanning the second and third centuries of the current era up until the last major persecution under Diocletian in the early fourth century. Concerning another period of time, the lecturer mentions nineteen weeks (fourteen and five). Often in exegesis of prophetic biblical texts, days are reckoned as years and a week as a period of seven years.[59] If these nineteen weeks were seen as weeks of years, they equal 126 years. This happens to be the exact number of years between the Council of Nicaea in 325 and the Council of Chalcedon in 451. This latter council was detested by many Egyptian Christians in the years following it; for they believed that the council was tainted with "Nestorian" heresy concerning the person of Christ.[60] Some Miaphysites (those who believe in one incarnate nature of the Word) considered the council to mark the beginning of the great eschatological

59 Interpretation of weeks as weeks of years was a common feature of patristic interpretation of Daniel 9:24-27. See Hippolytus, *Commentary on Daniel,* 4.30.5; 4.31.1-2; 4.32.1. In T.C. Schmidt, *Hippolytus of Rome: Commentary on Daniel and 'Chronicon'* (Piscataway, NJ: Gorgias, 2017), 161-162; Clement of Alexandria, *Stromata,* 1.21.142. PG 8:853; Origen, *On First Principles,* 4.1.5 ANF 4:353; *On Matthew,* 40. On Matt 24:15-18. PG 13:1656; Eusebius, *Eclogues on Daniel.* PG 22:1187-1191; Ammonius of Alexandria, *Fragments on Daniel.* On Dan 9:27. PG 85:1378.

60 On the conflict of Egyptian Christians with the decisions of the Council of Chalcedon and "Chalcedonian" Christians, see Davis, *Coptic Christology,* 49-54; and Davis, *Early Coptic Papacy,* 83-95. The Creed of the Council of Chalcedon is provided in Appendix 1.

apostasy spoken about in Scripture.[61] From the lecturer's further comments in Para 48, it is also likely that he viewed these 126 years as the time of false peace mentioned by the apostle Paul in 1 Thess 5:3. If this correspondence between the lecturer's numerology and the year of the Council of Chalcedon is more than coincidental, and is a reflection of what the author hinted at, the *Encomium* was preached after 451, the date of the Council of Chalcedon.

It should be noted that it is not unique for this lecturer to interpret passages in the Book of Revelation as signifying a church council, especially the Council of Chalcedon, as he seems to have done. According to one source, a sixth-century Coptic monk named Apa Apollo associated the opening of the pit of the abyss in Rev 9:1-2 as "the pit of the impiety which the rulers had gathered up who had come together to Chalcedon."[62] Another sixth-century encomium has the dragon, the ancient serpent Satan (cf. Rev 12:9) inspiring the Byzantine empress and emperor to assemble the Council of Chalcedon.[63] Still another Miaphysite commentary on the Book of Revelation, written in Egypt in the Syriac language and dated to the ninth or tenth century by Stan Larson but to about the year 700 by Schmidt,[64] interprets visions in Revelation as symbolic

61 W. H. C. Frend, *The Rise of the Monophysite Movement* (Cambridge, UK: Cambridge University Press, 1972), 184; Stan Larson, "The Earliest Syriac Commentary on the Apocalypse: Transcription, Translation, and Importance of Brit. Lib. MS. Add. 17,127," Thesis (Birmingham, UK: University of Birmingham, 1984), 249: "The third woe represents those who deny the true and orthodox faith and go astray and accept the doctrine of Satan, and follow and worship the Son of Perdition." Here the commentator is speaking of adherents of the two-nature Christology of the Council of Chalcedon as the doctrine of Satan and those who follow it as worshippers of Antichrist.

62 Stephen of Hnes, *Panegyric of Apollo*, 8. Cited in Askeland, "Sahidic Apocalypse," 279.

63 *Panegyric on Macarius*, 2.4-5. This text is cited and discussed in Askeland, "Sahidic Apocalypse," 279.

64 Larson, "The Earliest Syriac Commentary on the Apocalypse," 413; Schmidt, "The Last Book," 308. Youhanna Nessim Youssef ("The Commentary on the Apocalypse Councils and Eschatology," *Bulletin de la société d'archéologie copte* 49 [2010]:109-142) wrote on an Arabic fragment of the Syriac commentary. Unaware of Larson's work and that the entire commentary is extant, Youssef thought the fragment dated from the late sixth or early seventh century. Although the last council cited in the commentary is that of Constantinople in 533, Larson ("The Earliest Syriac Commentary on the Apocalypse," 412-413) makes a strong case that the commentary can be dated no earlier than the late seventh century. The text of the Apocalypse used in it is based upon Thomas of Harkel's translation completed about the year 615; and the apocryphal *Testament of our Lord*, used in and cited as Scripture in the commentary, was translated into Syriac about the year 686.

of the Council of Chalcedon. From Rev 2:18 to Rev 3:6, especially in the message to the church at Sardis, the commentator sees the words of Jesus as confounding "the proclaimers of the two natures" at the Council of Chalcedon and praising those who opposed it.[65]

Paragraph 34 may provide another hint that the enemies of the author were the Chalcedonians. The author writes, "Who is the beast other than the one whom God defeated, sending him down into the eternal abyss with his companions? He will approach many, so that they will fight against the servants of the Lord, and oppose them, and they will shed blood around the great city of Jerusalem." It could be that the lecturer is identifying the beast simply as Satan, whom God defeated and whom God cast down with the angels which followed him. But in Para 44 the lecturer says that the dragon and his angels were cast down from heaven to *earth*, not to the abyss. Or, the lecturer may see the beast as a future Antichrist whom God will send to the abyss at the Last Judgment. But the lecturer speaks of a beast whom God already defeated.[66] If Chalcedonians are the enemy of the lecturer, and this colored his interpretation of the beast, his comment could be a veiled reference to Juvenal, patriarch of Jerusalem, who was regarded as a traitor to the cause of Christ by Egyptian Miaphysites. Juvenal was a supporter of the Miaphysite party who changed sides at the Council of Chalcedon in 451. After Juvenal returned from Chalcedon, angry anti-Chalcedonian monks in Jerusalem refused to allow him to enter the city. Juvenal returned to Jerusalem with an army from Constantinople, and a massacre of anti-Chalcedonian monks occurred.[67] This historical episode seems to match the description in the *Encomium* where the beast fights against the servants of the Lord and blood is shed around the city of Jerusalem.

The lecturer may have referred to the historical episode about Juvenal and the monks of Jerusalem again in Para 39. There he says that "prophets were killed and stoned," but afterward "God humbled the impious man,

65 Larson, "Earliest Syriac Commentary," 69-81; Youssef, "The Commentary on the Apocalypse," 133-134.

66 Similarly, in Para 39 the lecturer says in the past tense that "God humbled the impious man."

67 V. C. Samuel, *The Council of Chalcedon Re-Examined* (Kent, UK: British Orthodox Press, 2001), 123-127; W. A. Wigram, *The Separation of the Monophysites* (London: Faith Press, 1923), 17-19.

and that man recognized that his renown became wicked before all."[68] Interestingly, Juvenal is identified by name and portrayed as an enemy in the aforementioned Miaphysite commentary on Revelation written in Egypt in the Syriac language. On Rev 2:12-17 its author censures Juvenal as one who lapsed and "joined with the reprobate council of Chalcedon."[69] The fact that he is mentioned in a Miaphysite commentary on Revelation written later than the *Encomium*, shows the disdain which those in that ecclesiastical community had for Juvenal, even centuries later.

Sixth-Century Events. In that same Para 34 the lecturer says that after God's servants are persecuted, the Lord gradually will give power to his people, and they will chase out the wicked and "defeat the enemy in twenty-eight weeks." Then "five more weeks will show what they did." Here is a mention of twenty-eight weeks and another five. If the author saw the weeks as weeks of years, the 28 weeks would equal 196 years, followed by another five weeks, or 35 years, to manifest the result of the victorious rise of the servants of God. While the narrative is in the future tense, it is possible that these calculations of weeks reflect past history from the standpoint of the lecturer. If the weeks of years began after the Roman persecutions ceased, like the author's comments on Rev 12:14 suggest (see above), the author may have had in mind the 196 years between the Edict of Toleration in the year 313 and the success of Severus, the powerful defender of the Miaphysites, in the royal court at Constantinople about the year 509. In 508 Severus, along with 200-300 of his anti-Chalcedonian monks, traveled to Constantinople and resided there for several years, from 508-511. During that time Severus was instrumental in getting the pro-Chalcedonian patriarch

68 However, I do recognize that this could also correspond with Cyrus, as Orlandi suggested, who persecuted anti-Chalcedonian monks in Egypt. He was elected patriarch of Alexandria in 632, but was deposed in 639. Frend (*Rise of the Monophysite Movement*, 349, 351) says that in the 620s in Egypt "'Cyrus the Caucasian' became a hated name" and that he "opened a reign of terror the like of which the Egyptians had not experienced since the Great Persecution." So, as Orlandi suggested, he could be the one referred to in Para 39 of the *Encomium* as "the impious man" whose "renown became wicked before all." There was also a massacre of Egyptian monks near Alexandria in 620 or a little thereafter by the Persians (See Frend, *Rise of the Monophysite Movement*, 342), but none of the secondary literature on the *Encomium* relates this massacre to statements in Para 34 & 39.

69 Larson, "Earliest Syriac Commentary," 65.

of Constantinople removed; and he himself became the spiritual advisor to the emperor Anastasius.[70] Then in 512 Severus, the champion at that time of the anti-Chalcedonians, was raised to the patriarchate of Antioch, in which position he assumed responsibility for the churches in Cilicia, Syria, Phoenicia, Arabia, and Mesopotamia. Also, at that time, the patriarchates of Antioch, Constantinople, and Alexandria were all held by non-Chalcedonians.[71] This "success" of the non-Chalcedonian cause is probably what the lecturer had in mind when he said that the enemy was defeated (Para 34). According to the lecturer, the additional five weeks or 35 years, would reveal the results of the victorious accomplishments of the servants of God. This could point to the Emperor Justinian's edict of condemnation of the "three chapters" issued in 544. In that edict Justinian condemned the person of Theodore of Mopsuestia, certain works of Theodoret of Cyrus, and a letter of Ibas of Edessa, all of which the Miaphysites considered to be Nestorian and apostate.[72] Also, in Para 48, in the lecturer's comment on *time, times, and half a time* (Rev 12:14), where he mentioned nineteen weeks (which I showed above hinted of a time up to the Council of Chalcedon in 451), he then mentions another "ninety-three days." If these 93 days represent years to be added to 451, they too bring the hearer to the year 544, exactly the year of Justinian's condemnation of the three chapters. If these major pro-Miaphysite events are what the lecturer hinted at in his numerology in Para 34 & 48,[73] then the *Encomium* was delivered after the condemnation of the three chapters in the year 544.

70 Brock and Fitzgerald, *Two Early Lives of Severos*, 3-4; Allen and Hayward, *Severus of Antioch*, 8; Samuel, *Council of Chalcedon*, 152-158; Iain R. Torrance, *Christology after Chalcedon: Serverus of Antioch and Sergius the Monophysite* (Norwich: Canterbury Press, 1988), 4; Frend, *Rise of the Monophysite Movement*, 216, 235.

71 Allen and Hayward, *Severus of Antioch*, 16; Samuel, *Council of Chalcedon*, 157.

72 Frend, *Rise of the Monophysite Movement*, 280.

73 One problem with the numerology pointing to Justinian's condemnation of the three chapters in 544 is that in 553 at the Council of Constantinople Justinian renewed the condemnation of the three chapters, but declared the Council of Chalcedon as the fourth ecumenical council, which was rejected by Miaphysites.

These correspondences between the lecturer's numerology and people, councils, and events of the fifth and sixth centuries which were significant to Egyptian Miaphysites, are offered by me knowing full well that I can be mistaken in my interpretations of these difficult statements. Therefore, further research on the numerology of the *Encomium* is greatly encouraged.[74]

Sixth-Century Controversy over the Resurrection and the Trinity. In Para 36 the *Encomium* mentions "those who have doubt concerning the resurrection of the Savior," or in MacCoull's translation "those who separated themselves from" Christ's resurrection.[75] This probably refers to the famous sixth-century controversy between Severus of Antioch and Julian of Halicarnassus when they were both living in exile in Alexandria.[76] The controversy took place during the years 524-526, but continued to be discussed in subsequent decades. It surrounded the question of whether or not Christ's body was incorruptible from the point of his Incarnation (Julian's position) or was incorruptible only from after his resurrection,

74 As Pieter G. R. de Villiers did with Oecumenius's commentary. See his "Numerical Symbolism in Oecumenius's Commentary on the Apocalypse," in Konrad Huber, Rainer Klotz, and Christoph Winterer, eds., *Tot Sacramenta Quot Verba* (Münster: Aschendorff, 2014):135-52.

75 MacCoull, "Pierpont Morgan," 37.

76 Several other controversies about the resurrection occurred in the sixth-century. One of them concerned the teaching of Origen (d. 231). Origen was a prolific writer whose conjectures concerning eschatology were considered unorthodox by many in the centuries following his death. Although he was not definitive about it, one of Origen's leanings was that after the resurrection, corporeality would be non-existent. (See his *On First Principles*, 2, 3.7.) One phase of the "Origenist" controversy arose in the mid-sixth century. At one point in the controversy, around 553, the emperor Justinian wrote fifteen anathemas against the Origenists. Anathema 10 of that work stated: "If anyone maintains that the body of the Lord, after the resurrection, is ethereal and spherical in form, and that the other resurrection bodies will be so also...let him be anathema." (Charles Joseph Hefele, *A History of the Councils of the Church*, Vol. 4 [Edinburgh: T & T Clark, 1895], 227-228) If the lecturer of the *Encomium* were referring to this sixth-century controversy, the Origenists were those who separated themselves from the resurrection of the Savior (cf. Para 36). For, if Christ rose bodily, so also will the rest of humanity. A few decades later, another controversy over the resurrection stemmed from the views of Eutyches, patriarch of Constantinople, not to be confused with the fifth-century monk of the same name condemned at Chalcedon. Eutyches believed that in the general resurrection God will not regroup the material particles of people's decomposed bodies, but will create all humans brand new. According to Samuel (*Council of Chalcedon*, 191), this opinion made Eutyches unpopular, and his opinion found almost no favor with anyone in his day. About the same time, the philosopher John Philoponus taught that at death, the body of humans "passes into corruption in matter *and* form," and possibly denied the resurrection of the flesh altogether. See Hefele, *History of the Councils of the Church*, 3:461.

before which it was mortal and corruptible (Severus's position).[77] If this is the controversy referred to in the *Encomium*, the lecturer took the side of Severus, and the Julianists were the people who had separated themselves from the Savior's resurrection. For followers of Severus, the corruptible and mortal bodies of humans will become incorruptible and immortal at the resurrection, the resurrection of Christ being a model of this. To think otherwise, that is, to say that Christ was incorruptible throughout his earthly life, and that he did not become incorruptible at his resurrection, as the followers of Julian reasoned, would be to separate their own future resurrection from Christ's resurrection.[78]

In Para 7, the lecturer says that there are no distinctions in each of the members of the Trinity. The lecturer is most likely not advocating Sabellianism (a collapsing of the true distinction of persons within the Trinity into modes of manifestation), but countering tritheism which arose among Miaphysites in Constantinople. Around 557 John Asconaghes taught that there were three "natures" in the Trinity, or essentially three Gods. These views were accepted by Sergius of Tella, Eugenius of Seleucia, Conon of Tarsus, and Athanasius, the grandson of empress Theodora. The disagreement was settled in Constantinople in 566, after which tritheism made inroads in Egyptian ecclesiastical and philosophical circles. In Egypt, the philosopher John of Philopenos allegedly taught "In the Trinity I count as many natures, essences, and Godheads, as I do hypostases."[79] By 569 this teaching was rejected and condemned by most

77 On the corruptible controversy, see Yonatan Moss, *Incorruptible Bodies: Christology, Society, and Authority in Late Antiquity* (Oakland: University of California Press, 2016), esp. 162; Davis, *Early Coptic Papacy*, 100-101; Samuel, *Council of Chalcedon*, 470-471; John Meyendorff, *Imperial Unity and Christian Divisions: The Church 450-680 A.D.* (Crestwood, NY: St Vladimir's Seminary Press, 1989), 254-256; Frend, *Rise of the Monophysite Movement*, 253-254; Wigram, *Separation of the Monophysites*, 121-122, 151-155.

78 See for example, Severus's *Synodical Letter to Theodosius* (Allen & Hayward, *Severus of Antioch*, 158-168 at 162), where he wrote: "For an impassible and immortal body does not admit of sufferings and death, but is considered to have suffered and died only in surmise, and as it were in an illusion of sleep. Now if the sufferings are considered to be false, and Emmanuel did not die our kind of death, then in every respect his resurrection also is to be considered false; and all those things which relate to our redemption, and the hope of resurrection which was promised to us, are lost."

79 Wigram, *Separation of the Monophysites*, 157.

Miaphysites, but surfaced in debates in the decades following the 560s.[80] When the lecturer, a Trinitarian speaking in response to tritheism, taught that there are no distinctions between the members of the Trinity (Para 7) and that we worship only one God (Para 32), he was very likely saying that there are not three *ousia* or natures in the Trinity, but only one. There is probably another refutation of tritheism in Para 32, when the lecturer says that the angels "prostrate to one God only," as opposed to three gods.

The *Encomium*'s allusion to the early-sixth century controversy over the incorruptibility of Christ and the tritheist controversy of the 560s suggest that this exegetical lecture was delivered no earlier than the 560s and probably a little after that time.

Those Sealed and Those Not Sealed. For the lecturer, those "sealed" by God are, in a general manner, those believers in Jesus who have been baptized, are repentant from sin, and walk in purity (Para 23). They received the seal when the Lamb marked each on his forehead with the sign of the seal (Para 40), hinting at the sign of the cross administered on the forehead in baptism. For the lecturer, virginity and the blood of martyrdom are also seals (Para 23 & 31).[81] By contrast, sinners and unbelievers are "far from the sign of the seal which is in Jesus Christ" (Para 23); they "carry the sign of Satan" (Para 29). These sinners "despise the image of God" (Para 29), meaning they are destructive to themselves, created in God's image. They do this by sinning against the Son of God, living in evil passions, not restraining themselves for God, and loving death instead of life (Para 19, 22-23, 25, 28).

However, in a more specific sense, the description of the lecturer's enemies as impious people, "antichrists" who bear the seal of Satan, and as people who mock the name of God and insult the "orthodox" saints (Para 13, 29, 35, 39), may also be reflective of his attitudes toward those who

80 Manlio Simonetti, "John Philoponus," in Angelo Di Berardino, ed., *Encyclopedia of Ancient Christianity*, 3 vols (Downers Grove, IL: InterVarsity, 2014), 2:449; Davis, *Early Coptic Papacy*, 109-110; Samuel, *Council of Chalcedon*, 197; Meyendorff, *Imperial Unity and Christian Divisions*, 256-257; Wigram, *Separation of the Monophysites*, 157; Hefele, *History of the Councils of the Church*, 3:460-461.

81 Cf. *Hymn 8* of Severus of Antioch (Allen and Hayward, *Severus of Antioch*, 169) says that the Virgin Mary has "the imprinted seal of virginity." The lecturer of the *Encomium* says that one who purifies his own body "will become a seal like John, whom Jesus loves for his purity" (Para 31).

held the two-nature Christology of the Council of Chalcedon. In this sense, these have joined together in despising the true "image of God," the Lord Jesus Christ.[82]

Conclusions about the Date of the Commentary. Evidence from the terminology of the *Encomium*, referring to John as the "theologian" and Mary as "theotokos," and from the mention of the *Trisagion* hymn, suggests that it most likely was not delivered earlier than the middle of the fifth century. In the lecturer's numerology, there are probably veiled references to the Council of Chalcedon, and in Para 34 & 39 to the massacre of monks in Jerusalem by Juvenal and the army which accompanied him shortly after Chalcedon. If so, the lecture took place after 451-452. In the numerology there may also be allusions to the success of Miaphysites under the leadership of Severus in the early sixth century and the condemnation of the "three chapters" by Justinian in 544. The sixth-century controversy about the incorruptibility of Christ's body, associated with Julian of Halicarnassus, is probably also referred to in the statement about those who separated themselves from the resurrection of the Savior. There is also evidence that the lecturer countered tritheistic views, which gained a foothold in Egypt in the 560s.

The lecturer and his audience of monks may have endured mockery and insults (Para 29 & 35), but they do not seem to be experiencing severe persecution in which their monastery and lives are at risk. The *Encomium* also does not hint that they are in the midst of fleeing from persecution. In fact, at the end of the presentation, the lecturer dismisses the monks to their cells and looks forward to an opportune time in which they can soon gather again and continue their study of the Book of Revelation. This shows that they are living under relatively peaceful circumstances. To me, this does not reflect the tumult of Cyrus's oppression in the 630s or of the Arab invasion of Egypt in the 640s.

82 Jesus Christ is called the image of God in 2 Cor 4:4; Col 1:15; Heb 1:3 and by Athanasius, *On the Incarnation*, 13, 20; Gregory of Nazianzus, *Theological Orations*, 3.17; 4.20 (Edward R. Hardy, ed., *Christology of the Later Fathers* [Philadelphia: Westminster Press, 1954], 67, 74, 172, 191). See also John Anthony McGuckin, trans., *St. Cyril of Alexandria, On the Unity of Christ*. Popular Patristic Series 13 (Crestwood, NY: St Vladimir's Seminary Press, 1995), 108.

The conflicts alluded to in the *Encomium* are more consistent with Egyptian Miaphysites' clashes with the Byzantines over the teaching and status of the Council of Chalcedon and with sixth-century internal disagreements among non-Chalcedonians in Egypt (on the resurrection and the Trinity) than with turmoil associated with the Arab invasion of the seventh century. The weight of evidence, therefore, suggests a date for the delivery of the *Encomium* in the 570s or 580s, when the views of Julianists and tritheists were still fresh and lively issues. This dating of the *Encomium* is confirmed by the fact that the lecturer claimed ignorance about where the Virgin Mary went after her death (Para 43). By the later part of the sixth century and definitely in the seventh century, it was almost universally held in the East that Mary was assumed to heaven. Brian E. Daley, who translated many patristic homilies on the dormition of Mary, wrote that "By the second half of the sixth century, it is clear that the story of Mary's transition from earth to heaven had come to be accepted as part of Christian tradition in both the Chalcedonian and the non-Chalcedonian Churches of the East."[83]

This dating of the *Encomium* to the 570s or 580s is only slightly earlier than the observations of MacCoull and Orlandi, the former who posited a late-sixth or early-seventh century date and the latter who suggested that the *Encomium* is from the mid-seventh century, shortly after the invasion of Egypt by the Arabs. By way of interaction with Orlandi's seventh-century dating of the *Encomium*, "those who despise the image of God" (Para 29) could simply refer to carnal sinners in general, as Orlandi admits,[84] or to those who hold that Christ has two natures (Chalcedonians), rather than Arab Muslims who rejected Christian imagery. From the context of Revelation 11, in the statement of the fools who said, "The kingdom of God has become that of the *animal* forever," the kingdom of the animal probably refers back to the kingdom of the beast (cf. Rev 11:7), although it could refer to the kingdom of man in contrast to the kingdom of God,

83 Brian E. Daley, trans., *On the Dormition of Mary. Early Patristic Homilies* (Crestwood, NY: St Vladimir's Seminary Press, 1998), 9.

84 Orandi, *Omelie copte*, 124. It probably does not refer to the iconoclast movement within the Byzantine empire in the eighth and ninth centuries.

since the lecturer earlier said that man was an animal. It does not necessarily reflect the kingdom of the Arabs.

Sources Used for the Commentary

The lecturer's main source is the Bible. Besides the quotations from and allusions to the Book of Revelation, the *Encomium* includes quotations from Deuteronomy, Psalms, Jeremiah, Malachi, Matthew, Romans, and 1 Thessalonians. There are many scriptural allusions to passages from Genesis, Exodus, 1 Kings, Ezra, Nehemiah, Job, Isaiah, Daniel, Zechariah, Mark, Luke, John, Acts, 1 & 2 Corinthians, Ephesians, Colossians, 1 & 2 Timothy, James, and 1 Peter. From the liturgical tradition the lecturer quotes the Creed and mentions the *Trisagion* hymn (Para 7 & 36).

The lecturer who delivered the *Encomium* does not cite by name any earlier Christian writers. The lecturer certainly was influenced by Eastern traditional interpretation, such as Mary giving birth without pain (Para 41) and John remaining a virgin (Para 31).[85] While other commentators on the Book of Revelation from the sixth and seventh century East often quoted from earlier writers on the Book of Revelation (from writers such as Hippolytus, Irenaeus, and Methodius),[86] the lecturer of the *Encomium* did not refer to any of these. Of course, a few patristic works on the Book of Revelation have been lost, e.g. the commentary of Didymus and

85 On Mary giving birth without pain, see Gregory of Nyssa, *Against Eunomius*, Hom. 2 (PG 45:492). On John as a virgin see the Coptic *The Mysteries of Saint John the Apostle the Holy Virgin* in E. A. Wallis Budge, ed., *Coptic Apocrypha in the Dialect of Upper Egypt* (London: Oxford University Press, 1913). More research to discover possible quotations or dependence of the author of the *Encomium* upon early Greek, Coptic, and Syriac writings is encouraged. The phrase "place of patience" is used in Para 23 & 29 of the *Encomium*. Is this phrase simply a stylistic feature of the lecturer or one derived from a literary or liturgical source?

86 Some of the many authors that Oecumenius cited from by name in his commentary on the Apocalypse are listed at the beginning and end of his commentary. See Weinrich, *Greek Commentaries on Revelation*, 1-2, 106-107; FC 112:20, 202-203. On Rev 13, the collection of *Scholia on the Apocalypse* quotes from Irenaeus's *Against Heresies* in Scholia 28 & 29. See Tzamalikos, *An Ancient Commentary on the Book of Revelation*, 193-195. Andrew of Caesarea (Weinrich, *Greek Commentaries on Revelation*, 114; FC 123:54) discusses his use of Irenaeus, Hippolytus, and Methodius in the prologue of his commentary.

homilies of Basil;[87] but if the lecturer knew of these and used them, he never referred to them or their authors explicitly.

What accounts for this absence? It is likely that the lecturer wanted to cover so much of the Book of Revelation in one lecture (i.e. the visions of Rev 7-12 in this lecture, and Rev 13-15 in the next lecture), that time did not afford for him to stop at certain passages to provide various interpretations that went before him, give his assessment of them, and then offer his own view. This seems to be in keeping with his purpose for the lecture, which he stated in the prologue. His lecture was intended to enlighten the hearts of his listeners rather than to test the intellects of those in his audience.

At the beginning of the sixth century, Oecumenius, a Miaphysite friend of Severus, wrote a Greek *Commentary on the Apocalypse*.[88] Although I have found no quotations from Oecumenius in the *Encomium*, there are a few similarities in interpretations of visions in Rev 7-12 between Oecumenius and the *Encomium*. One similarity is that the content of the trumpet blasts represent different punishments for different sins at the Last Judgment.[89] Also both Oecumenius and the lecturer, when commenting on the angels striking only a third part of the earth, sea, living creatures, sun, moon, and stars (cf. Rev 8), spoke of God's mercy and desire to forgive those who are repentant.[90] Another similarity is a discussion of God sparing punishment or lightening punishment for sinners who have not sinned grievously.[91] On Rev 11:15, which says that *the kingdom of this world has become that of the Lord*, both Oecumenius

87 Didymus, in his *Commentary on Zachariah*, 3.73, mentions that he had written a commentary on the Apocalypse. On ancient witnesses to sermons on the Apocalypse by Basil, see Tzamalikos, *Ancient Commentary on the Book of Revelation*, 22.

88 *Oecumenius. Commentary on the Apocalypse*. FC 112; Weinrich, *Greek Commentaries*. For Oecumenius as the Miaphysite recipient of letters of Severus, see John C. Lamoreaux, "The Provenance of Ecumenius' Commentary on the Apocalypse," *Vigiliae Christianae* 52 (1998):88-108 at 98 & 101. Eugenia Scarvelis Constantinou ("Andrew of Caesarea and the Apocalypse in the Ancient Church of the East: Studies and Translation," Thesis [Quebec: Université Laval, 2008], 14-21, esp. 17) disagrees and thinks the author of the commentary on the Apocalypse was a different Oecumenius who wrote at the end of the sixth century.

89 Compare Oecumenius on Rev 8:7; 9:1-4; 10:1 (FC 112:84, 87, 95) with Para 18 of the *Encomium*.

90 Compare Oecumenius on Rev 8:12-13 (FC 112:86) with Para 17, 19, & 21 of the *Encomium*.

91 Compare Oecumenius on Rev 9:1-6 (FC 112:88-89) with Para 25 of the *Encomium*.

and the author of the *Encomium* explain that God's kingdom has always existed and that God has always reigned.[92] Both authors believe that the two witnesses are Enoch and Elijah, the woman of Rev 12 is Mary, the crown of 12 stars on her head represent the apostles, and the offspring of the woman are the faithful.[93]

However, there are significant differences in interpretations between Oecumenius and the *Encomium*. Oecumenius believed that the 144,000 of Rev 7 were the Jewish people who had escaped the Roman siege of Jerusalem in 68-70 CE; the author of the *Encomium* saw them, at least on the literal level, as Jewish people of pre-Christian times.[94] For Oecumenius, the book in Rev 10 is one in which the deeds of exceedingly sinful people are recorded; for the author of the *Encomium* it is the book of the testament.[95] For Oecumenius, the desert of Rev 12:6,14 was Egypt to where Mary and Joseph fled when Jesus was a baby; for the author of the *Encomium* the desert was the place of Golgotha, where Mary witnessed the crucifixion of her Son, and the place in which Mary resides after her death.[96] For Oecumenius, the wings given to the woman (Rev 12:14) represented the angelic exhortation given to Joseph to take Mary and Jesus to Egypt; for the lecturer the two wings represented the two testaments.[97]

What accounts for the few similarities and many differences between the *Encomium* and the commentary of Oecumenius? The similarities suggest that the author of the *Encomium*, who knew at least some Greek,[98] could have read or listened to a reading of the commentary of Oecumenius at one time, and recalled some of its interpretations, especially those with which he agreed. Or, the similarities can be accounted for by the

92 Compare Oecumenius on Rev 11:15 (FC 112:105) with Para 39 of the *Encomium*.

93 Compare Oecumenius (FC 112:102, 107-109,117) with Para 37 & 41 of the *Encomium*.

94 Compare Oecumenius on Rev 7:1-6 (FC 112:76-78) with Para 9 of the *Encomium*.

95 Compare Oecumenius on Rev 10:2 (FC 112:96) with Para 28 of the *Encomium*.

96 Compare Oecumenius on Rev 12:6, 14 (FC 112:112, 116) with Para 43 & 47 of the *Encomium*.

97 Compare Oecumenius on Rev 12:14 (FC 112:116) with Para 47 of the *Encomium*.

98 See Para 19: "In fact, that star is onyx, according to the language of the Greeks." Greek words were also retained in the Coptic lecture in Para 9 & 41.

fact that Oecumenius and the lecturer both shared in common exegetical traditions current in the sixth-century East.[99] The significant differences between the two texts, on the other hand, show that the *Encomium* is a text with truly unique explanations of the Book of Revelation. The author of the *Encomium* did not simply use an earlier exegetical work on Revelation as a base text, and then edit, expand, or abridge it, as some later commentators in both the East and West have done.[100]

The *Encomium* contributes to exegesis of the Apocalypse in its unique interpretations of this biblical text. For example, the *Encomium* states that the 24 elders in Rev 4 represent the ten fingers, ten toes, nose, mouth, and ears of a human; and the silence in heaven in Rev 8:1 was God's silence before the creation of the world. The *Encomium* also stands as a witness of how Egyptian non-Chalcedonian Christians of the late-sixth century saw in the Book of Revelation their particular strivings with those who supported the Council of Chalcedon and with their fellow non-Chalcedonians whom they believed had erred in doctrine. Thus, the *Encomium* provides us with a fuller understanding of how Christians of late antiquity understood and used this very fascinating biblical text which, as Jerome once said, contains "as many mysteries as it does words."[101]

About the English Translation

In 2011, Francesca Lecchi, a student of mine from Italy who was studying at that time in the United States, provided me with a draft of the *Encomium* in English, having translated it from Orlandi's Italian translation. Shortly thereafter her translation was edited by Braeden Fallet

99 In the West, there was a similar phenomenon. The eighth-century Irish author of *On the Mysteries of the Apocalypse of John* most likely did not depend upon the earlier eighth-century *Exposition of the Apocalypse* by Bede who wrote in England. The similarities which exist between the two commentaries are attributed to both authors inheriting common insular exegetical traditions. See Francis X. Gumerlock, *Early Latin Commentaries on the Apocalypse* (Kalamazoo, MI: Medieval Institute Publications, 2016), 14.

100 In the East, Euthymus the Athonite and Nerses of Lambron used Andrew of Caesarea as their base text; in the West, Theodulf of Orleans used the *Handbook on the Apocalypse of the Apostle John* as his base text.

101 Jerome, *Letter* 53.9. NPNF, 2nd series, 6:102; CSEL 54:463; PL 22:548: *Apocalypsis Iohannis tot ibi sacramenta quot uerba.*

and myself. In 2016 Dr. Seth Fabian, a professor of Italian, edited the translation. In 2019 and 2020 I edited the translation again and added footnotes. Where MacCoull and Thomas Schmidt, in their studies of the *Encomium*, included sentences or phrases from it translated directly from the Coptic, I have included them in footnotes. In 2021 Professor Tito Orlandi graciously compared our English translation directly with the Sahidic Coptic and made very helpful suggestions.

PART

Translation of the Commentary

by Francesca Lecchi and Others

Incipit

An encomium delivered by Abba Cyril, archbishop of Alexandria, commenting on some passages of the Apocalypse of John, the apostle of Jesus Christ. In the peace of God, Amen.[1]

Prologue

[1] *The wind blows where it wills* (John 3:8) and will come to us in a ray of knowledge, teaching us the depth of the thoughts of *Scripture, inspired by God.* [2] So today he again[3] invites us, wanting to openly educate us and feed

1 Leslie S. B. MacCoull's translation of the heading from the Coptic manuscript ("Pierpont Morgan MS. Copt 591: The Apocalypse Commentary of Pseudo-Cyril of Alexandria," *Studia Patristica* 20 [1989], 33-39 at 33) reads: "An encomium which Apa Cyril, Archbishop of Rakote, pronounced, interpreting some small points from the Apocalypse of John the Apostle of Jesus Christ. In the peace of God, Amen." Similarly, Leo Depuydt's translation of the heading (*Catalogue of Coptic Manuscripts in the Pierpont Morgan Library* [Louvain: Peeters, 1993], 1:302) reads: "An encomium which Apa Cyril archbishop of Alexandria delivered explaining some matters in the Revelation of John the apostle of Jesus Christ. In God's peace. Amen."

2 Cf. 2 Tim 3:16.

3 This suggests that there may have been a previous lecture on the Apocalypse.

us with blessed nourishment. In fact, the words of God are nourishment,[4] of which we are never satisfied, especially those whose dwelling is with God, those who have put on the monk's robe, who made their body a sanctuary of his eternally glorious name.[5] From our words we will not receive the test of a disconcerting thought or one that empties our mind, but we shall make our own heart enlightened, and also you with us, you who have the true light.

[2] In fact the great John took our souls by the hand and led us to the meaning of his Apocalypse.[6] In this way then we receive light from the light of theology and from the perfume of the Holy Spirit, whose light will travel not only to the first celestial sphere, but to the end of the skies and finally to the end of the universe.[7] In fact when he started he did not look at things on earth nor did he reflect about them, but bodily he put his right hand on his corporeal temples and bowed his head as do those who reflect,[8] until he heard from God, who taught him everything, so that everyone could believe that it was the Holy Spirit who guided him in saying those things.[9]

[3] And it was not a minister that [the Holy Spirit] sent to him, nor a carnal servant that told him everything which had happened; but the Holy Spirit took him aside and led him there, showing him marvelous celestial thoughts,[10] and healing figures, and the wonderful thoughts, and

4 Cf. 1 Tim 4:6.

5 MacCoull's translation ("Pierpont Morgan," 34) from the Coptic reads: "especially (for) those of us who have their dwelling-place with God. These are they who wear the habit of monasticism, and who make their bodies a sanctuary for his glorious name forever."

6 T. C. Schmidt ("The Last Book: Revelation, Commentaries, and the Making of the New Testament," Diss.: Yale University, 220) translates the Coptic as: "John took our souls and led us to the understanding of his Apocalypse." Throughout their respective works, MacCoull and Schmidt have translated a few sentences of the *Encomium* from the Coptic.

7 Schmidt ("The Last Book," 217) translates the Coptic as "the first heaven, but the end of the heavens, and even the end of the universe."

8 Schmidt ("The Last Book," 208) translates the Coptic as "when John began [his vision], he did not look to the things on earth nor did he meditate upon them, but he physically put his hand on his forehead like those who meditate."

9 This is likely the lecturer's interpretation of John being "in the Spirit" in Rev 1:10 & 4:2.

10 Cf. Rev 4-6

the trumpets with a beautiful sound,[11] and the voices of benediction,[12] and the righteous planets,[13] and the dreadful things to consider,[14] and the incense of the saints and the prayer of the saints,[15] and the image of the Lamb between the righteous and pure lambs,[16] [and] the holy Mary mother of God.[17]

Revelation Chapter Four: [Man][18]

[4] Which mysteries did you not contemplate, O contemplator of the sacred mysteries?[19] **2** *I,* he says, *saw a throne staying in heaven.* Behold the mind of man. *And sitting on the throne* the Lamb,[20] which is the delight. **4** *Standing near the thrones twenty-four thrones, which are the twenty-four elders.* In fact, twenty are the fingers on a man, plus two eyes and his mouth and nose, which are by the brain.[21]

[5] *Sitting on the twenty-four thrones were twenty-four elders with crowns on their heads.* These then are the twenty nails that stay on the fingers to protect them from harm, and their nerves will not be harmed, nor will feel cold and make the body breathless and insensitive; and the tongue in the mouth professes [the faith]; and the two eyes provide the sight of the celestial things; and the nose [does its job] so that it can smell the perfume

11 Cf. Rev 8-9.

12 Cf. Rev 5:12; 7:12.

13 Cf. Rev 12:1.

14 Cf. Rev 13. Dan 7:7 & 19 describe the fourth beast as dreadful.

15 Cf. Rev 5:8; 8:3-4.

16 Cf. Rev 6:6; 7:17; 14:1-5.

17 Cf. Rev 12.

18 Tito Orlandi's subheading here (*Omelie copte* [Turin: Società Editrice Internazionale, 1981], 127) reads "L'uomo (apoc. 4)."

19 Schmidt ("The Last Book," 217) translates the Coptic here: "What mystery did you not contemplate, O contemplator of the sacred mysteries?"

20 Orlandi's Italian translation (*Omelie copte,* 127) has "the Lamb" as part of the lemma.

21 For "which are by the brain," MacCoull's translation ("Pierpont Morgan," 34) from the Coptic reads: "which surround the reason of man."

of the altar, so that they might bring the crown of their confession, the *things which* the righteous *God prepared for those* who will be worthy.[22]

[6] **10** *And they took off,* he says, *the twenty-four crowns from their heads and put them at the feet of him who was sitting on throne, saying:* **11** "*You are worthy, our Lord, to receive glory and honor and power and might.*" Also, you, O man, put your feet firmly on holy ground,[23] stretch out your hands,[24] confess with your mouth,[25] and remove from yourself any wickedness in your thoughts.[26] May your mind receive light from knowledge. And from now on, do not continue in sin;[27] and if you ask from God anything and it is not be given to you,[28] come to stone me wherever I shall be.

[7] **8** *And the four living creatures,* he says, *shouted throughout the whole time: "Holy, holy, holy is the Lord sabaoth.*[29]" The hymn is repeated three times, but its meaning is one. They offer the hymn of the holy, the lesson of the *Trisagion,*[30] taking it to the same God the Father almighty, meaning: The Son is *in the Father* and the Father is *in the Son*[31] with the Holy Spirit, without any distinction in each of them.[32]

---

22 Cf. 1 Cor 2:9.

23 Cf. Ex 3:5

24 Cf. Ps 143:6.

25 Cf. Rom 10:9

26 MacCoull's translation ("Pierpont Morgan," 34) reads: "You too, O man, take every evil out of yourself and your thoughts."

27 Cf. John 8:11.

28 Cf. John 15:7

29 That is, "Lord of hosts."

30 Based on Isa 6:3, the words of the hymn were "Holy God, Holy Mighty, Holy Immortal, have mercy on us." Some anti-Chalcedonians added "Thou who wast cruficied for us" before "have mercy on us" as a test of orthodoxy against Nestorianism. See V. C. Samuel, *The Council of Chalcedon Re-examined* (Kent, UK: British Orthodox Press, 2001), 145-146; W. H. C. Frend, *The Rise of the Monophysite Movement: Chapters in the History of the Church in the Fifth and Sixth Centuries* (Cambridge, UK: Cambridge University Press, 1972), 168.

31 Cf. John 14:11.

32 While in the Trinity there are distinctions of persons, the lecturer is emphasizing that there is no division of the divine *ousia* or substance in the Trinity. He may be teaching against "tritheists" among the Miaphysites. See the Introduction for a discussion of their persons and views.

[8] *And they never stop,* he says, *glorifying God.* How then should they fear the demons? In fact, no demons are near them in that place, and they are not tempted by anyone, not undermined by anyone, but they are always by God. They always attend to the hymns, and they listen to the help that comes to them by God. But they sing and glorify for you, man, that God might forgive your sins crimes. But you always persist in your evil, opening up your eyes in wickedness and your teeth and your eyelids in crime, your mouth in blasphemy, your heart in envy and in hatred and in hostility and in calumny, and you think your death is an absurdity. You would love to take part in a banquet full of meat from your brother. Perhaps there is no shame in your eyes, while the cherubim and seraphim bless for you, but you hasten to exalt yourself!

Revelation Chapter Seven

[9] But now we receive the instruction from what is written after these things, when the spirit of the contemplator and theologian was carried to heaven[33] into the highest things and dwelt above all our thoughts. Since man cannot contemplate these matters, no one who dwells under heaven can know or explain these things.[34] Therefore John, he in whose path the truth stands, says: **4** *I heard the number of those who were sealed, amounting to one hundred and forty-four thousand, from every tribe of the sons of Israel.* They sealed them so that the wrath that is coming upon everyone would not come on them too; for the *sins* of everyone *have reached* the sight of the Lord.[35] For, at the time of the one hundred and forty-four thousand, no one had been baptized, nor had any martyrs shed their blood, nor were there famous virgins, nor had any ascetics practiced any sort of asceticism, nor had any monks dedicated themselves to the monastic life, nor had any of those abstaining practiced abstinence, nor had those

33 Cf. Rev 4:1-2.

34 Cf. Rev 5:3-4.

35 Cf. Rev 18:5.

who give absolution[36] commanded, and those who commanded among them had not yet known the one who commands well. They still had not understood the mystery and its great sweetness. [37] But [the four angels in Rev 7:1-3] were going to seal those one hundred and forty-four thousand, each group receiving four thousand[38] in addition to the twelve, and the four thousand dividing into six tribes.[39] Each group is divided under three ancient fathers,[40] whose patriarchate was not solely theirs, but God gave it to them. And the priests come before those four thousand and the twelve, and grace comes from this, because it is one and simple. Consider what this mystery means to the Christian people: *Many will come from the east and from the west, and will sit down with Abraham, Isaac, and Jacob in the kingdom* (Matt 8:11).

[10] And after that he said: **9** *I saw a great multitude which no one could count, coming from every people, tribe, and language, before the Lamb. They were wearing white robes and were holding palm branches in their hands.* **10** *And they cried out in a loud voice: "Salvation belongs to God on the throne with the Lamb."* **11** *And all the angels were standing around the throne.* What is this crowd made of, if not the souls of the righteous who satisfied God in every lineage and tribe and language, those who prostrate in front of the Only-begotten of the Father, who placed his tent in the holy Virgin Mary, who conceived him in the flesh by the work of the Holy Spirit? And they all confess this: "Glory to you who sit on the throne of his kingdom." And who is the bishop, who consecrated those *elders* we have talked about (cf. Rev 7:11b), if not God who created the intelligible heaven and

36 Greek *synnomikoi*. Or perhaps "experts in the law."

37 The author interprets the 144,000 in reference to Jewish people in pre-Christian times, but later in the comment he infers that they are typological of Christian people.

38 A group of "four thousand" is mentioned three times in this paragraph and again in Para 14. The lecturer's source for this seems to be a Sahidic Coptic version of Rev 7:4 which translates to "And I heard the number of those who were sealed, fourteen ten thousands and four thousands out of every *tribe* of the sons of Israel." George William Horner, *The Coptic Version of the New Testament in the Southern Dialect Otherwise Called Sahidic and Thebaic*, Vol 7: The Catholic Epistles and the Apocalypse (Oxford: Clarendon, 1924), 335-37.

39 Interestingly four thousand divided by six tribes equals 666. Was this his way of expressing the imperfection of the Jewish law?

40 Cf. 1 Chron 23:6?

the body and blood of the Lamb? These [elders] are the ones who command them, who also sustain us so that we understand the perfection and purity of complete knowledge of ecclesiastical things. Understanding and wisdom come from the complete knowledge of the Lamb, who united his angels to men, so that the joy of their confession might be fulfilled.[41]

[11] **13** *Then,*[42] he said, *one of the elders responded, saying to me, "These in white robes, who are they and from where did they come?"* O great marvel and miracle![43] The citizens of heaven question those on earth about a profound concept. Indeed, man is an animal[44] which loves glory and which also loves power.

From where, he said, *did they come?* **14** *He answered saying, "Sir, you know." And he said to me: "These came out of the great tribulation, and have washed their robes and purified themselves in the blood of the Lamb."* What is this great tribulation if not the preoccupations of this life, full of upheavals, which all of us will leave to approach the throne of grace and wash our robes, even us, with the blood of the Lamb? That is, our souls which will leave this life and purify themselves for us through the One who purifies from every disease,[45] Jesus Christ. And we shall receive his body and his blood, which came out of his right side,[46] as salvation for the entire human race.

[12] And then he said: **15** *He who sits on the throne will shelter them.* **16** *Never again will they hunger; never again will they thirst, nor will the heat beat down on them,* **17** *but the Lamb, which is in the midst of the throne, will be their Shepherd.* And truly blessed are those who will be shepherded by the Lamb and those who will not be thirsty and hot anymore. For, how could they be thirsty if the spring of living water[47] is that which nourishes

41 Cf. Luke 12:8-9.

42 Orlandi (*Omelie copte*, 129, n. 13) wrote that the lack of comment on Rev 7:12 might indicate a lacuna.

43 Schmidt ("The Last Book," 213) translates this from the Coptic as "O great wonder and marvel!"

44 Italian *animale*. Or, perhaps "creature" or "beast."

45 Cf. Ps 103:3; Matt 9:35.

46 Cf. John 19:34.

47 Cf. Rev 7:17; John 4:10-11; 7:38.

them? Nor will they feel hot, for the *Sun of righteousness*[48] will be the one to enlighten them.

[13] He also said: *The Lamb, who is in the midst of the throne, will be their Shepherd; he will lead them to springs of the water of life and God will wipe away every tear from their eyes.* Blessed is the one whose tears God will wipe away from his eyes! And the one who will drink from that spring of living water will never thirst again.[49] Behold the One who spread out all his goods over the orthodox[50] and who is prepared to rule those who love him. And whoever wants help from the Son of God, let him abandon the wicked deeds of darkness and walk toward the light.[51] The one who wants to hear the trumpet of life has to stay firmly attached to the true life that comes from heaven.[52] Let us then be renewed by the word of truth.[53] In fact, John heard this and the Holy Spirit of God taught us this.

Revelation Chapter Eight

[14] I hear John again: **1** *When the seventh seal was opened there was silence in heaven for half an hour.* So how long did that silence last in heaven? So, did a tribunal take place or not? Did the face of everyone receive light from the bright light of the Lamb? What great unspeakable glory,[54] that a man of flesh heard the creation[55] in the firmament of heaven![56] God produced this great unspeakable glory, emitting his voice once so that those around him could shout until the twelve apparitions appear[57]

48 Mal 4:2.

49 Cf. John 4:14.

50 It is a way of saying the Son of God gave everything he had, even his own life, for his people.

51 Cf. Rom 13:12.

52 Cf. John 6:33.

53 Cf. James 1:18.

54 Cf. 1 Pet 1:8.

55 Italian *fondazione.*

56 The lecturer seems to associate this brief period of silence with the silence of God before the creation.

57 The vision of the twelve tribes in Rev 7:4-8.

and instantly produce thousands.[58] And the four thousand join in with these, and the peoples and tribes and languages[59] listen to what the Lamb did, and they bless God[60] who taught everyone the blessing which comes from heaven.

[15] **3** *Another angel*, besides the seven who were holding seven trumpets,[61] *came and stood on the altar, holding a golden censer in his hand. And they gave him incense, that he should offer it with the prayers of the saints at the golden altar which stood before the Lamb.* Let the priest be purified and he will become an angel of God. Let the people put their heart in God, and their prayer becomes incense on the altar, so that the angel of peace will kiss them on their lips and the perfume of the Spirit will come before the Lamb and will make them confident in the sight of God, being from that moment on without sin, without evil.

[16] **4** *And the smoke*, he says, *of the incense of the saints rises by the hands of the angels in the sight of God.* Contemplate and look at this mysterious thing that is revealed to us by John, who receives these mysteries, and find old and new things,[62] as God administers those things for us, teaching those things, one through the other. For, these angels and these priests, these people, this incense, this smoke, these prayers, these sacrifices will come to the altar of the Lamb from the mouth of the Christians.

[17] Then he said: **6** *And the seven angels who held the trumpets in their hand prepared to sound.* In what way did they prepare themselves? Who told them, "Get prepared!"? When did they get prepared? Of course, it was God who told them, "Get prepared!" They got prepared when Babylon the great raised its trumpet before it was humiliated[63] and before everyone received what was due him[64] from the hand of him who

58 The vision of the great multitude in Rev 7:9-10.

59 Cf. Rev 7:9.

60 Cf. Rev 7:10.

61 Cf. Rev 8:2. Orlandi (*Omelie copte*, 130) has this phrase as part of the lemma.

62 Cf. Matt 13:52.

63 Cf. Rev 18:2.

64 Cf. Rev 18:6-8.

lifts it, and before [the seven angels] repaid *everyone according to what he has done, both good and bad* (2 Cor 5:10). What did they sound [on their trumpets]? They sounded, "Do good and God will take away these evils from you." And after they had heard this, *they did not repent* (Rev 9:21).

[18] Look at what eventually happened because of those who sounded: **7** *The first started sounding, and there was thunder and lightning combined with blood, and it was sent to the earth, and a third part of the earth was burned.* Why did it burn? Because of the lust which is committed upon it by the sons of men.

8 *The second angel sounded, and a third part of the sea became blood,* **9** *and a third part of the living creatures in the sea died*—those [creatures] which humans seek as medicine—*and even the ships were destroyed.* Why did this happen? Because of those who deceive in business and who do not fear swearing by the name of God about what is false. Otherwise, what would be the evil of the fish and ships?

[19] **10** *And the third sounded, and a great star, blazing like a torch, fell from the sky, and came down on the springs and rivers,* **11** *and a third part of the waters became bitter. The name of the star is Ampsinthion,* that is, he who is terrible for some, but is bright for others. He who was punished in that moment is like fire among them. In fact, that star is onyx, according to the language of the Greeks. For, it is the joy of God when a man contemplates the things that will come upon him and repents and acts righteously before God.[65] In fact, at that time sin was grievous and God wanted to forgive their sins and their evil passions.

[20] **12** *The fourth angel sounded, and a third part of the sun was smitten, and a third part of the moon, and a third part of the stars, so that a third part of the day became dark, and a third part of the night.* So, there was no light left for men. Men sinned and all these evils came. In fact, the sun is a servant; the moon[66] is a servant; the stars are servants; man is a servant; and God is the One who created them. And if ruin comes upon only one servant, the others also sinned. But the God of all gave the celestial things

65 Cf. Luke 15:7, 10.

66 Corrected by Orlandi from *giorno* in *Omelie copte*, 132.

an arrangement outside of which nothing is able to stand. And so also the animals received the instinct that was given them.

[21] **13** *I looked,* he said, *and I heard an angel which was flying in the middle of the sky saying in a loud voice,* saying this: "*Woe three times*[67] *for those who dwell upon the earth.*" *(For, what will come)*[68] *from the rest of the angels who will sound?* "Woe," he said, "three times." Woe to the three ages of man, which [man] will spend wandering here and there without doing the will of the Lord in any of them, where the Lord would be merciful with him.

Revelation Chapter Nine

1 *I saw,* he said, *another star fall to the earth when the fifth angel sounded, and he was given the three keys to the pit of the abyss.*[69] What is the pit of the abyss, if not the place where there will be no visit for eternity, the place which all the sinners like me will inherit?

[22] Then he said: **3** *Locusts came into that place and were given power like scorpions of the earth have power.* **4** *And they were told to harm the fruits of the earth or all the trees, with the exception of only those people on whose forehead is the sign of the seal of God.* My dear ones, look at our fall and our ruin! Who are those locusts if not those to whom God gave the form of men and they changed it to the form of women, and grew hair as women would,[70] and chose for themselves their own shame? Those are the ones that the holy Apostle describes saying: *Those who change the character of their nature, going against their nature, were filled with love one for another, men with men, producing shame* (Rom 1:26-27). So, they prepared the pit of the abyss for themselves, but they will not go alone; they

67 This corresponds with the Sahidic translation of the Book of Revelation published by E. A. Wallis Budge (*Coptic Biblical Texts in the Dialect of Upper Egypt* [London: Oxford University Press, 1912], lxvii) which reads: "saying in a loud voice, Woe, three times" and that published by Horner (*Coptic Version of the New Testament*, 7:353) which reads: "saying in a great voice, Woe three times."

68 Orlandi (*Omelie copte*, 132) has this phrase in parentheses.

69 Corrected by Orlandi from *e gli diedero le chiavi del pozzo dell'abisso* in *Omelie copte*, 132.

70 Cf. Rev 9:8.

will drag others down with them.[71] So, woe to them seventy thousand times! And what is the power which was given to them if not the power of their tongue, to defame each other? They do not restrain themselves for God, nor for his priests who do his will.

[23] And he said: *They were told to harm the earth or its fruits or the trees with the exception of only those people upon whose forehead was the sign of the seal of God*, that is, those who received the seal of the blood of martyrdom and whose baptism purified the side of their body with all purity, those who are without envy, without hatred, without lust, those who did not beat, nor kill, nor defame, and who did not consign one another to death. These things and others similar to these go against the law and the law goes against them. Blessed are those who read[72] and understand, for that is the sign of the seal. Those are the ones to whom the Lamb sealed, who are the ones for whom the Lamb of God was sacrificed. Blessed are those who read and understand, for this is the place of patience. Blessed are those who read and understand that this is the salvation wherewith we received the seal, and we come to support one another in the fear of God. So, he who wishes to sin must know that he is far from the sign of the seal which is in Jesus Christ our Lord. Blessed, he said, are those who read and understand that the Lamb himself is the consubstantial One of the Father. He is the consubstantial One, whom the virgin bore, who marks each on his forehead with the sign of the seal. Blessed are those who read and understand that to the one who loves life[73] it will be granted, and to the one who loves death God will bring it upon him as he wished. For, his shepherd is king Death, called in Hebrew *Abbaton*.[74]

71 Cf. Rom 1:32. MacCoull ("Pierpont Morgan," 35-36) translates the comment: "Behold our fall and our destruction, O my beloved! What are these locusts which God adorned with the habit of maleness? They have changed to the habit of women; they have done their hair like women; they have chosen shamelessness with one another. These, again, are those whom the holy apostle has depicted for us, saying 'These are those who have changed the work/deeds of their nature for something against their nature.' They burned in their love for one another, males with males, doing the work of shamelessness. Again, these are those who prepared themselves for the pit of the abyss; and they do not go down alone: they take others with them."

72 Cf. Rev 1:3.

73 Cf. Ps 34:12.

74 Cf. Rev 9:11.

[24] And I can hear him after that: **13** *The sixth angel sounded, and I heard a voice from the horns of the altar, which is before God,* **14** *saying to the sixth angel who held the trumpet in hand: Release the four angels who are bound at the great river Euphrates.* **15** *And they were released, while every anger was ready to go according to the case or according to the occasion.* This is the evil that is destined to come at any hour and at any time. These, he said, are ready now, and in the days, and in the months, and in the year, to ruin a third part of mankind.

[25] And he said: **16** *The number of those* who went forth to ruin *amounted to two times ten thousand.*[75] Will these punishments perhaps happen to them, all in one way, and they will turn to repent?[76] God, in fact, brings to us this voice like this: "Know, O men, that the wrath is ready for those who sin not a single day or a month or a year, but at any moment the evil will come to him." And also, God does not punish anyone if his sins do not become great, and [if his sins do not] spring from him in all directions like horses ready for war.[77] And they count his sins and bring them to God,[78] sins being two times thousands of thousands, according to how the great John described them to us in the Apocalypse.

[26] **17** *They who ride on horses,* he said, *have breastplates the color of fire and of hyacinth,* that is, our sins, which are of different kinds, and which, even though we knew they were sins, we brought ourselves close to committing.

And he said: *The heads of the horses resembled those of lions, and out of their mouths came fire, smoke, and sulfur.* For that which will come out of

75 The Sahidic translation of the Book of Revelation published by Budge (*Coptic Biblical Texts*, lxvii) reads in English: "10000 X 10000 twice." The critical apparatus of George William Horner (*Coptic Version of the New Testament in the Southern Dialect, Otherwise Called Sahidic and Thebaic* [Oxford: Clarendon, 1911-1924], 7:362) confirms this: "ten th. of ten th. twice" and "two ten thousand of ten thousands they are."

76 The lecturer throughout these paragraphs on the trumpet blasts is hopeful that humans will repent, but this seems to be a rhetorical question expecting a negative answer, the one found in Rev 9:21: *Nor did they repent*... See Para 17 & 27.

77 Cf. Rev 9:17.

78 On angels bringing people's sins to God, see *The Apocalypse of Paul*, 7 in Edgar Hennecke, *New Testament Apocrypha*, 2 vols. Wilhlem Schneemelcher, ed.; R. McL. Wilson, trans. (Philadelphia: Westminster, 1965), 2:761: "For at that hour [i.e. sunset] all the angels go to the Lord to worship him and bring before him all the deeds of men, whether good or evil, which each of them does from morning until evening."

the mouth, we shall certainly render an account to God,[79] since **19** *their power was in their mouths and in their tails. In fact, their tails were like those of serpents having heads, and with them they inflict injury* upon men.

[27] **20** *The rest,* he said, *of mankind, who did not repent from these plagues, still did not repent of their actions, so as to cease from worshipping demons of gold, and of silver, and of wood, and of stone, which cannot see or feel or understand or walk or speak.* **21** *Nor did they repent of their murders, and of their wickedness, and of their lust.* And these sins come one after another, and we did not disregard any of them, nor did we find one before another. And the Holy Spirit showed all of these to the great John, so that they might recognize them and abstain from sin. But they did not repent from all these. And during that time Satan, *the serpent of old*[80] boasted about this: "Behold, I found what I was looking for. I dragged everyone in my nets, and I hit them, and no one can heal them. I kidnapped them and no one will save them from my hands." But God, merciful and pitiful, after he had seen our great misery, received our prayer, and turned the old into a new man.[81] And he wanted to take back to himself those who had been made prisoners,[82] so that they might repent and be attracted to him by the nets of his love toward mankind.

Revelation Chapter Ten

[28] Then he said: **1** *I looked and behold, another angel coming down from heaven, having great force. And a cloud clothed him, having a crown upon his head. And his face was as the sun and his feet looked like fiery pillars.* **2** *And I saw an open book in his hand, and he placed his right foot in the sea and his left on the shore.* **3** *And he shouted with a loud voice like a lion. When he shouted, the seven thunders thundered in their language.* [The thunders] spoke and what did they say? They said: "Those who will sin against the Son of God

79 Cf. Matt 12:36.

80 Cf. Rev 12:9.

81 Cf. 2 Cor 5:17; Eph 4:22-24; Col 3:9-10.

82 Cf. 2 Tim 2:26; Eph 4:8.

should be aware that they will perish, and the worm and fire of Gehenna[83] will inherit them." May all the tribes which committed evil against the Son of God mourn over themselves[84] and see him coming down having with him the light of his divinity; and his face will shine ten thousand times brighter than the sun. Let those who crucified him come and know that he is the *King of kings*[85], holding his testament in hand. And he will do according to what he said to the patriarchs. And he will be merciful with those whom he will want to be merciful;[86] and he will forgive those whom he will forgive, and will demonstrate great power by means of his strong arm, the Savior,[87] for those who hoped in his holy name. In fact, we heard that the seven churches of the seven cities[88] united with the five or seven churches,[89] so that the Holy Spirit might come upon the apostles of our Lord Jesus Christ, to which [apostles] he also made representation in the twelve tribes of the sons of Israel, in front of which the twenty thousand and four thousand[90] stood. And we put forth the four thousand[91] plus the five thousand who ate the five loaves of bread.[92] And the total is nine thousand in addition to those two thousand.[93] And from those the knowledge of grace was magnified among them. And we know the example of the necessary decision, which is that the one thousand and the ten

83 Cf. Mark 9:47-48; Isa 66:24.

84 Cf. Rev 1:7; Matt 24:30; Zech 12:10-14.

85 Rev 19:16.

86 Cf. Ex 33:19; Rom 9:15.

87 Cf. Isa 51:5; 52:10; 53:1; John 12:38.

88 Cf. Rev 1:11: Ephesus, Smyrna, Pergamum, Thyatira, Sardis, Philadelphia, and Laodicea.

89 Perhaps the seven churches to which the apostle Paul wrote, as stated in the Muratorian fragment. These are the churches of the Corinthians, Ephesians, Philippians, Colossians, Galatians, Thessalonians, and Romans. See Francis X. Gumerlock, *Revelation and the First Century* (Powder Springs, GA: American Vision, 2012), 40. If the "five" churches refer to the time of the lecturer, perhaps he refers to the five major "sees" of Rome, Constantinople, Antioch, Jerusalem, and Alexandria.

90 Cf. 1 Chron 23:4? For this group of four thousand, see Para 9 & 14.

91 Cf. Matt 15:38; 16:10.

92 Cf. Matt 14:17-21; 16:9.

93 Corrected by Orlandi to "two thousand" from *ventimila* in *Omelie copte*, 135.

thousand[94] will come to lift each other up, and will be placed in this same order, and will prostrate themselves before this same God Jesus Christ who created heaven and earth, and the same number from the number of Jericho will come.[95] They too [will come], whose meeting[96] was holy by means of a woman,[97] giving us the sign of the chosen order.

[29] **4** *I heard,* he said, *a voice which said to me: Seal up what the seven thunders said and do not write it down.* O Holy Spirit, for how long do you wish to seal up these words? Until those who despise the image of God will be ashamed and will turn back, and the light of his saints will appear, and they will proclaim his power and say, "We have known the place of love and patience. And we have known that the Lord listens to his saints; and he wants to give them eternal love and inheritance, so that those who carry the sign of Satan, and those who know both him and his evils, will not mock them."

[30] **5** *And the angel,* he said, *which I had seen on the sea, raised his hand to heaven.* **6** *And he swore by him who lives forever and ever, who created the heavens and all that is in them, the earth and all that is in it [saying]: Time will not be any more.*[98] **7** *But from the voice of the seventh angel, when*

---

94 Cf. Deut 33:2?

95 Possibly 345 in number as stated in Ezra 2:34 and Neh 7:36. Perhaps the lecturer sees the number twelve in it, since 3+4+5=12. For, just a few sentences above he mentioned the seven plus five (=12) churches, the twelve apostles, and the twelve tribes.

96 Italian *riunione*.

97 The woman is most likely Mary. See Para 23 & 41. I am not sure if the lecturer is referring to the meeting in the Upper Room where Mary was present (Cf. Acts 1:13-14), or the tradition of the falling asleep of Mary in which the twelve apostles were reunited and many others were gathered to witness Mary's dormition. I tend to lean toward this latter interpretation. For this tradition, see the various versions of the *Six Books* in Stephen J. Shoemaker, *Ancient Traditions of the Virgin Mary's Dormition and Assumption* (Oxford, UK: Oxford University Press, 2002), 370, 381, and the many homilies on the dormition of Mary in Brian E. Daley, *On the Dormition of Mary: Early Patristic Homilies* (Crestwood, NY: St Vladimir's Seminary Press, 1998), 71, 130, 174, 194, 210, 235, 252. If the lecturer is referring to sixth-century events, perhaps the woman is the empress Theodora, who sympathized with non-Chalcedonians and arranged for the ordination of Sergius of Tella and Theodore of Bostra, non-Chalcedonians, who in turn ordained many non-Chalcedonian bishops and priests throughout the East. See Samuel, *The Council of Chalcedon Re-Examined*, 177.

98 Italian *nessun altro tempo vi sarà* or "There will be no other time." This matches the Sahidic Coptic which says literally "there is not other time any more will be." See apparatus in Horner, *Coptic Version of the New Testament*, 7:371.

he sounds, the mystery of God will be completed, just as he announced to his servants the prophets. What then is "the mystery, just as he announced to his servants the prophets," if not the mystery which is three mysteries which he united to each other and placed together for us? These are the three orders of the Church of Christ, the mystery of the economy of holy baptism, the appearance of holy baptism, and the resurrection which gives life. In fact, the appearance of the body and blood of Christ is truly life[99] in every way. These are the words of redemption which were placed before us so that we might meditate upon them.

[31] And so he said: **8** *The voice which I had heard speaking with me said to me: Go and take the book that lies open in the hand of the angel.* They teach a mystery, greater than [any] mystery, to John the mystic. A bright person is one who will clearly see the Scriptures inspired by God.[100] In fact, this is a book of redemption, and also a book of value. And it is not possible for anyone to take this book and meditate upon it, except the one who will purify his own body[101] and will become a seal like John, whom Jesus loves for his purity. In fact, he is the one whose virginity[102] condemns the spirits of evil which exist under the heavens. He who desires to take that book from the hand of the angel should know that if they do not purify themselves and they do not eat it, they will not come to know its sweetness and its bitterness;[103] and they will not distinguish the one from

99 Cf. John 6:33, 35, 48, 51, 53-54.

100 Cf. 2 Tim 3:16.

101 Schmidt ("The Last Book," 202) translates this from the Coptic: "it is impossible for someone to obtain this book and meditate upon it except for those who will purify their own body."

102 Belief in John's virginity is expressed in many other texts of late antiquity including a Coptic work entitled *The Mysteries of Saint John the Apostle the Holy Virgin* (in Budge, ed., *Coptic Apocrypha in the Dialect of Upper Egypt* [London: Oxford University Press, 1913]), the earliest Greek narrative on the dormition of Mary in Shoemaker, *Ancient Traditions of the Virgin Mary's Dormition and Assumption*, 359; Jerome, *Against Jovinian*, 1.26 (NPNF, 2nd series 6:365); *Epistle* 55.5 (PL 22:564-65; NPNF, 2nd series 6:112); a Latin preface to the Apocalypse translated in Gumerlock, "Chromatius of Aquileia on John 21:22 and Rev. 10:11 Against a Legend about the Apostle John" in Ian Boxall and Richard Tresley, eds., *The Book of Revelation and Its Interpreters: Short Studies and an Annotated Bibliography* (Boulder, CO: Rowan and Littlefield, 2016), 61; Arator, *On the Acts of the Apostles*, 1.624-625; and a Latin *Assumption of Mary* mentioned in R. Alan Culpepper, *John, the Son of Zebedee: The Life of a Legend* (Edinburgh: T & T Clark, 2000), 234.

103 Cf. Rev 10:9-10.

the other, and they will not know that which they should, and they will bring bitterness on the death of the flesh, and life on the life of the soul.

Revelation Chapter Eleven

[32] And also he said: **1** *They gave me a reed which looked like a rod, saying: Arise and measure the temple of God and the altar*. In fact, all of them worship only one person,[104] and they prostrate to one God only.[105] For, the law and the lawyer will come from the temple of the Lord and the altar, and it is one spirit alone that they share. And the priest and the Levite and the sacrifice and the altar all come from the same God; and they will go back to him when they will come to find the sacrifice and the offer he promised them, saying: "*I will grant* you those" (Rev 11:3). The Holy Spirit said this through the mouth of David: *May our prayers be an abundant chant*.

2 *And the courtyard which stands outside the temple, leave it out and do not measure it, because it was given to the nations*. What people are the Hebrews, if not those who fulfill the will of the Lord? Accordingly, he said: *He is received in every people that will do righteousness* (Acts 10:35). And he is also the One who said: *There are many mansions in the house of my Father* (John 14:2). In fact, these are the celestial mansions full of the glory of God.

[33] *They will trample*, he said, *on the holy city for forty-two months*. Which one is the holy city, and what are the forty-two months? O city of Zion, raise your power! *Behold, your Savior comes to you* (Isa 62:11). And he came. It is he who orders numbers, counts the months, and brings them to five hundred Sabbaths. And their number [is] in addition to the seven and a half weeks,[106] which are subtracted from their number, according to the **3** *twelve hundred and sixty days* plus sixty. These, doubled

104 That is, the Incarnate Word who is one person with one nature. According to Miaphysites, there cannot be two natures in Christ, as Chalcedonians see Christ, without having two persons.

105 This is probably another statement in refutation of tritheists who flourished in the 560s in Miaphysite communities. See footnote on Para 7 and the Introduction.

106 Cf. Dan 9:25, 27.

twice, come to six hundred and thirty, which add to their number more than two years and three weeks. And we also add an extra week for Holy Easter, and we bring to them the knowledge of the nature of those whom we have just named.[107] And those who will do this computation will need to be *clothed in sackcloth* and to *prophesy*. And they will understand what is needed. He who puts on sackcloth is seeking repentance for his sins; he who seeks repentance seeks to please God; he who seeks to please God avoids punishment. In fact, we know that lustful and adulterous men, and those who commit evil deeds, will not be able to save themselves from the punishments which God established, which are terrible for the sons of men. He who wants to inherit these things will not have them[108] stolen from him. These are the flames of evil, which the prophet announced to us, so that they will not strike our bodies[109] and make our soul distant from God. And these are the things through which we have been robbed. But let us try to understand those whose minds were [given] knowledge and teaching. Those prophets thought about the problem; and you see how the Holy Spirit informed and still informs them.

[34] **5** *Whoever wants to harm them,* he says, *fire will come from their mouths and devour their enemies.*[110] *Whoever wants to harm them will die,* **6** *those who have the power to make it not rain on earth for all the days of their prophecy.*[111] Who will not be amazed at the mouth of the son of men who speaks and the whole firmament listens? *And they have power to turn the waters into blood and to strike the earth with every kind of plague that he wants.* 7 *And when they have finished their testimony, the beast which comes up from the abyss will make war with them.* Who is the beast other than the one whom God defeated,[112] sending him down into the eternal abyss with

107 Perhaps "those who carry the sign of Satan" mentioned in Para 29.

108 That is, virginity and purity. See Para 31.

109 Cf. Dan 3:27.

110 Orlandi corrected this to "enemies" from *teste* in *Omelie copte*, 138.

111 Orlandi's translation (*Omelie copte*, 138) has Rev 11:6 here as commentary rather than part of the biblical text.

112 MacCoull ("Pierpont Morgan," 36) translates it: "What, then, is the beast? The one whom God trod underfoot."

his companions? He will approach many, so that they will fight against the servants of the Lord,[113] and oppose them, and they will shed blood around the great city of Jerusalem.[114] But then God will give strength to his people, and they will be encouraged by the great power of the Lord, and will hunt and chase away the wicked. And *one* alone *will put a thousand to flight, and two will* fight against *ten thousand* (Deut 32:30). And they will defeat the enemy in twenty-eight weeks, and one hundred and three days will pass before he will see the light. And five more weeks will show what they did.

[35] So he said: **7** *The beast will overpower and kill them,* with the permission[115] of God. **8** *And their bodies will remain scattered in the public squares of the great city, Sodom, which is spiritually so called, and Egypt, where also the Lord was crucified.* **9** *And [some] from every people and tribe and language and nation will see the slain for three and a half days, and no one will bury their bodies in tombs.* **10** *And those who live on earth will see and rejoice and be happy and will bring gifts to one another, because these two prophets were slain, those who had tormented those who live on the earth.* Did you see, beloved, that God is patient for some time, and then he lifts up his power for some days and shows everyone that he is the only true God, and that no one is like him[116] in exerting his power and his miracles for us at the right time?[117] Furthermore, [he does this] so that the antichrists will not think about other insults or ways [of persecuting the saints].

[36] Listen to great John saying: **11** *After three and a half days the spirit of life came and entered them, and great fear fell upon them. And those who saw them were frightened.* And what is this other fear and this other

113 MacCoull ("Pierpont Morgan," 36) translates it: "He will give his woe to a multitude who will fight with the servants of the Lord."

114 Cf. Rev 11:7-8.

115 Italian *l'accordo* or "agreement."

116 Cf. Jer 10:6.

117 In the phrase "miracles for us at the right time" does the lecturer have in mind the missionary activity of the non-Chalcedonian Jacob Baradeus, who over three decades in the sixth-century (542-577) ordained many non-Chalcedonian bishops and priests and allegedly performed miracles?

tremor, that men should rise after they die and go to their relatives[118] and stand freely in front of those who see them? O miracle of the living God! O knowledge of the true God! Who then is the God who can do that? Shame on those who have doubt concerning the resurrection of the Savior![119] And we confess that Jesus Christ was crucified and died for our sins, and on the third day he rose again from the dead. He ascended into heaven, and sat at the right hand of his Father. And then he will come again to judge the living and the dead, and to judge *each according to what he has done* (Rom 2:6), both the good and the wicked, so that all peoples and tribes and every language[120] will know that he is the one who was crucified before the ages.[121]

[37] Then John the theologian said: **12** *And they went up to heaven in a cloud, while their enemies looked on.* O Enoch and Elijah, a bright cloud rose for your glory! But let us see what happened on that day.

13 *There was a severe earthquake and seven thousand people both fell and died.* You have seen how many God punishes for his saints, those who pleased God day and night.[122] A great solid city was destroyed like wax, because in it they tempted those who obeyed and served him, so that all the crowds recognized God;[123] and David the prophet came in the midst with his harp and said: *Who is God but our God, and who is the Lord other than our Lord?* (Ps 18:31)

118 Cf. 1 Kings 17:23; Acts 9:41.

119 Cf. Rev 13:8. MacCoull ("Pierpont Morgan," 37) translates this creedal statement from the Coptic as follows: "Let those who separated themselves from the resurrection of the Saviour [sic] be ashamed. But we, we confess that Jesus Christ was crucified, and died for our sins; and he rose from the dead on the third day, he went into heaven, he sat down on the right hand of his Father, and thus he will come to judge the living and the dead, and to judge one by one according to what they have done, whether good or evil, until every people and tribe and language knows that this is the Crucified."

120 Cf. Rev 11:9.

121 Cf. Rev 13:8.

122 Cf. Rev 7:15. In this sentence, it may be that the lecturer is simply commenting on the earthquake in the biblical passage. However, it could be a veiled reference to the earthquake in Antioch in 526 which killed an estimated 250 thousand people including an infamous enemy of non-Chalcedonians, Euphrasius. In the 520s Euphrasius waged a persecution against anti-Chalcedonians and according to Pauline Allen and C. T. R. Hayward (*Severus of Antioch* [New York: Routledge, 2004], 27) "perished in the great earthquake in Antioch in 526."

123 Cf. Rev 11:13.

[38] *The rest of those* who were not killed *were terrified and glorified the god of heaven.*[124] In fact, *the gods who did not create heaven and earth, let them perish from the earth* (Jer 10:11), for *they are not gods* (Jer 16:20).

And behold, thus **14** *the second woe is fulfilled*, according to that which the Holy Spirit told our father John. In fact, with the other punishments the impious men finally recognize the fear, terror, and tremor that will follow, until the great city,[125] full of every trade of earth,[126] will become deserted[127] and the enemies of God will perish at their own hands, and also the sons of the sons of their sons; for their end is ruin. They will come out of one lament and enter into a worse lament, one more difficult to bear.

[39] After that he said: **15** *And the seventh angel sounded, and there were loud voices which said: The kingdom of the world has become that of our Lord and of his Christ; and he will reign forever and ever.* O John, wise in the things of God, did the kingdom of God become God's only that day? Before heaven and earth and what is in heaven and what is on earth existed, he is God and King and Savior with his Son, Jesus Christ our Lord and with the Holy Spirit. "I know it well," he says, "and I also taught you the truth of all this." But while God allows the enemy freedom, so that his elect might be revealed,[128] he left room for the enemy and his acolytes, letting them do whatsoever they wanted,[129] insomuch as the prophets were killed and the legislators stoned, and even the great name of God was mocked, so that many people said in their folly: "The kingdom of God has become that of the animal[130] forever." And after this, God humbled the impious man, and that man recognized that his renown became

124 Although in the previous paragraph the lecturer says that they recognized God, from his comment on this passage, here he may understand the passage as saying that they glorified a false god of the heavens.

125 Cf. Rev 17:18; 18:10, 16, 18-19, 21.

126 Cf. Rev 18:12-13.

127 Cf. Rev 17:16; 18:22-23.

128 Cf. 1 Cor 11:19.

129 Cf. 2 Tim 2:26.

130 Italian: *dell'animale*. This could refer to the kingdom of man. In Para 11 the lecturer called man an *animal* which loves glory and power. Or it could refer to the kingdom of the beast, a reference back to Rev 11:7.

wicked before all and that those who had joined with the wicked one realized that they had walked in his territory. Then they will see the servants of God glorified and the servants of the enemy put to shame.[131]

[40] Then everyone will shout: *The kingdom of the world has become that of the Lord and of his Christ forever and ever.* God established a glorious throne for his elect. God made his servants secure, and with peace received those who know mercy. Those who walked with the wicked, their power ceased in their body.[132] They placed their hope in a servant's spirit,[133] and it was an evil spirit that breathed in their mouth. And if they turn and will recognize their ruin, then they will turn and call on the name of the Lord, but the Lord will not listen.[134] But they will hear that terrible voice, "He who is ignorant is ignorant of him."[135] In fact, woe to them, for they are not sealed on their forehead with the sign of the seal, the one which the Lamb granted to us. In fact, it was not our virtues which granted it to us, but his great love.

131 MacCoull ("Pierpont Morgan," 36) translates this, saying that "those who adhered to the enemy will regret that they walked in his ways. Then they will see the servants of God being glorified and the servants of the enemy being ashamed."

132 Cf. Ps 9:6.

133 That is, they placed their hope in a creature, i.e. a servant, or perhaps in human strength. For a discussion of humans and other created things as God's servants, see Para 20.

134 This seems unlike the teaching of the lecturer, who throughout the *Encomium* encourages repentance and preaches that God is merciful to forgive and receive the penitent. Perhaps, based on an interpretation that Rev 11:15 refers to the Last Judgment, he is teaching that at the Last Judgment it will be too late for sinners to repent and become part of God's sealed people.

135 Cf. Matt 7:23.

Revelation Chapter Twelve

[41] And again after that, and after the adoration and confession of the elders,[136] and after there were *voices and peals of thunder* (Rev 11:19) and afflictions and great peals of thunder, **1** *a great sign appeared in heaven*. Next, let us see what the sign was: *A woman, clothed with the sun, having the moon under her feet, and having twelve stars as a crown on her head,* **2** *being pregnant and being in labor* but without pain,[137] *cried out to give birth*. What woman is this other than the one whose name we said a while ago?[138] In fact, she knows her sons who come from her. She purified the ones who surround us, having appeared to receive the mediator between us and the Lord of all,[139] the One by which the whole world is enlightened,[140] according to the testimony of the twelve stars, among which are the sun and the moon and the stars with their energy, (a testimony) of the mystery that appeared. From these, their voices came equally among them, as the rest of the stars. I call the apostles "stars." In fact, they truly are stars, whose light extends over the whole earth.

Therefore, we can now understand this woman. In fact, she does not need us to say her name with our mouth. Everyone knows her, and all the names we could not even think about will suit her, like "city," or "appointed time," or "virgin," or "security," or "nurse," or "mother," or "stage," or "place of rest," or "place of light," or "*Menabon*,"[141] or "mother of Christ," or "pure treasure." In fact, she is the *theotokos*,[142] holy Mary, who generated

136 Cf. Rev 11:16-18.

137 On the tradition that Mary gave birth without pain, see Gregory of Nyssa, *Against Eunomius*, Hom. 2 (PG 45:492).

138 In Para 3 & 10.

139 Cf. 1 Tim 2:5.

140 Cf. John 1:9.

141 A Greek name which was not understood by Orlandi. Perhaps "nurturer."

142 "God-bearer" or "Mother of God," a term applied to Mary with the canonical authority of the Ecumenical Council of Ephesus in 431.

the greatest light of all the earth,[143] our Lord Jesus Christ and our God, our Savior.[144]

42. And then he said: **3** *Another sign appeared in heaven, a great fiery dragon with seven heads and ten horns. And there were seven diadems upon its horns.* And he said: **4** *He drew under his tail the twelve stars and hurled them to the earth. And the dragon stood in front of the woman so that when he would see her give birth, he would devour her son.* **5** *And she bore a male son, who will shepherd all the people with a rod of iron.* But [God] did not allow it[145]; for it was not yet the time for him to hang upon the cross to be crucified for our kind, so that we were safe and the people admired us. But [the dragon] is the one who insidiously abused our kind with many, and made them his members. And after they came to know that there was no possibility of harming [Christ], all the nations followed [Christ]. And he shepherded them with an iron rod. And no harm will come to him; for he is the Son of God. Therefore, then they *snatched him up to God*; for he comes from God and he is his Only-begotten.

[43] And then he said: *To his throne.* **6** *The woman fled to the desert into a place prepared for her by God, where she might be nourished for 1260 days.* These 1260 days make up three primitive weeks, which he picked among them, producing them. And the ten thousand thrones and the

143 Cf. John 8:12.

144 MacCoull ("Pierpont Morgan," 37) translates the paragraph from the Coptic as follows: "Therefore let us now understand this woman, for there is no need to put her aside in our mouth: for everyone knows her, and every name comes from her. Who does not conceive of her as city (*polis*), or *prothesmia* (appointed time), or virgin, or birth, or midwife (MECIW), or mother, or MONH (*mansio*) or place of rest or place of light or (nurturer?), or mother of Christ or pure treasure. For she is the Mother of God, holy Mary, who gave birth to the great light of the whole *oikoumene*, our Lord Jesus Christ, our God and our Saviour [sic]." Schmidt (*The Last Book*, 174), translates the last sentence from the Coptic: "She is the Theotokos, holy Mary, who gave birth to the greatest light of all the universe, our Lord Jesus Christ and our God, our Savior."

145 God did not allow the Christ child to be devoured.

numbers,[146] and the place where the virgin went, no man made of flesh knows it up to now.[147]

[44] Then he said: **7** *There was a war in heaven. Michael and his angels fought against the dragon.* And the dragon is Satan and his angels, demons,[148] who were shamefully driven out of heaven for doing evil with their father, the devil.[149] **8** In fact, they did not have power and did not find a place for themselves in heaven.[150] **9** Therefore, he is *the ancient serpent,* ancient in his malignity and wicked perfidy, ancient in his destruction, the one from which all evil came, the one through which all evil was produced, the one who descended upon the earth.

[45] After that he said: **10** *I heard a loud voice from heaven say to me: Look at what happened. In fact, now has come the salvation and the power and the kingdom of God.* Here Michael fights and wins. Did perhaps a war arise against the archangel? Had he perhaps had a need to attack in battle? No, never. But the enemy, after rebelling, wanted to capture the whole of mankind. So, Michael fought with him. In fact, Michael the archangel always fights for the whole of mankind, helping it, being for

146 On the lecturer's interpretation of the number of 42 months, see Para 33. On his interpretation elsewhere of the number of 1260 days, see Para 48. Here the lecturer seems to view the 1260 days as a figure of synecdoche, a part designated the whole time between Mary's assumption, which is presumed but not stated definitively, and the Second Coming of Christ.

147 MacCoull ("Pierpont Morgan," 37) translates the last phrase: "The place to which the virgin fled, no man of flesh knows it up until now." The hesitancy on the part of the lecturer to definitely claim where the virgin went is reminiscent of Epiphanius's caution in *Panarion,*78.23.9 (PG 42:715-716), written in the 370s: "The holy virgin may have died and been buried—her falling asleep was with honor, her death in purity, her crown in virginity. Or she may have been put to death-as the scripture says, 'And a sword shall pierce through her soul'-her fame is among the martyrs and her holy body, by which light rose on the world, [rests] amid blessings. Or she may have remained alive, for God is not incapable of doing whatever he wills. No one knows her end." Translation from Shoemaker, *Ancient Traditions of the Virgin Mary's Dormition and Assumption,* 14. See also pseudo-Jerome, *Epistle to Paula et Eustochius,* 9.2 (PL 30:127-28): "Many of us are in doubt as to whether she [Mary] was taken up together with her body or died, her body left behind...Since nothing is impossible for the Lord, we do not deny that it [her assumption to heaven in body and soul] happened to Mary although, being cautious, with belief conserved, it is important to think with pious desire rather than, ill-advised, to define, without peril, what is not known." Translation from Priscilla Throop, trans., *Yes and No: The Complete English translation of Peter Abelard's Sic et Non,* 2nd ed. (Charlotte, VT: MedievalMS, 2008), 214-15.

148 Orlandi's translation (*Omelie copte,* 142) has "and his angels, demons" as part of the biblical text.

149 Cf. John 8:44.

150 This is a paraphrase of Rev 12:8.

them a defender before God who created us. Therefore, blessed is he who will die clean of the violence of that dragon. A great evil happened to us, my beloved, since the wicked enemy, the enemy of truth, was driven down near to us. But let us drive away from us his wicked actions, so that he will not drag us down into destruction with him.

[46] And let us see what one from heaven said. In fact, they say that after [Michael and his angels] drove the wicked down, they drove down *the accuser of the brethren, the one who accuses the brethren before God*. If he accuses the incorporeal, who do not fall [into sin] at all, how much greater will the accusation be against us, we with whom every malady of passion surrounds our soul and our body? May it never be that his blows strike us and make us fall!

And some of you say, "Why then does God let the evil one tempt us beyond our power?" I will say to them: "If God did not let the evil one attack us this way, how and in which way could the righteous receive their rewards? And also, how could the devil be punished, together with those who walk in his wicked actions? And also, if neither the righteous nor sinners were made manifest,[151] whom would God judge on the day of true judgment?[152] And how would the resurrection be fulfilled? Lastly, who could say that God's judgments are not fair judgments?[153] In fact, *God is light* (1 John 1:5), and all the things of God are light.

[47] Therefore, he taught us his blessed illumination: **13** *After the dragon saw that he had been hurled upon the earth, he ran to the woman who had given birth to her firstborn male.* **14** *And the woman was given two wings of a bird.* Which woman is that, other than the holy Virgin Mary, who gave birth to the only-begotten of the Father? Which wings are those,

151 Cf. 1 Cor 11:19.

152 This answer is similar to Tyconius's comment on Rev 2:24 (FC 134:52) in answer to the question of why God allows relentless attacks of Satan. His answer was: "Otherwise, for what reason does the Lord threaten and teach that evil doers receive punishments appropriate to their evils? Or how would the righteous become more praiseworthy, if they overcame something they did not hear or see?"

153 Cf. Rom 9:14, 19-20.

other than the New and Old Testament?[154] Which Paraclete[155] is that, other than the Holy Spirit who is ready to come upon the waters,[156] *so that she might fly to the desert, the place where she would be nourished for a time, for times, and for half a time?* And what is the desert other than the place where they crucified the Son of God?[157]

[48] Grace and virginity left the synagogue of the Jews; and they came to us, to the holy church. And it received the sacrifices of the blessed bishops and their prayers and offerings; and it nourished itself with those. And [it received] the perfume of the altar, and the hymns of the saints, until the "time" was fulfilled. And then the martyrs gave their body to the fire and to another great number of tortures until their bodies filled the whole world, and another "time" was fulfilled. And then the martyrs went to God. And after that, a false peace will begin to exist in the middle of a time, so that everyone *will say*, "This is the time of *peace." After that, sudden destruction will come* (1 Thess 5:3), until the 1260 days will fulfill the number of the fourteen weeks and other three, which remain in the five.[158] These will fulfill the two and three and a half days, coming to the number in the fulfillment of "times," which are included in the words spoken by the seven thunders, about which they said to our father John: *Seal up what the seven thunders said and do not write it down* (Rev 10:4).

154 This interpretation of the two wings as the Testaments is in the seventh-century Greek *Commentary on the Apocalypse* by Andrew of Caesarea. FC 123:145.

155 Cf. John 14:16, 26. The bird in Rev 12:14 is associated with the Holy Spirit, who is associated with a dove in Matt 3:16; Mark 1:10; and Luke 3:22.

156 Cf. Gen 1:2.

157 Golgatha, where Mary witnessed the crucifixion. Cf. John 19:25-29.

158 The author interpreted the first "time" of Rev 12:14 as the time of the establishment of the church, when the church replaced the Jews as the people of God. Another "time" was that of the persecutions of the second and third centuries. The "half a time" the lecturer associates with the time of peace in 1 Thess 5:3, perhaps the time after Diocletian persecution and the cessation of persecution under Constantine. The destruction that would soon come, he seems to refer to the teaching of the Council of Chalcedon. If he viewed a week as seven years (a week of years), the nineteen weeks (fourteen and five) in his comment equal 126 years, the exact time between the Council of Nicaea (325) and the Council of Chalcedon (451). Many Coptic Christians of Egypt favored the teaching that Christ has one nature (Miaphysitism) and rejected the teachings of Chalcedon that Christ has two natures, human and divine, because of their suspicions that such teaching was the same as or similar to what the Nestorians allegedly taught, that there were two persons in Christ.

[49] And after that he said: **15** *And the serpent sent out from his mouth water like a river upon the woman, so that she might be submerged.* Look carefully at the great power of God, how the power of the dragon is not enough to fight with him, nor do his flames burn those who hope in his name. **16** *But the earth swallowed the water,* he said, *which came from the mouth of that dragon.* **17** *And the dragon was enraged at the woman and went off to wage a war against the rest of her offspring, those who observe the commandments of God and maintain the testimony of Jesus* the Christ, our Lord, until we pass from this life, which is full of every evil.[159]

Conclusion

[50] But I see that the greater part of you criticizes my insufficiency[160] saying, "Now the time has come for us [to be dismissed]. Therefore, give us peace so that we might go where we have to go." In fact, I came among you as a friend or a brother. I then pray that you know that as soon as God gives us another tranquil time,[161] you will come to learn what comes after that [in the Apocalypse].

[Revelation Chapter Thirteen]

1 And you will know what the *beast* is which he saw rising *from the sea with ten horns*[162] and *seven heads,* with a *blasphemous name* written *on the heads,* **2** *and similar to a leopard.* **11-12** And also, you will learn about the *beast,* similar to the *first beast,* with *two horns.* **18** For, in that *is the place of wisdom.*

159 Cf. Job 14:1.

160 He may be referring to his insufficiency to finish in a timely manner, or perhaps it is simply an expression of humility.

161 A time when the monks are freed from their duties.

162 Corrected by Orlandi from *code* in *Omelie copte,* 144.

[Revelation Chapter Fourteen]

1 And also [you will learn about] *the Lamb* who was standing on the hill of *Zion*, **2** and the voice that he heard similar to a harp, **3** singing a new sound *before the throne* of God *and the four living creatures*.[163]

[51] **6** And also [you will learn about] the *gospel* that was in the hand of the *angel* who was preaching an *eternal* peace: **7** *Fear* the Lord *God; for the moment of his judgment has come*. **8** And also [you will learn about] the *other angel*, the second one, *saying*: the great *Babylon has fallen*. **9** And [you will learn about] the other angel announcing the worship of the beast or its image; **13** and [you will learn about] what he says: *Blessed* will be those who will die *from now on in* the name of *the Lord*. **14** And [you will learn about] the fiery *cloud* which he saw, on which was a *man* of light. **17** And [you will learn about] *another angel* who *came out of the temple* of the Lord. **18** And [you will learn about] he who is coming *out of the altar* and about the borderline of the *sea of glass* (Rev 15:2).[164]

[52] Then finally, when we know the solution to these three other issues,[165] the Spirit of God will give us permission to return to our homes, and will give us an appointed time, and will teach us the rest[166] through the grace of our Lord Jesus Christ, to whom all glory is due, with his good Father and the Holy Spirit, who gives life and is consubstantial, now and forever, throughout all the ages. Amen.

163 MacCoull ("Pierpont Morgan," 38) translates some of this paragraph as follows: "So that you may know what is the beast which he (John) saw coming out of the sea, having ten horns and seven heads, with a name written upon his heads...and the (other) beast...and the voice like a kithara...and the four living creatures..."

164 MacCoull ("Pierpont Morgan," 38) translates some of this paragraph as follows: "...and the gospel in the hand of the angel...and the other angel saying 'Fallen, fallen is Babylon the great'...and those saying 'Blessed are those who die from henceforth in the name of the Lord' (a textual variant), and the white cloud which he saw with the man of light upon it,...and the sea of glass."

165 He seems to be referring to issues in the text upon which he will teach next time they meet. These are probably the visions of the beasts (Rev 13:1-18), of the Lamb (Rev 14:1-5), and of the angels (Rev 14:6-15:4).

166 MacCoull ("Pierpont Morgan," 38) translated a portion of the sentence as follows: "the Spirit of God will give us a CYrrNWMH so we can go away into our house, and he will give us an appointed time and inform us about the rest."

PART

3

Transcription of the Commentary

by Tito Orlandi

Introduction

Clavis Coptica #0107: Homily *In Apocalypsin*, attributed to Cyril, archbishop of Alexandria (412-444), from the manuscript New York, The Morgan Library & Museum, Department: Medieval and Renaissance Manuscripts, MS M.591 foll. 11-49, written in the year 861 for the monastery of St. Michael the Archangel of Alli in the Fayum (cf. the colophon in Van Lantschoot *Colophons* n. XI p. 20-22).

The homily (called *egkomion* in the manuscript, which is equivalent to a homily) was chosen together with many other texts by the Copts around the IX century, with a view to form an ordered collection to be read in the weekly liturgical ceremonies. The texts were copied in codices written between the IX and XII centuries, when Coptic was gradually replaced by (Christian) Arabic. This replacement also occurred in the liturgy. The attention of the scholars who organized the choice was devoted only to their content, so that the titles placed in the manuscripts before them, including the name of the supposed author, the subject treated, and the circumstances of their composition, are completely unreliable and historically inaccurate. Each text (and the present homily is no exception) must be evaluated with critical examination in order to establish its real origin and character because, of course, the choice mentioned above was made between documents of various origin, many from the golden period of the Christian literature. Later Coptic texts may restore lost works of ancient Greek authors or give an idea of the development of Coptic original literature, much of which is also lost.

The text is reproduced in so-called paleographic transcription, respecting the layout of the manuscript of two columns per page, and without any intervention on the orthography or the correctness of words. The text is also partially present in a fragment of 8 pages of another manuscript (Paris Bibl. Nationale, copte 131,3 foll. 58-61), which we have used to reconstruct some scarcely legible passages, without producing a critical edition. Only we have added some interlinear notes between <...>.

Transcription

<page 22>

<column right>

= = = = = = = = = =

ⲞⲨⲈⲄⲔⲞⲘⲒⲞⲚ Ⲉ
ⲀϤⲦⲀⲨⲞϤ ⲚϬⲒ Ⲁ
ⲠⲀ ⲔⲨⲢⲒⲖⲖⲞⲤ
ⲠⲀⲢⲬⲒⲈⲠⲒⲤⲔⲞ
ⲠⲞⲤ Ⲛ̅ⲢⲀⲔⲞⲦⲈ
ⲈϤϨⲈⲢⲘⲎⲚⲈⲨⲈ
ⲚϨⲈⲚⲔⲞⲨⲒ̈ ⲈⲂⲞⲖ
ϨⲚ ⲦⲀⲠⲞⲔⲀⲖⲨⲘ
ⲮⲒⲤ Ⲛ̅ⲒⲰϨⲀⲚ
ⲚⲎⲤ· ⲠⲀⲠⲞⲤⲦⲞ
ⲖⲞⲤ ⲘⲠⲈⲬ̅Ⲥ̅ Ⲓ̅Ⲥ̅
ϨⲚ ⲞⲨⲈⲒⲢⲎⲚⲎ
ⲚⲦⲈ ⲠⲚⲞⲨⲦⲈ
ϨⲀⲘⲎⲚ :~

= = = = = = = = = =

ⲠⲈⲠ̅Ⲛ̅Ⲁ̅ ⲞⲨⲚ Ⲙ
ⲠⲚⲞⲨⲦⲈ ⲚⲒⲂⲈ
ⲈⲠⲘⲀ ⲈⲦϤⲞⲨ
ⲀϢϤ· ⲀⲨⲰ Ϥ
ⲚⲎⲨ ϢⲀⲢⲞⲚ Ϩ̅Ⲛ̅
ⲞⲨⲀⲔⲦⲒⲚ Ⲛ̅Ⲅ̅
ⲚⲰⲤⲒⲤ· ⲈϤⲦⲤⲀ
ⲂⲞ ⲘⲘⲞⲚ ⲈⲠϢⲒⲔ
ⲚⲚⲚⲰⲎⲘⲀ Ⲛ
ⲚⲈⲄⲢⲀⲪⲎ ⲚⲚⲒ
ⲂⲈ ⲚⲦⲈ ⲠⲚⲞⲨⲦⲈ
ⲠⲀⲖⲒⲚ ⲞⲚ ⲈⲒⲤ
ϨⲎⲦⲈ ⲞⲚ Ⲙ
ⲠⲞⲞⲨ· ϤⲦⲰϨⲘ
ⲘⲘⲞⲚ· ⲈϤⲞⲨⲰϢ
ⲈⲠⲈⲆⲈⲨⲈ ⲘⲘⲞⲚ

<page 23>
<column left>
ⲡⲁⲣⲣⲏⲥⲓⲁⲥⲧⲓ
ⲕⲟⲥ· ⲁⲩⲱ ⲉ̄ⲥⲁ
ⲛⲟⲩϣⲛ ϩⲛ ⲧⲉ
ⲧⲣⲟⲫⲏ ⲙⲙⲁ
ⲕⲁⲣⲓⲟⲛ· ⲟⲩⲧ
ⲣⲟⲫⲏ ⲅⲁⲣ ⲧⲉ ⲛⲉ
ϣⲁϫⲉ ⲙⲡⲛⲟⲩ
ⲧⲉ· ⲙⲡⲉ ⲗⲁⲁⲩ
ⲥⲓ ⲙⲙⲟⲟⲩ ⲉⲛⲉϩ
ⲙⲁⲗⲓⲥⲧⲁ ⲛⲉⲛ
ⲧⲁ ⲡⲉⲩⲙⲁⲛⲟⲩⲱ
ϣⲱⲡⲉ· ⲙⲛ ⲡ
ⲛⲟⲩⲧⲉ· ⲛⲁⲓ̈ ⲛ
ⲧⲁⲩⲫⲱⲣⲓ̈ ⲙⲡⲉⲥ
ⲭⲏⲙⲁ ⲛ̄ⲧⲙⲛⲧ
ⲙⲟⲛⲟⲭⲟⲥ· ⲁⲩⲱ
ⲛⲉⲛⲧⲁⲩⲣ̄ ⲡⲉⲩ
ⲥⲱⲙⲁ ⲛⲟⲩⲑⲩ
ⲥⲓⲁⲥⲧⲏⲣⲓⲟⲛ ⲙ
ⲡⲉϥⲣⲁⲛ ⲉⲧϩⲁ ⲉ
ⲟⲟⲩ ⲛ̄ϣⲁⲉⲛⲉϩ·
ϩⲣⲁⲓ̈ ϩⲙ ⲡⲉⲛϣⲁ
ϫⲉ ⲉⲛⲛⲁϫⲓ ⲡⲓ
ⲣⲁ ⲁⲛ ⲛⲟⲩⲛⲟⲏ
ⲙⲁ· ⲉϥⲧⲁⲣⲁⲥⲥⲉ
ⲏ̄ ⲉϥⲕⲉⲛⲉⲥⲑⲉ
ⲙ̄ⲡⲉⲛⲛⲟⲩⲥ·
ⲁⲗⲗⲁ ⲉⲛⲛⲁⲧⲣⲉ
ⲡⲉⲛϩⲏⲧ ⲙⲙⲓⲛ
ⲙⲙⲟⲛ ϫⲓ ⲟⲩⲟ
ⲉⲓⲛ· ⲁⲩⲱ ⲛ̄ⲧⲱ
ⲧⲛ ϩⲱⲧⲧⲏⲩⲧⲛ
ⲛⲙⲙⲁⲛ· ⲛⲉⲧⲉ

<column right>
ⲟⲩⲛ̄ⲧⲁⲩ ⲙⲙⲁⲩ
ⲙ̄ⲡⲟⲩⲟⲉⲓⲛ ⲙ
ⲙⲉ· ⲁⲡⲛⲟϭ
ⲅⲁⲣ ⲓⲱϩⲁⲛⲛⲏⲥ
ⲁⲙⲁϩⲧⲉ ⲛⲧϭⲓϫ
ⲛ̄ⲧⲉⲛⲯⲩⲭⲏ
ⲁϥⲉⲓⲛⲉ ⲙⲙⲟⲛ
ⲉϫⲙ ⲡⲛⲟⲏⲙⲁ
ⲛ̄ⲧⲉϥⲁⲡⲟⲕⲁ
ⲗⲩⲙⲯⲓⲥ· ⲧⲁⲓ̈
ϩⲱⲱⲥ ⲧⲉ ⲑⲉ ⲉⲥϫⲓ
ⲟⲩⲟⲉⲓⲛ ⲉⲃⲟⲗ ϩ̄ⲙ
ⲡⲟⲩⲟⲉⲓⲛ ⲛⲧⲉ
ⲑⲉⲱⲗⲟⲅⲓⲁ· ⲙⲛ
ⲧⲁⲧⲃⲥ ⲙ̄ⲡⲉⲡ̅ⲛ̅ⲁ̅
ⲉⲧⲟⲩⲁⲁⲃ· ⲧⲁⲓ̈
ⲉⲧⲉⲣⲉ ⲡⲉⲥⲟⲩⲟⲉⲓ̄
ⲛⲏⲩ ⲁⲛ ⲉϫⲙ ⲡ
ϣⲟⲣⲡ ⲛⲥⲧⲉⲣⲉ
ⲱⲙⲁ ⲙⲙⲁⲧⲉ
ⲁⲗⲗⲁ ⲟⲛ ⲡϫⲱⲕ
ⲛⲛⲉⲙⲡⲏⲩⲉ·
ⲁⲩⲱ ϩⲁⲡⲗⲱⲥ
ϣⲁ ⲁⲣⲏϫϥ ⲙ
ⲡⲕⲁϩ· ϩⲙ ⲡⲧ
ⲣⲉϥⲁⲣⲭⲉⲓ ⲅⲁⲣ ⲛ
ⲧⲁϥϭⲱϣⲧ ⲁⲛ
ⲉⲛⲉϩⲃⲏⲩⲉ ⲙⲡ
ⲕⲁϩ· ⲏ̄ ⲡⲕⲁϩ
ⲁϥⲑⲉⲱⲗⲟⲅⲓ· ⲡ
ⲣⲟⲥ· ⲣⲟⲟⲩ· ⲁⲗⲗⲁ
ⲛⲧⲁϥⲕⲁ ⲧⲉϥ
ϭⲓϫ ⲛⲟⲩⲛⲁⲙ ϩⲁ

<page 24>
<column left>
ⲡⲉϥⲥⲙⲁⲩ ⲥⲱ
ⲙⲁⲧⲓⲕⲟⲥ· ⲁϥ
ⲣⲓⲕⲉ ⲙⲡⲉϥϩⲟ
ⲛⲑⲉ ⲛⲛⲉⲧⲑⲉⲱ
ⲣⲉⲓ· ϣⲁⲛⲧⲟⲩ
ⲡⲓⲑⲉ ⲙⲙⲟϥ ⲉ̄ⲃⲟⲗ
ϩⲓ̈ⲧⲙ ⲡⲛⲟⲩⲧⲉ
ⲉⲧⲁⲙⲟϥ ⲉϩⲱⲃ
ⲛⲓⲙ· ϫⲉⲕⲁⲥ ⲉ
ⲣⲉ ⲟⲩⲟⲛ ⲛⲓⲙ ⲛⲁ
ⲡⲓⲥⲧⲉⲩⲉ ϫⲉ ⲡⲉ
ⲡ̄ⲛ̄ⲁ̄ ⲉⲧⲟⲩⲁⲁⲃ
ⲡⲉⲧϫⲓ ⲙⲟⲉⲓⲧ
ϩⲏⲧϥ ϣⲁ ⲛⲁⲓ
ⲧⲏⲣⲟⲩ· ⲛⲟⲩϥⲃⲁⲓ̈
ϣⲓⲛⲉ ⲁⲛ ⲡⲉⲛⲧⲁϥ
ⲧ̄ⲛ̄ⲛⲟⲟⲩϥ ⲛⲁϥ·
ⲛⲟⲩϣⲙϣⲓⲧ ⲁⲛ
ⲛⲥⲱⲙⲁⲧⲓⲕⲟⲛ
ⲡⲉⲛⲧⲁϥϫⲱ ⲛⲁϥ
ⲛⲛⲁⲓ̈ ⲧⲏⲣⲟⲩ ⲛ̄
ⲧⲁⲩϣⲱⲡⲉ·
ⲁⲗⲗⲁ ⲉⲣⲉ ⲡⲉⲡ̄ⲛ̄ⲁ̄
ⲉⲧⲟⲩⲁⲁⲃ ϥⲓ ⲙ
ⲙⲟϥ ⲉⲡⲉⲓⲥⲁ· ⲉϥⲉⲓ
ⲛⲉ ⲙⲙⲟϥ ⲉⲡⲁⲓ
ⲉϥⲧⲥⲁⲃⲟ ⲙⲙⲟϥ
ⲉⲛⲉⲡⲟⲩⲣⲁⲛⲓⲟⲛ
ⲛⲛⲟⲏⲙⲁ ⲛⲑⲁⲩ
ⲙⲁ· ⲙ̄ⲛ̄ ⲛⲉⲡⲣⲟ
ⲥⲱⲡⲟⲛ ⲛⲑⲉⲣⲁ
ⲡⲓⲁⲧⲓⲕⲟⲛ· ⲙ̄ⲛ̄
ⲛⲟⲏⲙⲁ ⲛϣⲡⲏⲣⲉ

<column right>
ⲙⲛ ⲛⲉ ⲥⲁⲗⲡⲓⲅⲝ
ⲉⲛⲉⲥⲉ ⲧⲉⲩⲥⲙⲏ
ⲙⲛ ⲛⲉϩⲣⲟⲟⲩ ⲛⲥ
ⲙⲟⲩ· ⲙⲛ ⲛⲉ
ⲫⲱⲥⲧⲏⲣ ⲛⲉⲟⲟⲩ
ⲁⲩⲱ ⲛⲉⲫⲱⲥ
ⲧⲏⲣ ⲛⲛⲇⲓⲕⲁⲓ
ⲟⲥ· ⲙⲛ ⲛⲉⲧⲟ ⲛ
ϩⲟⲧⲉ ⲉⲑⲉⲱⲣⲉⲓ
ⲙⲙⲟⲟⲩ· ⲙⲛ ⲛⲉ
ϣⲟⲩϩⲏⲛⲉ ⲛⲛⲉ
ⲧⲟⲩⲁⲁⲃ· ⲙ̄ⲛ̄
ⲡⲥⲟⲡⲥ ⲛⲛⲉⲧⲟⲩ
ⲁⲁⲃ· ⲙ̄ⲛ̄ ⲑⲓ
ⲕⲱⲛ ⲙ̄ⲡⲉϩⲓⲉⲓⲃ
ⲡⲉ ⲉⲃⲟⲗ ϩ̄ⲛ̄ ⲧⲉ
ϩⲓⲁⲓⲃⲉ ⲙⲙⲉ· ⲁⲩⲱ
ⲛⲁⲧⲧⲱⲗⲙ· ⲧⲉ
ⲑⲉⲱⲇⲟⲕⲟⲥ ⲉⲧⲟⲩ
ⲁⲁⲃ ⲙⲁⲣⲓⲁ·
ⲁϣ ⲙⲙⲏⲥⲧⲏⲣⲓ
ⲟⲛ· ⲡⲉⲧⲙⲡⲉⲕⲑⲩ
ⲱⲣⲉⲓ ⲙⲙⲟϥ· ⲱ
ⲡⲑⲉⲱⲣⲁⲧⲓⲕⲟⲥ
ⲛⲛⲉⲙⲙⲏⲥⲧⲏ
ⲣⲓⲟⲛ ⲉⲧⲟⲩⲁⲁⲃ
ⲁⲛⲟⲕ ⲡⲉϫⲁϥ ⲁⲓ
ⲛⲁⲩ ⲉⲩⲑⲣⲟⲛⲟⲥ
ⲉϥⲕⲏ ⲉϩⲣⲁⲓ̈ ϩⲛ ⲧ
ⲡⲉ· ⲁⲩⲱ ⲉⲓⲥ ⲡ
ⲛⲟⲩⲥ ⲙⲡⲣⲱⲙⲉ
ⲁⲩⲱ ⲛⲉϥϩⲙⲟⲟⲥ ϩⲓ̈
ϫⲙ ⲡⲉⲑⲣⲟⲛⲟⲥ ⲛ

<page 25>
<column left>
ϬⲒ ⲠⲈϨⲒⲈⲒⲂ· ⲈⲦⲈ
ⲦⲀÏ ⲦⲈ ⲦⲘⲚⲦ
ⲂⲀÏϨⲎⲦ· ⲈⲨⲘ
ⲠⲔⲰⲦⲈ ⲘⲠⲈⲐ
ⲢⲞⲚⲞⲤ· ⲚϬⲒ ϪⲞⲨ
ⲦⲀϤⲦⲈ Ⲛ̄ⲐⲢⲞⲚⲞⲤ
ⲈⲦⲈ ⲚⲀÏ ⲚⲈ Ⲡ
ϪⲞⲨⲦⲀϤⲦⲈ ⲘⲠ
ⲢⲈⲤⲂⲨⲦⲈⲢⲞⲤ·
ⲠⲈϪⲞⲨⲰⲦ ⲄⲀⲢ
ⲚⲈ ⲚⲦⲎⲎⲂⲈ Ⲙ
ⲠⲢⲰⲘⲈ· ⲀⲨⲰ
ⲠⲈϤⲂⲀⲖ ⲤⲚⲀⲨ
ⲘⲚ ⲦⲈϤⲦⲀⲠⲢⲞ
ⲘⲚ ϢⲀⲀⲦϤ·
ⲈⲨⲘ̄ⲠⲔⲰⲦⲈ Ⲙ
ⲠⲚⲞⲨⲤ· ⲈⲨϨ
ⲘⲞⲞⲤ Ϩ· ⲠϪⲞⲨⲦⲀϤ
ⲦⲈ ⲚⲐⲢⲞⲚⲞⲤ Ⲛ̄
ϬⲒ ⲠϪⲞⲨⲦⲀϤ
ⲦⲈ ⲘⲠⲢⲈⲤⲂⲨⲦⲈ
ⲢⲞⲤ· ⲈⲢⲈ ϨⲈⲚⲔ
ⲖⲞⲘ ϨⲒϪⲚ ⲚⲈⲨ
ⲀⲠⲎⲨⲈ· ⲚⲀÏ
ⲞⲚ ⲚⲈ ⲠⲈϪⲞⲨⲰⲦ
ⲚⲈⲒⲈⲒⲂ· ⲈⲨϨⲒϪⲚ
ⲚⲈⲚⲦⲎⲎⲂⲈ· ⲈⲨ
ⲤⲔⲨⲠⲀⲌⲈ ⲘⲘⲞ
ⲞⲨ ϪⲈ ⲚⲚⲈⲨϪⲒ
ϨⲘⲘⲈ· ⲚⲤⲈⲀⲚϨⲀ
ⲖⲒⲤⲔⲈ ⲚϬⲒ ⲚⲈⲨ
ⲚⲈⲨⲢⲞⲚ· Ⲏ̄ Ⲛ̄ⲤⲈ
ϪⲒ Ⲟ̄ϬⲂⲈⲤ· ⲚⲤⲈⲢ

<column right>
ⲠⲤⲰⲘⲀ ⲚⲀⲦⲠ
ⲚⲞⲎ· ⲀⲨⲰ ⲚⲤⲈ
ⲀⲀϤ ⲚⲀⲤⲐⲎⲚⲎⲤ
ⲀⲨⲰ ⲠⲖⲀⲤ ⲚⲦ
ⲦⲀⲠⲢⲞ· ⲈϤⲈⲜⲞⲘⲞ
ⲖⲞⲄⲈⲒ· ⲀⲨⲰ Ⲡ
ⲔⲈⲤⲚⲀⲨ ⲚⲂⲀⲖ ⲈⲨ
ⲠⲀⲢⲀⲦⲎⲢⲈⲒ ⲈⲠ
ϬⲰϢⲦ ⲈⲂⲞⲖ
ⲈⲚⲈⲠⲞⲨⲢⲀⲚⲒⲞ̄
ⲀⲨⲰ ⲠϢⲀⲚⲦϤ
ⲈⲦⲢⲈϤϬⲰ ⲈϤ
ϢⲰⲖⲘ· ⲈⲠⲈⲤ
ϮⲚⲞⲨⲂⲈ ⲘⲠⲈⲐⲎ
ⲤⲒⲀⲤⲦⲎⲢⲒⲞⲚ· Ⲛ
ⲤⲈⲪⲰⲢⲈⲒ ⲘⲠⲈⲔ
ⲖⲞⲘ Ⲛ̄ϨⲞⲘⲞⲖⲞ
ⲄⲒⲤⲘⲞⲤ· ⲚⲀÏ Ⲛ̄
ⲦⲀ ⲠⲚⲞⲨⲦⲈ ⲘⲘⲈ
ⲤⲂⲦⲰⲦⲞⲨ ⲚⲚⲈ
ⲦⲘⲠϢⲀ ⲘⲘⲞⲞⲨ
ⲈⲚⲈ ϢⲀⲨⲚⲞⲨϨⲈ
ⲠⲈϪⲀϤ ⲘⲠⲈⲨ
ϪⲞⲨⲦⲀϤⲦⲈ ⲚⲔ
ⲖⲞⲘ ϨⲒϪⲚ ⲚⲈⲨⲀ
ⲠⲎⲨⲈ· ⲚⲤⲈⲔⲀⲀⲨ
ϨⲀⲢⲀⲦⲞⲨ· ⲚⲚⲈⲞⲨ
ⲈⲢⲎⲦⲈ· ⲘⲠⲈⲦϨ
ⲘⲞⲞⲤ ϨⲒϪ̄Ⲛ̄ ⲠⲈ
ⲐⲢⲞⲚⲞⲤ· ⲈⲨϪⲰ
ⲘⲘⲞⲤ ϪⲈ ⲔⲘⲠϢⲀ
ⲠϪⲞⲈⲒⲤ· ⲈϪⲒ ⲘⲠⲈ
ⲞⲞⲨ· Ⲙ̄Ⲛ̄ ⲠⲦⲀÏⲞ̄

<page 26>
<column left>
Ⲙ̅Ⲛ̅ ⲠⲀⲘⲀϨⲦⲈ
Ⲙ̅Ⲛ̅ ⲦϬⲞⲘ :~
ⲚⲦⲞⲔ ⲆⲈ ϨⲰⲰⲔ
Ⲱ ⲠⲢⲰⲘⲈ ⲦⲀϪ
ⲢⲈ ⲚⲈⲔⲞⲨⲈⲢⲎⲦⲈ
ⲈϪⲚ ⲞⲨⲔⲀϨ ⲈϤ
ⲞⲨⲀⲀⲂ· ⲠⲰⲢϢ
ⲈⲂⲞⲖ Ⲛ̅ⲚⲈⲔϬⲒϪ
ϨⲞⲘⲞⲖⲞⲄⲒ̈· ϨⲚ
ⲦⲈⲔⲦⲀⲠⲢⲞ·
ϤⲒ ⲠⲞⲚⲎⲢⲞⲚ ⲚⲒⲘ
Ⲛ̅ⲤⲀⲂⲞⲖ ⲘⲘⲞⲔ
Ⲙ̅Ⲛ̅ ⲚⲈⲔ ⲘⲈⲈⲨⲈ
ⲘⲀⲢⲈ ⲠⲈⲔⲚⲞⲨⲤ
ϪⲒ ⲞⲨⲞⲈⲒⲚ ϨⲚ̅ ⲦⲈⲄ
ⲚⲰⲤⲒⲤ· Ⲙ̅ⲠⲈⲢ
ⲦⲀϬⲔ ⲈⲠⲚⲞⲂⲈ ϪⲒ̅
ⲠⲈⲒⲚⲀⲨ· ⲀⲨⲰ
ϨⲰⲂ ⲚⲒⲘ ⲈⲦⲈⲔⲚⲀ
ⲈⲦⲒ ⲘⲘⲞⲞⲨ Ⲛ̅Ⲧ̅Ⲙ̅
ⲠⲚⲞⲨⲦⲈ· ⲈⲘⲠⲈϤ
ⲦⲀⲀⲨ ⲚⲀⲔ· ⲀⲘⲞⲨ
ⲚⲄϨⲒⲰⲚⲈ Ⲉ̅ⲢⲞⲒ̈ ϨⲘ
ⲠⲘⲀ Ⲉ̅ⲚⲈⲒⲚ̅ϨⲎⲦϤ
ⲀⲨⲰ ⲠⲈϤⲦⲞⲞⲨ Ⲛ̅
ⲌⲰⲞⲚ ⲠⲈϪⲀϤ
ⲈⲚⲈⲨⲰϢ ⲈⲂⲞⲖ
ⲚⲞⲨⲞⲈⲒϢ ⲚⲒⲘ
ϪⲈ ϤⲞⲨⲀⲀⲂ· ϤⲞⲨ
ⲀⲀⲂ· ϤⲞⲨⲀⲀⲂ· Ⲛ
ϬⲒ ⲠϪⲞⲈⲒⲤ ⲤⲀⲂⲀ
ⲰⲐ· ⲠϨⲨⲘⲚⲞⲤ
ⲘⲈⲚ ⲞⲨϢⲞⲘⲚ̅Ⲧ̅

<column right>
Ⲛ̅ⲤⲞⲠ ⲠⲈ· ⲠⲈϤ
ⲚⲞⲎⲘⲀ ⲆⲈ Ⲛ
ⲦⲞϤ· ⲞⲨⲘⲞⲚⲀⲤ
ⲠⲈ· ⲈⲨⲦⲀⲨⲞ̅ Ⲙ
ⲠϨⲀⲄⲒⲀⲤⲘⲞⲤ
ⲚⲦⲖⲈⲜⲒⲤ· ⲚⲦⲢⲒⲤ
ϨⲀⲄⲒⲞⲤ· ⲈⲨⲈⲒ
ⲚⲈ ⲘⲘⲞϤ ⲈϪⲘ̅
ⲠⲒⲚⲞⲨⲦⲈ ⲚⲞⲨ
ⲰⲦ· ⲠⲈⲒⲰⲦ
ⲠⲠⲀⲚⲦⲰⲔⲢⲀ
ⲦⲰⲢ· ⲈϤⲦⲀ
ⲘⲞ ⲘⲘⲞⲚ ϨⲘ
ⲠⲀⲒ̈ ϪⲈ ⲠϢⲎ
ⲢⲈ ϨⲘ ⲠⲈⲒⲰⲦ
ⲀⲨⲰ ⲠⲈⲒⲰⲦ
ϨⲘ ⲠϢⲎⲢⲈ ⲘⲚ
ⲠⲈⲠ̅Ⲛ̅Ⲁ̅· ⲈⲦⲞⲨⲀⲀⲂ·
ⲈⲦⲈ Ⲙ̅Ⲛ̅ ⲠⲰⲢϪ
ϨⲚ ⲞⲨⲀ ⲘⲘⲞⲞⲨ
ⲈⲘⲈⲨⲔⲀⲢⲰⲞⲨ Ⲉ
ⲚⲈϨ ⲠⲈϪⲀϤ ⲈⲨⲤ
ⲘⲞⲨ ⲈⲠⲚⲞⲨⲦⲈ
ⲀⲢⲀ ⲈⲦⲂⲈ ⲞⲨ ⲈⲨⲢ̅
ϨⲞⲦⲈ ϨⲎⲦⲞⲨ Ⲛ̅Ⲛ̅
ⲆⲀⲒⲘⲞⲚⲒⲞⲚ· ⲞⲨ
ⲆⲈ ⲄⲀⲢ Ⲙ̅Ⲛ̅ ⲆⲀⲒ
ⲘⲰⲚ ϢⲞⲞⲠ
ϨⲀϨⲦⲎⲨ ϨⲘ Ⲡ
ⲘⲀ ⲈⲦⲘⲘⲀⲨ
Ⲛ̅ⲤⲈⲠⲒⲢⲀⲌⲈ Ⲙ
ⲘⲞⲞⲨ ⲀⲚ ϨⲒⲦ̅Ⲛ̅
ⲖⲀⲀⲨ· ⲚⲤⲈⲈⲠⲒ

<page 27>
<column left>
ⲃⲟⲩⲗⲉⲩⲉ ⲉⲣⲟⲟⲩ
ⲁⲛ ϩⲓⲧⲛ ⲗⲁⲁⲩ·
ⲁⲗⲗⲁ ⲥⲉϩⲏⲛ ⲉ
ϩⲟⲩⲛ ⲉⲡⲛⲟⲩⲧⲉ
ⲛⲟⲩⲟⲉⲓϣ ⲛⲓⲙ
Ⲥⲉⲡⲣⲟⲥⲩⲭⲉ ⲉⲛⲉⲩ
ϩⲩⲙⲛⲟⲥ ⲛⲟⲩⲟ
ⲉⲓϣ ⲛⲓⲙ· ⲥⲉⲥⲱ
Ⲧⲙ ⲉⲧⲃⲟⲏⲑⲓⲁ ⲉⲧ
ⲡⲏϩ ϣⲁⲣⲟⲟⲩ ⲉ
ⲃⲟⲗ ϩⲓⲧⲙ ⲡⲛⲟⲩ
ⲧⲉ· ⲁⲗⲗⲁ ⲉⲩ
Ϩⲱⲥ ⲉⲩⲥⲙⲟⲩ· ⲉⲩ
ϯⲉⲟⲟⲩ ⲉⲧⲃⲏⲏⲧⲕ
ⲱ ⲡⲣⲱⲙⲉ· ⲧⲁ
ⲣⲉ ⲡⲛⲟⲩⲧⲉ ⲕⲱ
ⲛⲁⲕ ⲉⲃⲟⲗ ⲛⲛⲉⲕ
ⲛⲟⲃⲉ· ⲙ̄ⲛ ⲛⲉⲕⲁ
ⲛⲟⲙⲓⲁ· ⲛⲧⲟⲕ
Ⲇⲉ ϩⲱⲱⲕ· ⲕⲙⲏ̄
ⲉⲃⲟⲗ ϩⲛ ⲛⲉⲕⲡⲉ
ⲑⲟⲟⲩ ⲙⲙⲏⲛⲉ
ⲉⲁⲕϫⲉⲣ ⲛⲉⲕⲃⲁⲗ
ϩⲛ ⲧⲕⲁⲕⲓⲁ :~
ⲛⲉⲕⲟⲃϩⲉ· ⲙⲛ ⲛⲉⲕ
ⲃⲟⲩϩⲉ ϩⲛ ⲧⲁⲛⲟ
ⲙⲓⲁ· ⲧⲉⲕⲧⲁⲡ
Ⲣⲟ ϩⲛ ⲛⲉϥⲗⲁⲥⲫⲏ
ⲙⲓⲁ· :~ ⲡⲉⲕϩⲏⲧ
ϩⲙ ⲡⲕⲱϩ· ⲙⲛ
ⲡⲙⲟⲥⲧⲉ· ⲙⲛ ⲡ
ϯⲧⲱⲛ· ⲙⲛ ⲧⲕⲁ
ⲧⲁⲗⲁⲗⲓⲁ· ⲉⲁⲡ

<column right>
ⲙⲟⲩ ϣⲱⲡⲉ
ⲛⲑⲉ ⲛⲛⲉⲓϩⲱⲃ
ⲛⲥⲱⲃⲉ ⲙⲡⲉⲕ
ⲙ̄ⲧⲟ ⲉⲃⲟⲗ :~
Ⲟⲩⲧⲣⲁⲡⲉⲍⲁ ⲉⲥ
ⲙⲉϩ ⲉⲃⲟⲗ ϩⲛ ⲛⲁⲃ
ⲙⲡⲉⲕⲥⲟⲛ· ⲁⲕ
ⲙⲉⲣⲉ ⲟⲩⲱⲙ ⲉⲃⲟⲗ
ⲛϩⲏⲧⲥ· ⲙⲏ ⲙ̄ⲛ
ϣⲓⲡⲉ ϩⲛ ⲛⲉⲕⲃⲁⲗ
Ⲉⲣⲉ ⲛⲉⲭⲉⲣⲟⲩⲃⲓⲛ
ⲙⲛ ⲛⲥⲉⲣⲁⲫⲓⲛ
ⲥⲙⲟⲩ ⲉⲧⲃⲏⲏⲧⲕ
Ⲛⲧⲟⲕ ϩⲱⲱⲕ
ⲛⲅϭⲉⲡⲏ ⲛⲅⲧⲟⲩ
ⲛⲟⲥⲕ· ⲡⲗⲏⲛ
Ⲙⲁⲣⲉ ⲡⲉϩⲣⲏⲧⲟⲛ
ⲧⲁⲙⲟⲛ ⲉⲛⲉⲧ
ⲛⲏⲩ· ⲙⲛⲛⲥⲁ ⲛⲁⲓ
Ϩⲙ ⲡⲧⲣⲉⲩϫⲓ ⲟⲛ
ⲙⲡⲉⲡ̄ⲛ̄ⲁ̄ ⲙⲡⲉ
ⲑⲉⲱⲣⲁⲧⲓⲕⲟⲛ
ⲁⲩⲱ ⲛⲑⲉⲟⲗⲟⲅⲟⲥ
ⲉϩⲣⲁⲓ ⲉⲧⲡⲉ ϣⲁ
ⲛⲉⲧϫⲟⲥⲉ ⲉⲙⲁ
ⲧⲉ ⲉⲡⲉϩⲟⲩⲟ
ⲁϥⲣ̄ ϩⲓⲧⲡⲉ ⲛⲛⲉ
ⲧⲛⲙⲉⲉⲩⲉ ⲉⲣⲟⲟⲩ
ⲧⲏⲣⲟⲩ· ϫⲉ ⲙⲉⲣⲉ
ⲣⲱⲙⲉ ⲛⲓⲙ ⲑⲉ
ⲱⲣⲉⲓ ⲙⲙⲟⲟⲩ·
Ⲛⲁⲓ ⲙⲉⲛ ⲙⲛⲗⲁⲁⲩ
ϩⲁⲡⲉⲥⲏⲧ ⲛⲧⲡⲉ

<page 28>
<column left>
ⲛⲁϣ ⲉⲓⲙⲉ ⲉⲣⲟⲟⲩ
ⲏ̄ ⲛϥϩⲉⲣⲙⲏⲛⲉⲩⲉ
ⲙⲙⲟⲟⲩ :~
Ⲡⲉϫⲁϥ ⲅⲁⲣ ⲛϭⲓ ⲡⲉ
ⲧⲉⲣⲉ ⲧⲙⲉ ϣⲟⲟⲡ
ϩⲛ ⲛⲉϥϩⲓⲟⲟⲩⲉ
ⲧⲏⲣⲟⲩ ⲓ̈ⲱϩⲁⲛ
ⲛⲏⲥ· ϫⲉ ⲁⲓ̈ⲥⲱ
ⲧⲙ ⲉⲧⲏⲡⲉ ⲛ̄ⲛ̄
ⲧⲁⲩⲥⲫⲣⲁⲅⲓⲍⲉ
ⲙⲙⲟⲟⲩ· ⲥⲉⲉⲓⲣⲉ
ⲙⲙⲛⲧⲁϥⲧⲉ ⲛⲧ
ⲃⲁ· ⲙⲛ ϥⲧⲟⲟⲩ
Ⲛϣⲟ· ⲉⲃⲟⲗ ϩⲙ
ⲫⲓⲗⲏ ⲛⲓⲙ· ⲛⲧⲉ
ⲛϣⲏⲣⲉ ⲙⲡⲓ̄ⲏ̄ⲗ̄
ⲛⲧⲁⲩⲥⲫⲣⲁⲅⲓⲍⲉ
ⲛⲛⲁⲓ̈ ϫⲉⲕⲁⲥ ⲛ
ⲛⲉ ⲧⲟⲣⲅⲏ ⲉⲧⲧⲏϣ
ⲉϣⲱⲡⲉ ⲛⲟⲩⲟⲛ
ⲛⲓⲙ ϣⲱⲡⲉ ⲙ
ⲙⲟⲟⲩ ϩⲱⲟⲩ· ⲉⲧ
ⲃⲉ ϫⲉ ⲁⲛⲛⲟⲃⲉ
ⲛⲟⲩⲟⲛ ⲛⲓⲙ· ⲉⲓ
ⲙⲡⲉⲙⲧⲟ ⲉⲃⲟⲗ
ⲙⲡϫⲟⲉⲓⲥ·
Ⲉⲡⲓⲇⲏ ⲙⲡⲉⲩⲟ
ⲉⲓϣ ⲙⲡⲙⲛ
ⲧⲁϥⲧⲉ ⲛⲧⲃⲁ
ⲙⲛ ⲡⲉϥⲧⲟⲟⲩ
ⲛϣⲟ· ⲉⲛⲉ ⲙ
ⲡⲁⲧⲟⲩⲃⲁⲡⲧⲓ
ⲍⲉ ⲛⲟⲩⲟⲛ·

<column right>
Ⲉⲛⲉ ⲙⲡⲁⲧⲙ̄ⲙⲁⲣ
ⲧⲩⲣⲟⲥ· ⲡⲱϩⲧ
ⲉⲃⲟⲗ ⲙⲡⲉⲩⲥⲛⲟϥ
Ⲉⲛⲉ ⲙⲡⲁⲧⲉ ⲥⲁ
ⲉⲓⲧ ⲙⲡⲁⲣⲑⲉⲛⲟⲥ
ϣⲱⲡⲉ :~
Ⲉⲛⲉ ⲙⲡⲁⲧⲉ ⲁⲥⲕⲓ
ⲧⲏⲥ ⲁⲥⲕⲉⲓ :~
Ⲉⲛⲉ ⲙⲡⲁⲧⲉ ⲙⲙⲟ
ⲛⲟⲭⲟⲥ ⲡⲟⲗⲓⲧⲉⲩⲉ·
Ⲉⲛⲉ ⲙⲡⲁⲧⲉ ⲉⲅ
ⲣⲁⲧⲏⲥ ⲉⲅⲣⲁ
ⲧⲉⲩⲉ :~
Ⲉⲛⲉ ⲙⲡⲁⲧⲉ ⲥⲩⲛ
ⲛⲟⲙⲓⲭⲟⲥ ⲁⲣⲭⲉⲓ
Ⲁⲩⲱ ⲛⲉⲛⲧⲁⲩⲁⲣ
ⲭⲉⲓ ϩⲛ ⲛⲁⲓ̈ ⲛⲉⲙ
ⲡⲁⲧⲟⲩⲥⲟⲩⲛ ⲡⲉ
ⲧⲟⲩⲁⲣⲭⲉⲓ ⲉⲣⲟϥ
ⲕⲁⲗⲱⲥ :~
Ⲉⲛⲉ ⲙⲡⲁⲧⲟⲩⲛⲟⲓ
ⲙⲡⲙⲏⲥⲧⲏⲣⲓⲟ̄
ⲙⲛ ⲡⲉϥⲛⲟϭ ⲛ
ϩⲗⲟϭ· ⲁⲗⲗⲁ ⲉⲩ
Ⲛⲁⲥⲫⲣⲁⲅⲓⲍⲉ ⲙ
ⲡⲉⲓⲙⲛⲧⲁϥⲧⲉ
ⲛⲧⲃⲁ ⲙⲛ ⲡⲉⲓ
ϥⲧⲟⲟⲩ ⲛϣⲟ
ϣⲁⲣⲉ ⲑⲩⲗⲉⲥⲓⲥ
ⲑⲩⲗⲉⲥⲓ̈ⲥ ϣⲡ
ϥⲧⲟⲟⲩ ⲛϣⲟ ⲉ
ⲣⲟⲥ· ⲉϩⲣⲁⲓ ⲉ
ⲙⲛⲧⲥⲛⲟⲟⲩⲥ·

<page 29>
<column left>
ⲁⲩⲱ ϣⲁⲣⲉ ⲡⲉϥ
ⲧⲟⲟⲩ ⲛϣⲟ· ⲡⲱϣ
ⲉⲣⲛ ⲥⲟ ⲙⲫⲩⲗⲏ·
ϣⲁⲥⲡⲱϣ ⲉϫⲛ̄
ϣⲟⲙⲛⲧ ⲛⲓⲱⲧ
ⲛⲁⲣⲭⲁⲓⲟⲥ· ⲛⲁϊ
ⲛⲧⲁ ⲧⲉⲩⲙⲛⲧⲡⲁⲧ
ⲣⲓⲁⲣⲭⲏⲥ ϣⲱⲡⲉ
ⲛⲁⲩ ϩⲁⲣⲓϩⲁⲣⲟⲟⲩ
ⲁⲛ· ⲁⲗⲗⲁ ⲡⲛⲟⲩ
ⲧⲉ ⲡⲉⲛⲧⲁϥⲭⲁ
ⲣⲓⲍⲉ ⲙⲙⲟⲥ ⲛⲁⲩ
ⲁⲩⲱ ⲡⲉⲕⲗⲏⲣⲟⲥ
ⲉⲓ ⲛⲛⲁϩⲣⲙ ⲡⲉϥ
ⲧⲟⲟⲩ ⲛϣⲟ ϩⲓ ⲙⲛⲧ
ⲥⲛⲟⲟⲩⲥ· ⲁⲩⲱ
ⲛⲧⲉ ⲧⲉⲭⲁⲣⲓⲥ ϣⲱ
ⲡⲉ ⲉⲟⲩⲉⲓ ⲛⲟⲩⲱⲧ
ⲧⲉ ⲛϩⲁⲡⲗⲟⲩⲛ
ⲁⲛⲁⲩ ϫⲉ ⲉⲣⲉ ⲡⲉⲓ
ⲙⲏⲥⲧⲩⲣⲓⲟⲛ
ⲡⲁⲓ ⲥⲩⲙⲁⲛⲉ ⲙ
ⲡⲗⲁⲟⲥ ⲛⲛⲉⲭ
ⲣⲏⲥⲧⲓⲁⲛⲟⲥ ϫⲉ ⲟⲩ
ⲛⲉⲩⲛ ⲟⲩⲟⲛ ⲛⲏⲩ
ⲉⲃⲟⲗ ϩⲛ ⲛⲉⲙⲙⲁ̄
ϣⲁ· ⲙⲛ ⲛⲉⲙⲁⲛ
ϩⲱⲧⲡ· ⲛⲥⲉⲛⲁ
ϫⲟⲩ ⲙⲛ ⲁⲃⲣⲁ
ϩⲁⲙ· ⲙⲛ ϊⲥⲁⲕ
ⲙⲛ ⲓⲁⲕⲱⲃ ϩⲣⲁϊ
ϩⲛ ⲧⲙⲛⲧⲉⲣⲟ·
ⲙⲛⲛⲥⲁ ⲛⲁϊ ⲟⲛ

<column right>
ⲡⲉϫⲁϥ· ϫⲉ ⲁⲓ
ⲛⲁⲩ ⲉⲩⲛⲟϭ ⲙⲙⲏ
ⲏϣⲉ ⲉⲛⲁϣⲱϥ
ⲉⲙⲛⲗⲁⲁⲩ ⲛⲁϣ
ⲟⲡϥ· ⲉⲃⲟⲗ ϩⲛ ϩⲉⲑ
ⲛⲟⲥ ⲛⲓⲙ· ϩⲓ ⲫⲩ
ⲗⲏ ϩⲓ ⲁⲥⲡⲉ· ⲙⲡ̄ⲙ
ⲧⲟ ⲉⲃⲟⲗ ⲙⲡⲉϩⲓ
ⲉⲓⲃ· ⲉⲩϭⲟⲟⲗⲉ ⲛ
ϩⲉⲛⲥⲧⲟⲗⲏ ⲛⲟⲩ
ⲱⲃϣ· ⲉⲣⲉ ϩⲉⲛ
ⲃⲁ ϩⲛ ⲛⲉⲩϭⲓϫ·
ⲉⲩⲁϣⲕⲁⲕ ⲉⲃⲟⲗ
ϩⲛ ⲟⲩⲛⲟϭ ⲛⲥⲙⲏ
ϫⲉ ⲡⲟⲩϫⲁϊ ⲙⲡ
ⲛⲟⲩⲧⲉ ⲉⲧϩⲙⲟⲟⲥ
ϩⲓ ⲡⲉⲑⲣⲟⲛⲟⲥ ⲙⲛ
ⲡⲉϩⲓⲉⲓⲃ· ⲁⲩⲱ
ⲛⲁⲅⲅⲉⲗⲟⲥ ⲧⲏⲣⲟⲩ
ⲛⲉⲩ ⲙⲡⲕⲱⲧⲉ
ⲙⲡⲉⲑⲣⲟⲛⲟⲥ·
ⲁϣ ⲡⲉ ⲡⲛⲟϭ ⲙ
ⲙⲏⲏϣⲉ ⲛⲥⲁ
ⲛⲉⲯⲩⲭⲏ ⲛⲛⲇⲓ
ⲕⲁⲓⲟⲥ· ⲛⲁϊ ⲛⲧⲁⲩ
ⲣ ⲁⲛⲁϥ ⲙⲡⲛⲟⲩ
ⲧⲉ ⲉⲃⲟⲗ ϩⲛ ⲅⲉⲛⲟⲥ
ⲛⲓⲙ· ϩⲓⲫⲩⲗⲏ ϩⲓ
ⲁⲥⲡⲉ· ⲉⲩⲡⲣⲟⲥⲕⲩ
ⲛⲉⲓ ⲙⲡⲙⲟⲛⲟ
ⲅⲉⲛⲏⲥ ⲙⲡⲉⲓⲱⲧ
ⲡⲉⲛⲧⲁϥⲡⲏⲥⲥⲉ
ⲛⲧⲉϥⲥⲕⲩⲛⲏ ϩⲛ ⲧ

<page 30
<column left>
ⲡⲁⲣⲑⲉⲛⲟⲥ ⲉⲧⲟⲩ
ⲁⲁⲃ ⲙⲁⲣⲓⲁ ⲧ̅ⲛ̅
ⲧⲁⲥⲱ ⲙⲙⲟϥ ϩ̅ⲛ̅
ⲟⲩⲡ̅ⲛ̅ⲁ̅ ⲉϥⲟⲩⲁⲁⲃ
ⲙⲛ ⲟⲩⲥⲁⲣⲝ ⲉⲩⲉ
ⲝⲟⲙⲟⲗⲟⲅⲉⲓ ⲛⲁϥ
ⲧⲏⲣⲟⲩ ϫⲉ ⲡⲉⲟⲟⲩ
ⲛⲁⲕ ⲡⲉⲧϩⲙⲟⲟⲥ
ϩⲓϫⲙ ⲡⲉⲑⲣⲟⲥ<sic> ⲛ
ⲧⲉϥⲙⲛⲧⲉⲣⲟ :~
ⲏ ⲛⲓⲙ ⲡⲉ ⲡⲉⲡⲓⲥ
ⲕⲟⲡⲟⲥ ⲛⲧⲁϥⲡⲉ
ϣⲛ ⲛⲉⲓⲡⲣⲉⲥⲃⲩ
ⲧⲉⲣⲟⲥ ⲛⲧⲁⲛϣⲁ
ϫⲉ ⲉⲣⲟⲟⲩ· ⲉⲓⲙⲏ
ⲧⲉⲓ ⲡⲛⲟⲩⲧⲉ ⲡⲉⲛ
ⲧⲁϥⲧⲁⲙⲓⲟ ⲡⲛⲟ
ⲏⲣⲟⲛ ⲛ̅ⲧⲡⲉ :~
ⲁⲩⲱ ⲡⲥⲱⲙⲁ ⲙ̅ⲛ̅
ⲡⲉⲥⲛⲟϥ ⲙⲡⲉϩⲓ
ⲉⲓⲃ· ⲉⲛⲉ ⲛⲧⲟⲟⲩ
ⲡⲉⲧⲟⲩⲁⲣⲭⲉⲓ ⲉ
ⲣⲟⲟⲩ· ⲉⲩⲕⲁⲧⲁⲛⲓ
ⲍⲉ ⲙⲙⲟⲛ ϩⲱⲱⲛ
ⲉⲧⲣⲉⲛⲛⲟⲓ̈ ⲙⲡ
ⲧⲉⲗⲓⲟⲛ· ⲁⲩⲱ
ⲡⲟⲩⲱⲡ ⲛⲛⲉⲕⲕ
ⲗⲏⲥⲓⲁⲥⲧⲓⲕⲟⲛ
ⲙⲡⲥⲟⲟⲩⲛ ⲧⲏⲣϥ
ⲡⲛⲟⲩⲥ· ⲧⲥⲟⲫⲓⲁ
ϩⲛⲉⲃⲟⲗ ϩⲙ ⲡⲥⲟ
ⲟⲩⲛ ⲧⲏⲣϥ ⲙⲡⲉ
ϩⲓⲉⲓⲃ ⲡⲉ· ⲡⲁⲓ̈

<column right>
ⲛⲧⲁϥϩⲉⲧⲣ ⲛⲉϥ
ⲁⲅⲅⲉⲗⲟⲥ ⲙⲛ ⲛⲉ
ⲣⲱⲙⲉ· ϣⲁⲛ
ⲧⲉ ⲡⲣⲁϣⲉ ⲛ̅ⲧⲉⲓ
ⲉⲝⲟⲙⲟⲗⲟⲅⲏⲥⲓⲥ
ϫⲱⲕ ⲉⲃⲟⲗ :~
ⲁϥⲟⲩⲱϣⲃ ⲡⲉ
ϫⲁϥ ⲛ̅ϭⲓ ⲟⲩⲁ ⲉ
ⲃⲟⲗ ϩ̅ⲛ̅ ⲛⲉⲡⲣⲉⲥ
ⲃⲩⲧⲉⲣⲟⲥ ⲉϥϫⲱ
ⲙⲙⲟⲥ ⲛⲁⲓ ϫⲉ
ⲛⲓⲙ ⲛⲉ ⲛⲁⲓ̈ ⲉⲧ
ϭⲟⲟⲗⲉ ⲛⲛⲓⲥⲧⲟ
ⲗⲏ ⲛⲟⲩⲱⲃϣ
ⲁⲩⲱ ⲛⲧⲁⲩⲉⲓ ⲉ
ⲃⲟⲗ ⲧⲱⲛ :~
ⲱ ϣⲡⲏⲣⲉ ⲛⲛⲟϭ
ⲁⲩⲱ ⲛⲑⲁⲩⲙⲁ·
ⲛⲉⲣ̅ⲙ̅ⲡⲉ ⲉⲩϫⲛⲟⲩ
ⲛⲛⲉⲣⲙⲕⲁϩ ⲉⲩ
ⲛⲟⲏⲙⲁ· ⲛ̅ⲛⲟϭ
ⲡⲣⲱⲙⲉ ⲅⲁⲣ ⲟⲩⲥⲱ
ⲱⲛ ⲡⲉ ⲙⲙⲁⲓ̈
ⲉⲟⲟⲩ· ⲁⲩⲱ ⲙ
ⲙⲁⲓ̈ⲁⲣⲭⲉⲓ ϩⲓⲟⲩ
ⲥⲟⲡ· ⲁⲣⲁ ⲡⲉ
ϫⲁϥ ⲛⲧⲁⲩⲉⲓ ⲉⲃⲟⲗ
ⲧⲱⲛ· ⲁϥⲟⲩⲱ
ϣⲃ ⲉϥϫⲱ ⲙⲙⲟⲥ
ϫⲉ ⲡϫⲟⲉⲓⲥ ⲛ̅
ⲧⲟⲕ ⲉⲧⲥⲟⲟⲩⲛ
ⲡⲉϫⲁϥ ⲛⲁⲓ̈ ϫⲉ
ⲛⲁⲓ̈ ⲛⲉⲛⲧⲁⲩⲉⲓ

<page 31>
<column left>
ⲉⲃⲟⲗ ϩⲛ ⲧⲛⲟϭ ⲛ
ⲑⲗⲓⲯⲓⲥ· ⲉⲁⲩⲉⲓⲱ
ⲛⲛⲉⲩⲥⲧⲟⲗⲏ· ⲁⲩⲱ
ⲁⲩⲧⲃⲃⲟⲟⲩ ϩⲙ̄
ⲡⲉⲥⲛⲟϥ ⲙⲡⲉϩⲓ
ⲉⲓⲃ· ⲁϣ ⲧⲉ ⲧ
ⲛⲟϭ ⲛⲑⲗⲓⲯⲓⲥ ⲛ̄
ⲥⲁ ⲛⲣⲟⲟⲩϣ ⲙⲡⲓ
ⲁⲓⲱⲛ ⲉⲧⲙⲉϩ ⲙ
ⲡⲉⲣⲓⲥⲡⲁⲥⲙⲟⲥ·
ⲡⲁⲓ ⲉⲧⲛⲛⲁⲕⲁⲁϥ
ⲛⲥⲱⲛ ⲧⲏⲣⲛ·
ⲁⲩⲱ ⲛⲧⲛϯ ⲙ
ⲡⲉⲛⲟⲩⲟⲓ ⲉⲡⲉⲑ
ⲣⲟⲛⲟⲥ ⲛ̄ⲧⲉⲭⲁⲣⲓⲥ
ⲛⲧⲛⲉⲓⲱ ⲛⲛⲥ
ⲧⲟⲗⲏ ϩⲱⲱⲛ ϩⲙ
ⲡⲉⲥⲛⲟϥ ⲙⲡⲉ
ϩⲓⲉⲓⲃ· ⲉⲧⲉ ⲛⲁⲓ
ⲛⲉ ⲛⲉⲙⲯⲩⲭⲏ
ⲉⲩⲛⲏⲩ ⲉⲃⲟⲗ ϩⲙ
ⲡⲉⲓⲃⲓⲟⲥ· ⲛⲥⲉ
ⲕⲁⲑⲁⲣⲓⲍⲉ ⲙⲙⲟ
ⲟⲩ ⲛⲁⲛ· ϩⲓⲧⲙ̄
ⲡⲉⲧⲕⲁⲑⲁⲣⲓⲍⲉ
ⲛϣⲱⲛⲉ ⲛⲓⲙ
ⲓ̄ⲥ̄ ⲡⲉⲭ̄ⲥ̄· ⲁⲩⲱ
ⲛⲧⲛϫⲓ ⲉⲃⲟⲗ ϩ̄ⲙ
ⲡⲉϥⲥⲛⲟϥ· ⲙⲛ
ⲡⲉϥⲥⲱⲙⲁ· ⲡⲁⲓ
ⲛⲧⲁϥⲉⲓ ⲉⲃⲟⲗ ϩⲙ
ⲡⲉϥⲥⲡⲓⲣ ⲛⲟⲩ
ⲛⲁⲙ· ⲉⲩⲥⲱⲧⲉ

<column right>
ⲙⲡⲅⲉⲛⲟⲥ ⲧⲏⲣ̄ϥ
ⲛⲛⲣⲱⲙⲉ·
ⲁⲩⲱ ⲟⲛ ⲡⲉϫⲁϥ ϫⲉ
ⲡⲉⲧϩⲙⲟⲟⲥ ϩⲓ
ϫⲙ ⲡⲉⲑⲣⲟⲛⲟⲥ
ⲛⲁⲣ ϩⲁⲓ̈ⲃⲥ ⲉⲣⲟⲟⲩ
ⲛⲥⲉⲛⲁϩⲕⲟ ⲁⲛ
ⲟⲩⲇⲉ ⲛⲥⲉⲛⲁⲉⲓⲃⲉ
ⲁⲛ· ⲟⲩⲇⲉ· ⲙⲛ ⲕⲁⲩ
ⲙⲁ ⲛⲁϩⲉ ⲉϫⲱⲟⲩ
ⲁⲗⲗⲁ ⲡⲉϩⲓⲉⲓⲃ ⲉ
ⲧⲛⲧⲙⲏⲧⲉ ⲙ
ⲡⲉⲑⲣⲟⲛⲟⲥ ⲡⲉⲧ
ⲛⲁⲙⲟⲟⲛⲉ ⲙⲙⲟ
ⲟⲩ· ⲁⲩⲱ ⲛⲁⲓ̈ⲁⲧⲟⲩ
ⲁⲗⲏⲑⲱⲥ ⲛⲛⲉⲧⲟⲩ
ⲛⲁⲙⲟⲟⲛⲉ ⲙⲙⲟⲟⲩ
ϩⲓⲧ̄ⲙ ⲡⲉϩⲓⲉⲓⲃ·
ⲁⲩⲱ ⲛⲉⲧⲉ ⲙⲛϩⲕⲟ
ⲛⲁϣⲱⲡⲉ ⲛⲁⲩ
ⲟⲩⲇⲉ ⲕⲁⲩⲙⲁ· ⲉⲩ
ⲛⲁⲉⲓⲃⲉ ⲅⲁⲣ ⲛⲁ
ϣⲛϩⲉ· ⲉⲧⲡⲩ
ⲅⲏ ⲙⲙⲟⲩⲛⲱⲛϩ
ⲡⲉⲧⲙⲟⲟⲛⲉ ⲙ
ⲙⲟⲟⲩ· ⲙⲛ ⲕⲁⲩ
ⲙⲁ ⲛⲁϣⲱⲡⲉ
ϩⲓϫⲱⲟⲩ· ⲡⲣⲏ
ⲅⲁⲣ ⲛ̄ⲧⲇⲓⲕⲁⲓⲟ
ⲥⲩⲛⲏ· ⲡⲉⲧⲛⲁ
ⲣ̄ ⲟⲩⲟⲉⲓⲛ ⲉⲣⲟⲟⲩ
ⲡⲉϫⲁϥ ⲟⲛ ϫⲉ ⲡⲉ
ϩⲓⲉⲓⲃ ⲉⲧⲛⲧⲙⲏⲧⲉ

<page 32>
<column left>
ⲘⲠⲈⲐⲢⲞⲚⲞⲤ ⲚⲀ
ⲘⲞⲞⲚⲈ ⲘⲘⲞⲞⲨ
ⲚϤϪⲒⲦⲞⲨ ⲈϨⲢⲀⲒ
ⲈϪⲚ ⲚⲘⲠⲨⲄⲎ
ⲘⲘⲞⲨⲚⲰⲚϨ
ⲚⲦⲈ ⲠⲚⲞⲨⲦⲈ
ⲂⲰⲦⲈ ⲚⲚⲈⲨⲢⲘ
ⲈⲒⲞⲞⲨⲈ ⲈⲂⲞⲖ Ϩ̄Ⲛ̄
ⲚⲈⲨⲂⲀⲖ :~
Ⲱ ⲚⲀⲒⲀⲦϤ ⲘⲠⲈ
ⲦⲈⲢⲈ ⲠⲚⲞⲨⲦⲈ
ⲚⲀⲂⲰⲦⲈ ⲚⲚⲈϤ
ⲢⲘⲈⲒⲞⲞⲨⲈ ⲈⲂⲞⲖ
ϨⲚ ⲚⲈϤⲂⲀⲖ·
ⲀⲨⲰ ⲠⲈⲦⲚⲀⲤⲰ
ⲈⲂⲞⲖ ϨⲚ ⲦⲠⲨⲄⲎ
ⲘⲘⲞⲨⲚⲰⲚϨ Ⲉ
ⲦⲘⲘⲀⲨ Ⲛ̄ϤⲚⲀ
ⲈⲒⲂⲈ ⲀⲚ ϢⲀ ⲈⲚⲈϨ
ⲈⲒⲤ ⲠⲈⲦⲈⲢⲈ ⲚⲈϤ
ⲀⲄⲀⲐⲞⲚ ⲦⲎⲢⲞⲨ
ⲠⲞⲢϢ ⲈⲂⲞⲖ ϨⲀ
ⲢⲰⲞⲨ ⲚⲚⲞⲢⲐⲞ
ⲆⲞⲜⲞⲤ· ⲈϤⲤⲂⲦⲰⲦ
ⲈⲬⲞⲢⲎⲄⲈⲒ Ⲛ
ⲚⲈⲦⲘⲈ ⲘⲘⲞϤ
ⲠⲈⲦⲞⲨⲰϢ ⲆⲈ
ⲈⲦⲢⲈ ⲠϢⲎⲢⲈ Ⲙ
ⲠⲚⲞⲨⲦⲈ ϢⲰ
ⲠⲈ ⲚⲀϤ Ⲛ̄ⲂⲞⲎ
ⲐⲞⲤ· ⲘⲀⲢⲈϤⲈⲒ
ⲈⲂⲞⲖ ϨⲚ ⲚⲈϤϨ
ⲂⲎⲨⲈ ⲈⲐⲞⲞⲨ ⲘⲠ

<column right>
ⲔⲀⲔⲈ· ⲚⲤⲈⲘⲞⲞ
ϢⲈ ⲈϨⲞⲨⲚ ⲈⲠⲞⲨ
ⲞⲈⲒⲚ· ⲠⲈⲦⲞⲨ
ⲰϢ ⲈⲤⲰⲦⲘ ⲈⲦ
ⲤⲀⲖⲠⲒⲄⲜ Ⲙ̄ⲠⲰ
ⲚϨ· ⲘⲀⲢⲈϤⲦⲀϪ
ⲢⲞϤ ⲈϪⲘ ⲠⲰⲚϨ
ⲚⲀⲖⲎⲐⲒⲚⲞⲚ Ⲛ̄
ⲦⲀϤⲈⲒ ⲈⲂⲞⲖ ϨⲚ Ⲧ
ⲠⲈ· ⲀⲢⲒ ⲂⲢⲢⲈ
ⲞⲨⲚ ϢⲀⲢⲞⲚ ⲘⲠ
ϢⲀϪⲈ ⲚⲦⲘⲈ·
ⲒⲰϨⲀⲚⲚⲎⲤ ⲄⲀⲢ
ⲀϤⲤⲰⲦⲘ ⲈⲚⲀⲒ̈
ⲀⲨⲰ ⲠⲈⲠ̄Ⲛ̄Ⲁ̄ ⲈⲦⲞⲨ
ⲀⲀⲂ ⲘⲠⲚⲞⲨⲦⲈ
ⲀϤⲦⲤⲀⲂⲞⲚ ⲈⲚⲀⲒ
†ⲤⲰⲦⲘ ⲞⲚ ⲈⲢⲞϤ
Ⲛ̄ϬⲒ ⲒⲰϨⲀⲚⲚⲎⲤ
ϪⲈ ⲚⲦⲈⲢⲞⲨ<sic>ⲰⲚ
ⲚⲦⲘⲈϨⲤⲀϢϤⲈ
ⲚⲤⲪⲢⲀⲄⲒⲤ· ⲀⲨ
ⲔⲀⲢⲰϤ ϢⲰⲠⲈ
ϨⲚ ⲦⲠⲈ ⲚⲀⲞⲨϬⲒⲤ
ⲞⲨⲚⲞⲨ· ⲀⲢⲀ Ⲛ
ⲦⲀ ⲦⲒⲈϨⲎⲬⲒⲀ ϢⲰ
ⲠⲈ ϨⲚ ⲦⲠⲈ ϢⲀⲚ
ⲦⲈ ⲞⲨ ϢⲰⲠⲈ·
ⲀⲢⲀ ⲚⲦⲀ ⲞⲨⲘⲀⲚ
†ϨⲀⲠ ⲤⲰⲢ ⲈⲂⲞⲖ
ϪⲒⲚ ⲘⲘⲞⲚ ⲚⲦⲀ
ⲠⲈⲠⲢⲞⲤⲞⲠⲞⲚ
ⲘⲠⲞⲨⲀⲠⲞⲨⲀ ϪⲒ

<page 33>
<column left>
ⲟⲩⲟⲉⲓⲛ· ϩⲙ ⲡⲟⲩ
ⲟⲉⲓⲛ_ⲛⲗⲁⲙⲡ
ⲣⲟⲛ ⲙ̄ⲡⲉϩⲓⲉⲓⲃ·
Ⲱ ⲡⲉⲓⲛⲟϭ ⲛⲉⲟⲟⲩ
ⲛⲁⲧϣⲁϫⲉ ⲉⲣⲟϥ
ⲛⲧⲉ ⲟⲩⲣⲙⲛⲥⲁ
ⲣⲝ ⲥⲱⲧⲙ ⲉⲧⲕⲁ
ⲧⲁⲥⲧⲁⲥⲓⲥ ϩⲙ ⲡⲉ
ⲥⲧⲉⲣⲉⲱⲙⲁ ⲛⲧ
ⲡⲉ· ⲡⲛⲟⲩⲧⲉ
Ⲡⲉⲛⲧⲁϥⲧⲣⲉ ⲡⲉⲓ
ⲛⲟϭ ⲛⲉⲟⲟⲩ ϣⲱ
ⲡⲉ ⲛⲁⲧϣⲁϫⲉ ⲉ
ⲣⲟϥ· ϩⲙ ⲡⲧⲣⲉϥ
ϯ ⲛⲧⲉϥⲥⲙⲏ ⲛⲟⲩ
ⲥⲟⲡ· ⲁⲩⲱ ⲛϥ
ⲧⲣⲉ ⲛⲉⲧⲙⲡⲉⲩ
ⲕⲱⲧⲉ ϯ ⲙⲡⲉⲩ
ϩⲣⲟⲟⲩ· ϣⲁⲛⲧⲉ
ⲙⲛⲧⲥⲛⲟⲟⲩⲥⲉ ⲙⲡ
ⲣⲁⲧⲉⲥⲓⲁ <! ??> ⲥⲱⲣ ⲉ
ⲃⲟⲗ ⲛⲥⲉϯ ⲛⲟⲩⲧ
ⲃⲁ ⲛⲧⲉⲩⲛⲟⲩ·
ⲁⲩⲱ ⲛⲧⲉ ⲕⲉ ϥⲧⲟ
ⲟⲩ ⲛϣⲟ ⲡⲱϣ
ⲉϫⲱⲟⲩ :~
Ⲛⲧⲉ ⲛⲗⲁⲟⲥ· ⲙ̄ⲛ
ⲛⲉⲫⲩⲗⲏ· ⲙⲛ
ⲛⲁⲥⲡⲉ· ⲥⲉⲧⲙ
ⲛⲉⲛⲧⲁ ⲡⲉϩⲓⲉⲓⲃ
ⲁⲁⲩ ⲛⲥⲉⲥⲙⲟⲩ
ⲉⲡⲛⲟⲩⲧⲉ· ⲡⲉⲛ
ⲧⲁϥⲧⲥⲁⲃ[ⲉ ⲟⲩⲟⲛ]

<column right>
ⲛⲓⲙ ⲉⲡⲉⲥⲙⲟⲩ
ⲡⲏ ⲉⲃⲟⲗ ϩⲛ ⲧⲡⲉ
Ⲁϥⲉⲓ ⲛϭⲓ ⲕⲉ ⲁⲅ
ⲅⲉⲗⲟⲥ ⲭⲱⲣⲓⲥ
ⲡⲥⲁϣϥ· ⲉⲧⲉⲣⲉ
ⲡⲥⲁϣϥⲉ ⲛⲥⲁⲗ
ⲡⲓⲅⲝ ⲛⲧⲟⲟⲧⲟⲩ
ⲁϥⲁϩⲉⲣⲁⲧϥ ϩⲓ̈
ϫⲙ ⲡⲉⲑⲏⲥⲓⲁⲥ
ⲧⲏⲣⲓⲟⲛ· ⲉⲣⲉ ⲟⲩ
ϣⲏ ⲛⲛⲟⲩⲃ ⲛⲧⲟ
ⲟⲧϥ· ⲁⲩϯ ⲛⲁϥ
ⲛⲟⲩϣⲟⲩϩⲏⲛⲉ·
ⲉⲧⲣⲉϥⲧⲁⲁϥ ⲉϩ
ⲣⲁⲓ ⲙⲛ ⲛⲉϣⲗⲏⲗ
ⲛⲛⲉⲧⲟⲩⲁⲁⲃ· ⲉ
ϫⲙ ⲡⲉⲑⲏⲥⲓⲁⲥ
ⲧⲏⲣⲓⲟⲛ ⲛⲛⲟⲩⲃ
ⲉⲧⲙⲡⲉⲙⲧⲟ ⲉⲃⲟⲗ
ⲙⲡⲉϩⲓⲉⲓⲃ :~
Ⲙⲁⲣⲉ ⲡⲟⲩⲏⲏⲃ ϭⲉ
ⲧⲃⲃⲟϥ· ⲁⲩⲱ ϥⲛⲁ
ϣⲱⲡⲉ ⲛⲁⲅⲅⲉⲗⲟⲥ
ⲛⲧⲉ ⲡⲛⲟⲩⲧⲉ·
Ⲙⲁⲣⲉ ⲡⲗⲁⲟⲥ ⲕⲁ
ⲡⲉϥϩⲏⲧ ϩⲓ ⲡⲛⲟⲩ
ⲧⲉ· ⲁⲩⲱ ϣⲁⲣⲉ
ⲡⲉⲩϣⲗⲏⲗ ϣⲱ
ⲡⲉ ⲛϣⲟⲩϩⲏⲛⲉ
ϩⲓϫⲙ ⲡⲉⲑⲏⲥⲓⲁⲥ
ⲧⲏⲣⲓⲟⲛ· ϫⲉ ⲉⲣⲉ
ⲡⲁⲅⲅⲉⲗⲟⲥ ⲛϯ
ⲣⲏⲛⲏ· ⲛⲁ ⲁⲥⲡⲁ

<page 34>
<column left>
ⲍⲉ ⲙⲙⲟⲟⲩ ⲉⲧⲉⲩ
ⲧⲁⲡⲣⲟ· ⲛ̄ⲧⲉ ⲡⲉⲥ
ϯⲛⲟⲩⲃⲉ ⲙⲡⲉ
ⲡ̄ⲛ̄ⲁ̄· ⲉⲓ ⲉⲃⲟⲗ· ⲙ̄
ⲡⲙⲧⲟ ⲉⲃⲟⲗ ⲙ̄ⲡⲉ
ϩⲓⲉⲓⲃ· ⲛϥⲧⲣⲉⲩ
ⲡⲁⲣⲣⲏⲥⲓⲁⲍⲉ ⲙ
ⲙⲟⲟⲩ ⲙ̄ⲡ̄ⲙ̄ⲧⲟ ⲉ̄
ⲃⲟⲗ ⲙⲡⲛⲟⲩⲧⲉ
ⲛ̄ⲥⲁⲑⲏ· ϩⲙ ⲡ
Ⲧⲣⲉⲩϣⲱⲡⲉ ⲛⲁⲧ
ⲛⲟⲃⲉ ⲉⲩⲥⲁϩⲏⲩ
ⲉⲃⲟⲗ· ⲙⲡⲡⲉⲑⲟ
ⲟⲟⲩ· ⲁⲩⲱ ⲁϥ
Ϫⲓⲥⲉ ⲉϩⲣⲁϊ ⲡⲉϫⲁϥ
ⲛ̄ϭⲓ ⲡⲕⲁⲡⲛⲟⲥ
ⲛⲛϣⲟⲩϩⲏⲛⲉ
ⲛⲛⲉⲧⲟⲩⲁⲁⲃ·
ⲉⲃⲟⲗ ϩⲓⲧⲛ ⲧϭⲓϫ
ⲙⲡⲁⲅⲅⲉⲗⲟⲥ ⲙ
ⲡⲉⲙⲧⲟ ⲉⲃⲟⲗ ⲙ
ⲡⲛⲟⲩⲧⲉ :~
Ⲑⲉⲱⲣⲉⲓ ⲛⲧⲉⲧⲛ
ⲛⲁⲩ ⲉϩⲱⲃ ⲙⲙⲏⲥ
ⲧⲏⲣⲓⲟⲛ· ⲉϥⲟⲩ
ⲟⲛϩ ⲛⲁⲛ ⲉⲃⲟⲗ ϩⲓ̈
ⲧⲛ ⲓⲱϩⲁⲛⲛⲏⲥ
ⲡⲉⲓⲃⲁϊⲙⲏⲥⲧⲏ
ⲣⲓⲟⲛ· ⲛ̄ⲧⲉⲧⲛ
ϭⲓⲛⲉ ⲛ̄ⲛⲉⲓⲁⲥ
ⲙⲛ ⲛⲓⲃⲣⲣⲉ· ⲉⲣⲉ
ⲡⲛⲟⲩⲧⲉ ⲟⲓⲕⲟ
ⲛⲟⲙⲉⲓ ⲙⲙⲟⲟⲩ

<column right>
ⲛⲁⲛ· ⲉϥⲧⲁⲙⲟ
Ⲙⲙⲟⲛ ⲉⲣⲟⲟⲩ ⲙⲛ
ⲛⲉⲩⲉⲣⲏⲩ· ϫⲉ
ⲛⲉⲓⲁⲅⲅⲉⲗⲟⲥ
ⲙⲛ ⲛⲉⲓⲟⲩⲏⲏⲃ
ⲡⲉⲓⲗⲁⲟⲥ ⲛⲉⲓϣⲟⲩ
ϩⲏⲛⲉ· ⲛⲉⲓⲕⲁⲡ
ⲛⲟⲥ· ⲛⲉⲓϣⲗⲏⲗ·
ⲛⲉⲓⲑⲩⲥⲓⲁ· ⲉⲩ
ⲛⲏⲩ ϣⲁ ⲡⲉⲑⲏ
ⲥⲓⲁⲥⲧⲏⲣⲓⲟⲛ ⲙ
ⲡⲉϩⲓⲉⲓⲃ· ϩⲛ ⲧ
ⲧⲁⲡⲣⲟ ⲛⲛⲉⲭ
ⲣⲏⲥⲧⲓⲁⲛⲟⲥ·
ⲉⲓⲧⲁ ⲟⲛ ⲡⲉϫⲁϥ
ϫⲉ ⲁⲩⲱ ⲡⲥⲁϣϥ
ⲛⲁⲅⲅⲉⲗⲟⲥ· ⲉⲧⲉ
ⲣⲉ ⲧⲥⲁϣϥⲉ ⲛ
ⲥⲁⲗⲡⲓⲅⲝ ⲛⲧⲟⲟⲧⲟⲩ
ⲁⲩⲥⲉⲃⲧⲱⲧⲟⲩ ⲉⲧ
ⲣⲉⲩⲥⲁⲗⲡⲓⲍⲉ·
Ⲛⲧⲁⲩⲥⲃⲧⲱⲧⲟⲩ
ⲛⲁϣⲛϩⲉ· ⲛⲓⲙ
ⲡⲉⲛⲧⲁϥϫⲟⲟⲥ
ⲛⲁⲩ ϫⲉ ⲥⲃⲧⲉ ⲧⲏⲩ
ⲧⲛ· ⲏ ⲁϣ ⲡⲉ ⲡ
ⲛⲁⲩ ⲛⲧⲁⲩⲥⲃⲧⲱ
ⲧⲟⲩ ⲙⲙⲟϥ· ⲁⲣⲏⲩ
Ⲡⲛⲟⲩⲧⲉ ⲡⲉⲛⲧⲁϥ
ϫⲟⲟⲥ ⲛⲁⲩ ϫⲉ ⲥⲃ
ⲧⲉ ⲧⲏⲩⲧⲛ· ⲛ̄
Ⲧⲁⲩⲥⲃⲧⲱⲧⲟⲩ ⲙ
ⲡⲛⲁⲩ ⲛⲧⲁ ⲧⲃⲁ

<page 35>
<column left>
ⲂⲨⲖⲞⲚ ⲚⲚⲞϬ ϪⲒ
ⲤⲈ ⲘⲠⲈⲤⲦⲀⲠ Ⲙ
ⲠⲀⲦⲞⲨⲐⲂⲂⲒⲞⲤ·
ⲀⲨⲰ ⲘⲠⲀⲦⲈ ⲠⲞⲨⲀ
ⲠⲞⲨⲀ ϪⲒ ⲚⲚⲈ
ⲦⲈ ⲚⲞⲨϤ ⲚⲈ ⲈⲂⲞⲖ
ϨⲚ ⲦϬⲒϪ ⲘⲠⲈⲦ
ⲦⲞⲨⲚⲞⲤ· ⲀⲨⲰ
ⲚⲤⲈⲦⲞⲨⲈⲒⲞ Ⲙ
ⲠⲞⲨⲀⲠⲞⲨⲀ· ⲠⲢⲞⲤ
ⲚⲈⲚⲦⲀϤⲀⲀⲨ
ⲈⲒⲦⲈ ⲀⲄⲀⲐⲞⲚ· ⲈⲒⲦⲈ
ⲠⲈⲐⲞⲞⲨ :~
ⲚⲦⲀⲨⲤⲀⲖⲠⲒⲌⲈ ⲆⲈ
ⲞⲚ ϪⲈ ⲞⲨ· ⲚⲦⲀⲨ
ⲤⲀⲖⲠⲒⲌⲈ ϪⲈ ⲀⲢⲒ
ⲠⲀⲄⲀⲐⲞⲚ ⲚⲦⲈ
ⲠⲚⲞⲨⲦⲈ ϤⲒ ⲚⲚⲒ
ⲠⲞⲚⲎⲢⲒⲀ ⲚⲤⲀⲂⲞⲖ ⲘⲘⲰⲦⲚ̄·
ⲀⲨⲰ ⲚⲦⲈⲢⲞⲨⲤⲰ
ⲦⲘ ⲘⲠⲞⲨⲘⲈⲦⲀ
ⲚⲞⲒ̈· ⲀⲚⲀⲨ ϪⲈ Ⲛ
ⲦⲀ ⲞⲨ ϢⲰⲠⲈ Ⲙ
ⲠϨⲀⲈ· ϨⲒⲦⲚ̄ ⲚⲈⲦ
ⲤⲀⲖⲠⲒⲌⲈ :~
ⲠϢⲞⲢⲠ ⲀϤϢⲰ
ⲠⲈ ⲈϤⲤⲀⲖⲠⲒⲌⲈ
ⲀϤϢⲰⲠⲈ Ⲛ̄ϬⲒ ⲞⲨ
ⲀⲖⲘⲠⲈ ⲘⲚ ⲞⲨ
ⲔⲰϨⲦ· ⲈϤⲦⲎϨ
ⲘⲚ ⲞⲨⲤⲚⲞϤ· ⲀⲨⲰ
ⲀⲨⲚⲞϪϤ ⲈϪⲘ Ⲡ

<column right>
ⲔⲀϨ· ⲀⲨⲰ ⲠⲞⲨ
ⲈⲚⲈϢⲞⲘⲚⲦ
ⲘⲠⲔⲀϨ ⲀϤⲦⲀ
ⲔⲞ· ⲚⲦⲀϤⲢⲰ
ⲔϨ· ⲈⲦⲂⲈ ⲞⲨ· ⲈⲦ
ⲂⲈ ⲘⲠⲞⲢⲚⲒⲀ· Ⲉ
ⲦⲞⲨⲈⲒⲢⲈ ⲘⲘⲞⲞⲨ
ϨⲒϪⲰϤ ⲚϬⲒ Ⲛ
ϢⲎⲢⲈ ⲚⲚⲢⲰⲘⲈ
ⲀϤⲤⲀⲖⲠⲒⲌⲈ ⲚϬⲒ
ⲠⲘⲈϨⲤⲚⲀⲨ ⲚⲀⲄ
ⲄⲈⲖⲞⲤ· ⲀⲨⲰ
ⲠⲞⲨⲚϢⲞⲘⲚⲦ
ⲚⲐⲀⲖⲀⲤⲤⲀ· ⲀϤ
Ⲣ ⲤⲚⲞϤ· ⲀⲨⲘⲞⲨ
ⲚϬⲒ ⲠⲞⲨⲈⲚϢⲞ
ⲘⲚⲦ ⲚⲚⲌⲰⲞⲚ
ⲚⲐⲀⲖⲀⲤⲤⲀ·
ⲚⲀⲒ̈ ⲈⲦⲈⲢⲈ ⲚⲢⲰ
ⲘⲈ ϬⲒⲚⲈ ⲘⲘⲞⲞⲨ
ⲈⲨⲐⲨⲢⲀⲠⲒⲀ·
ⲀⲨⲰ ⲚⲔⲈ ⲈϪⲎⲨ
ⲀⲨⲦⲀⲔⲞ· Ⲛ̄ⲦⲀ
ⲚⲀⲒ̈ ⲆⲈ ⲞⲚ ϢⲰ
ⲠⲈ ⲈⲦⲂⲈ ⲞⲨ· ⲈⲦ
ⲂⲈ ⲚⲈⲦⲈⲒⲢⲈ Ⲛ̄
ⲚⲈⲒⲘ̄Ⲛ̄ⲦⲈϢⲰⲦ
ⲚⲔⲢⲞϤ· ⲚⲤⲈ
ϮⲤⲀ ⲀⲚ ⲈⲰⲢⲔ Ⲙ
ⲠⲢⲀⲚ ⲘⲠⲚⲞⲨ
ⲦⲈ ⲚⲚⲞⲨϪ·
ⲈⲚⲈ ⲘⲘⲞⲚ ⲞⲨ
ⲠⲈ ⲠⲠⲈⲐⲞⲞⲨ Ⲛ

<page 36>
<column left>
ⲚⲈⲚⲦⲂⲦ ⲘⲚ ⲚⲈ
ⲈϪⲎⲨ :~
ⲀⲨⲰ ⲠⲘⲈϨϢⲞ
ⲘⲚⲦ ⲀϤⲤⲀⲖⲠⲒ̈
ⲌⲈ· ⲀⲨⲰ ⲀϤϨⲈ
ⲈⲂⲞⲖ Ϩ̄Ⲛ̄ ⲦⲠⲈ Ⲛ
ϬⲒ ⲞⲨⲚⲞϬ ⲚⲤⲒⲞⲨ
ⲈϤϪⲈⲢⲞ ⲚⲐⲈ ⲚⲞⲨ
ⲖⲀⲘⲠⲀⲤ· ⲀϤⲈⲒ
ⲈⲠⲈⲤⲎⲦ ⲈϪⲚ ⲚⲘ
ⲠⲨⲄⲎ ⲘⲘⲞⲞⲨ
ⲘⲚ ⲚⲒⲢ̄Ⲣ̄ⲰⲞⲨ
ⲀⲨⲰ ⲠⲞⲨⲚϢⲞ
ⲘⲚⲦ· ⲚⲚⲘⲘⲞ
ⲞⲨ· ⲀϤⲤⲒϢⲈ· Ⲡ
ⲢⲀⲚ ⲘⲠⲤⲒⲞⲨ Ⲉ
ⲦⲘⲘⲀⲨ· ⲠⲈ ⲀⲘ
ⲮⲒⲚⲐⲒⲞⲚ· ⲈⲦⲈ
ⲠⲀⲒ̈ ⲠⲈ ⲠⲈⲦⲞ ⲚϨⲞ
ⲦⲈ Ⲛ̄ⲚⲀϨⲢ̄Ⲛ̄ ϨⲞⲒ̈
ⲚⲈ· ⲠⲈⲦⲞ ⲚⲞⲨ
ⲞⲈⲒⲚ ϢⲀ ϨⲈⲚⲔⲞ
ⲞⲨⲈ· ⲠⲈⲦⲈ ϢⲀⲨ
ⲔⲞⲖⲀⲌⲈ ⲘⲘⲞϤ Ⲙ
ⲠⲈⲨⲞⲈⲒϢ ⲈⲦⲘ
ⲘⲀⲨ· ⲚⲦⲞϤ ⲠⲈ
ⲦⲞ ⲚϢⲀϨ ϨⲘ ⲠⲈⲨ
ⲔⲰⲦⲈ :~
ⲠⲤⲒⲞⲨ ⲄⲀⲢ ⲈⲦⲘ
ⲘⲀⲨ Ⲛ̄ⲦⲞϤ ⲠⲈ Ⲡ
ⲖⲀⲦⲰⲚⲒⲜ· ⲔⲀ
ⲦⲀ ⲦⲀⲤⲠⲈ ⲚⲚⲈϨ
ⲢⲰⲘⲀⲒⲞⲤ· ⲠⲢⲀ

<column right>
ϢⲈ ⲄⲀⲢ ⲘⲠⲚⲞⲨ
ⲦⲈ ⲠⲈ· ⲈⲢϢⲀⲚ
ⲞⲨⲢⲰⲘⲈ ⲐⲈⲰⲢⲒ̈
ⲚⲚⲈⲦⲚⲎⲨ ⲈϪⲰϤ
Ⲛ̄Ϥ̄ⲘⲈⲦⲀⲚⲞⲒ̈ Ⲛ̄Ϥ̄
ⲈⲒⲢⲈ ⲘⲠⲠⲈⲦⲚⲀ
ⲚⲞⲨϤ ⲘⲠⲘⲦⲞ ⲈⲂⲞⲖ
ⲘⲠⲚⲞⲨⲦⲈ :~
ⲘⲠⲈⲨⲞⲈⲒϢ ⲄⲀⲢ ⲈⲦⲘ
ⲘⲀⲨ ⲚⲈⲢⲈ ⲠⲚⲞⲂⲈ
ⲞϢ ⲠⲈ· ⲚⲈⲢⲈ Ⲡ
ⲚⲞⲨⲦⲈ ϨⲰⲰϤ ⲞⲨ
ⲰϢ ⲈⲔⲰ ⲈⲂⲞⲖ
ⲚⲚⲈⲨⲚⲞⲂⲈ· ⲘⲚ
ⲚⲈⲨⲠⲀⲐⲞⲤ ⲈⲐⲞⲞⲨ
ⲠⲘⲈϨϤⲦⲞⲞⲨ ⲚⲀⲄ
ⲄⲈⲖⲞⲤ· ⲀⲨ<?>ⲤⲀⲖⲠⲒ
ⲌⲈ· ⲀⲨⲰ ⲠⲞⲨⲚ̄
ϢⲞⲘⲚⲦ ⲘⲠⲢⲎ
ⲀϤϢⲰⲰϬⲈ· ⲀⲨⲰ
ⲠⲞⲨⲚϢⲞⲘⲚⲦ Ⲙ
ⲠⲞⲞϨ· ⲘⲚ ⲠⲞⲨⲚ
ϢⲞⲘⲚⲦ ⲚⲚⲤⲒⲞⲨ
ϪⲈ ⲈⲢⲈ ⲠⲞⲨⲚϢⲞ
ⲘⲚⲦ ⲘⲠⲈϨⲞⲞⲨ Ⲣ
ⲔⲀⲔⲈ· ⲘⲚ ⲠⲞⲨⲚ
ϢⲞⲘⲚⲦ ⲚⲦⲈⲨ
ϢⲎ· ⲚⲦⲈⲦⲘ ⲞⲨ
ⲞⲈⲒⲚ ϬⲈ ϢⲰⲠⲈ
ⲚⲚⲢⲰⲘⲈ :~
ⲚⲦⲀ ⲚⲢⲰⲘⲈ ⲢⲚⲞ
ⲂⲈ· ⲀⲚⲒⲠⲈⲐⲞⲞⲨ
ⲦⲎⲢⲞⲨ ϢⲰⲠⲈ·

<page 37>
<column left>
ⲡⲣⲏ ⲅⲁⲣ ⲟⲩϩⲙϩⲁⲗ ⲡⲉ·
ⲡⲟⲟϩ· ⲟⲩϩⲙϩⲁⲗ ⲡⲉ·
ⲛⲉⲥⲓⲟⲩ· ϩⲛϩⲙ
ϩⲁⲗ ⲛⲉ :~
ⲡⲣⲱⲙⲉ ⲟⲩϩⲙ
ϩⲁⲗ ⲡⲉ· ⲁⲩⲱ
ⲡⲛⲟⲩⲧⲉ ⲡⲉⲛ
ⲧⲁϥⲧⲁⲙⲓⲟⲟⲩ·
ϩⲙ ⲡⲧⲣⲉ ⲡⲧⲁⲕⲟ
ⲇⲉ ϣⲱⲡⲉ ⲛⲟⲩ
ϩⲙϩⲁⲗ ⲛⲟⲩⲱⲧ
ⲁⲡⲕⲉⲥⲉⲉⲡⲉ ⲉⲣ
ⲛⲟⲃⲉ :~ ⲁⲗⲗⲁ
ⲛⲓⲉⲡⲟⲩⲣⲁⲛⲓⲟⲛ ⲟⲩ
ⲧⲱϣ ⲡⲉⲛⲧⲁϥ
ⲉⲓ ⲛⲁⲩ· ⲉⲃⲟⲗ ϩⲓⲧⲙ
ⲡⲛⲟⲩⲧⲉ ⲙⲡⲧⲏ
ⲣϥ· ⲡⲉⲧⲉ ⲙⲛⲟⲩ
ⲟⲛ ϣⲟⲟⲡ ⲛⲥⲁⲃⲏⲗ
ⲗⲁϥ· ⲁⲩⲱ ⲧⲁⲓ̈ ⲧⲉ
ⲑⲉ ⲛⲧⲁ ⲛⲕⲉⲍⲱ
ⲟⲛ ⲣ ⲧⲩⲭⲏ· ⲡ
ⲣⲟⲥ ⲡⲉⲛⲧⲁϥⲉⲓ ⲉ
ⲃⲟⲗ ϣⲁⲣⲟⲟⲩ·
ⲁⲓⲛⲁⲩ ⲡⲉϫⲁϥ
ⲁⲩⲱ ⲁⲓ̈ⲥⲱⲧⲙ
ⲉⲩⲁⲅⲅⲉⲗⲟⲥ ⲉϥ
ϩⲏⲗ ϩⲛ ⲧⲙⲏⲧⲉ
ⲛⲧⲡⲉ· ⲉϥϫⲱ
ⲙⲙⲟⲥ ϩⲛ ⲟⲩⲛⲟϭ
ⲛⲥⲙⲏ· ⲉϥϫⲱ
ⲙⲙⲟⲥ ⲛⲧⲉⲓϩⲉ·
ϫⲉ ⲟⲩⲟⲓ̈ ⲛϣⲟⲙⲛⲧ

<column right>
ⲛⲥⲟⲡ ⲛ̄ⲛⲉⲧⲟⲩ
ⲏϩ ϩⲓϫⲙ ⲡⲕⲁϩ
ⲉⲃⲟⲗ ϩⲙ ⲡⲕⲉⲥⲉ
ⲉⲡⲉ ⲛⲛⲁⲅⲅⲉⲗⲟⲥ
ⲉⲧⲛⲁⲥⲁⲗⲡⲓⲍⲉ·
ⲟⲩⲟⲓ̈ ⲡⲉϫⲁϥ ϣⲁ
ϣⲟⲙⲛⲧ ⲛⲥⲟⲡ·
ⲟⲩⲟⲓ̈ ⲛⲧϣⲟⲙⲧⲉ
ⲛϩⲩⲗⲏⲅⲓⲁ ⲙⲡ
ⲣⲱⲙⲉ ⲉⲧϥⲛⲁ
ⲁⲁⲩ ⲉϥⲡⲉⲣⲓⲥⲡⲁ
ⲉⲡⲉⲓⲥⲁ ⲙⲛ ⲡⲁⲓ̈
ⲙⲡⲉϥⲉⲓⲣⲉ ⲙⲡⲟⲩ
ⲱϣ ⲙⲡϫⲟⲉⲓⲥ
ϩⲛ ⲟⲩⲉⲓ ⲙⲙⲟⲟⲩ
ϫⲉ ⲉⲣⲉ ⲡϫⲟⲉⲓⲥ
ⲛⲁ ⲛⲁϥ :~
ⲁⲓ̈ⲛⲁⲩ ⲡⲉϫⲁϥ ⲉ
ⲕⲉ ⲥⲓⲟⲩ ⲉⲁϥϩⲉ ⲉ
ϫⲙ ⲡⲕⲁϩ· ϩⲙ
ⲡⲧⲣⲉ ⲡⲙⲉϩϯⲟⲩ
ⲛⲁⲅⲅⲉⲗⲟⲥ ⲥⲁⲗ
ⲡⲓⲍⲉ· ⲁⲩⲱ ⲁⲩ
ϯ ⲛⲁϥ ⲛⲛϣⲟⲙⲧ
ⲛⲧϣⲱⲧⲉ ⲙⲡ
ⲛⲟⲩⲛ :~
ⲁϣ ⲇⲉ ⲟⲛ ⲧⲉ ⲧ
ϣⲱⲧⲉ ⲙⲡⲛⲟⲩⲛ
ⲛⲥⲁ ⲡⲙⲁ· ⲉⲧⲙ
ⲡϣⲁⲉⲛⲉϩ ⲡⲉⲧ
ϭⲓⲛⲉ ⲁⲛ ⲙⲡⲉϥ
ϣⲓⲛⲉ· ⲡⲙⲁ ⲉϣⲁ
ⲣⲉ ⲛⲣⲉϥⲣⲛⲟⲃⲉ

<page 38>
<column left>
ⲧⲏⲣⲟⲩ ⲛⲧⲁⲙⲓ̈
ⲛⲉ ⲕⲗⲏⲣⲟⲛⲟⲙⲉⲓ
ⲙⲙⲟϥ· ⲁⲩⲱ
Ⲟⲛ ⲡⲉϫⲁϥ ϫⲉ ⲁ
ϩⲉⲛϣϫⲏ ⲉⲓ ⲉϩ
ⲣⲁⲓ̈ ϩⲙ ⲡⲙⲁ ⲉⲧⲙ
ⲙⲁⲩ· ⲁⲩⲱ ⲁⲩ
ϯ ⲛⲁⲩ ⲛⲟⲩⲉⲝⲟⲩ
ⲥⲓⲁ· ⲛⲑⲉ ⲉⲧⲉ ⲟⲩ
ⲛⲧⲁⲩ ⲉⲝⲟⲩⲥⲓⲁ
ⲙⲙⲁⲩ ⲛϭⲓ ⲛⲟⲩ
ⲟⲟϩⲉ ⲙⲡⲕⲁϩ· ⲉ
ⲁⲩϫⲟⲟⲥ ⲛⲁⲩ ⲉⲧⲁ
ⲕⲟ ⲛⲛⲕⲁⲣⲡⲟⲥ
ⲙⲡⲕⲁϩ· ⲙⲛ
ϣⲏⲛ ⲛⲓⲙ· ⲉⲓⲙⲏ
ⲧⲉ ⲛⲛⲣⲱⲙⲉ ⲙ
ⲙⲁⲧⲉ· ⲉⲣⲉ ⲙⲙⲁ
ⲉⲓⲛⲧⲉⲥⲫⲣⲁⲅⲓⲥ
ⲙⲡⲛⲟⲩⲧⲉ ϩⲓ
ϫⲛ ⲧⲉⲩⲧⲉϩⲛⲉ :~
Ⲁⲛⲁⲩ ⲉⲡⲉⲛϩⲉ· ⲙ̄ⲛ̄
ⲡⲉⲛⲧⲁⲕⲟ· ⲱ ⲛⲁ
ⲙⲉⲣⲁⲧⲉ· ⲁϣ
ⲛⲉ ⲛⲉϣϫⲏ ⲉⲧⲙ̄
ⲙⲁⲩ· ⲛⲥⲁ ⲛⲉⲛⲧⲁ
ⲡⲛⲟⲩⲧⲉ ⲕⲟⲥ
ⲙⲉⲓ ⲙⲉⲛ ⲙⲙⲟⲟⲩ
ϩⲙ ⲡⲉⲥⲭⲏⲙⲁ ⲛⲧ
ⲙⲛⲧϩⲟⲟⲩⲧ·
ⲁⲩⲡⲱⲱⲛⲉ ⲉⲡⲉⲥ
ⲭⲏⲙⲁ ⲛ̄ⲛⲉϩⲓⲟⲙⲉ
ⲁⲩⲥⲙⲓⲛⲉ ⲛⲁⲩ ⲛϩ̄ⲛ̄

<column right>
ⲃⲱ ⲛⲑⲉ ⲛⲛⲁ ⲛⲉ
ϩⲓⲟⲙⲉ· ⲁⲩⲥⲉⲧⲡ
ⲧⲁⲥⲭⲏⲙⲱⲥⲩ
ⲛⲏ ⲛⲁⲩ ⲙⲙⲓⲛ
ⲙⲙⲟⲟⲩ :~
Ⲛⲁⲓ̈ ⲟⲛ ⲛⲧⲁ ⲫⲓⲉ
ⲣⲟⲥ ⲛⲁⲡⲟⲥⲧⲟⲗⲟⲥ
ⲥⲱⲅⲣⲁⲫⲉⲓ ⲛⲁⲛ
ϩⲁⲣⲟⲟⲩ ⲉϥϫⲱ ⲙ
ⲙⲟⲥ· ϫⲉ ⲛⲁⲓ̈ ⲛ̄
ⲧⲁⲩϣⲓⲃⲉ ⲙⲡϩⲱⲃ
ⲛⲧⲉⲩⲫⲩⲥⲓⲥ ⲉⲩ
ⲡⲁⲣⲁ ⲧⲉⲩⲫⲩⲥⲓⲥ·
ⲁⲩⲙⲟⲩϩ ϩⲙ ⲡⲉⲩ
ⲙⲉ ⲉϩⲟⲩⲛ ⲉⲛⲉⲩ
ⲉⲣⲏⲩ· ϩⲉⲛϩⲟⲟⲩⲧ
ⲙⲛ ϩⲉⲛϩⲟⲟⲩⲧ
ⲉⲩⲣϩⲱⲃ ⲉⲧⲁⲥⲭⲩ
ⲙⲟⲥⲩⲛⲏ· ⲛⲁⲓ ⲟⲛ
Ⲛⲉⲛⲧⲁⲩⲥⲟⲃⲧⲉ ⲛⲁⲩ
ⲛⲧϣⲱⲧⲉ ⲙⲡ
ⲛⲟⲩⲛ· ⲁⲩⲱ ⲛⲉⲩ
ⲃⲏⲕ ⲁⲛ ⲉⲡⲉⲥⲏⲧ
ⲙⲁⲩⲁⲁⲩ· ⲁⲗⲗⲁ
ⲉⲩϥⲓ ⲛϩⲉⲛⲕⲟⲟⲩⲉ
ⲛⲙⲙⲁⲩ· ⲉⲧⲃⲉ
Ⲡⲁⲓ̈ ⲟⲩⲟⲓ̈ ⲛⲁⲩ ϣⲁ
ⲥⲁϣϥ ⲛ̄ⲧⲃⲁ ⲛ̄
ⲥⲁⲡ·   ⲁϣ ⲟⲩⲛ
Ⲧⲉ ⲧⲉⲝⲟⲩⲥⲓⲁ ⲛ
ⲧⲁⲩⲧⲁⲁⲥ ⲛⲁⲩ
ⲛⲥⲁ ⲧⲉⲝⲟⲩⲥⲓⲁ ⲙ̄
ⲡⲉⲩⲗⲁⲥ· ⲉⲩⲕⲁⲧⲁ

<page 39>
<column left>
ⲗⲁⲗⲉⲓ ⲛⲥⲁ ⲛⲉⲩ
ⲉⲣⲏⲩ· ⲛⲥⲉϯⲥⲁ
ⲁⲛ ⲉⲧⲃⲉ ⲡϫⲟⲉⲓⲥ
ⲟⲩⲇⲉ ⲛⲉϥϣⲙ
ϣⲓⲧ ⲉⲧⲉⲓⲣⲉ ⲙ
ⲡⲉϥⲟⲩⲱϣ·
ⲡⲉϫⲁϥ ⲟⲛ ϫⲉ ⲁⲩ
ϫⲟⲟⲥ ⲛⲁⲩ ⲉⲧⲁ
ⲕⲉ ⲡⲕⲁϩ· ⲙ̄ⲛ̄
ⲛⲕⲁⲣⲡⲟⲥ· ⲙ̄ⲛ̄
ⲛⲉⲛϣⲏⲛ· ⲉⲓ
ⲙⲏⲧⲉⲓ ⲛⲛⲣⲱ
ⲙⲉ· ⲙⲙⲁⲉⲓⲛ ⲛ
ⲧⲉⲥⲫⲣⲁⲅⲓⲥ ⲙ
ⲡⲛⲟⲩⲧⲉ ϩⲓϫⲛ̄
ⲧⲉⲩⲧⲉϩⲛⲉ· ⲉⲧⲉ
ⲛⲉⲛⲧⲁⲩⲥⲫⲣⲁ
ⲅⲓⲍⲉ ⲙⲙⲟⲟⲩ ⲛⲉ
ϩⲙ ⲡⲉⲥⲛⲟϥ ⲛⲧ
ⲙⲛⲧⲙⲁⲣⲧⲩ
ⲣⲟⲥ· ⲁⲩⲱ ⲛⲉⲛ
ⲧⲁ ⲡⲉⲩⲃⲁⲡⲧⲓⲥ
ⲙⲁ· ⲧⲃⲃⲉ ⲡⲕⲱ
ⲧⲉ ⲙⲡⲉⲩⲥⲱⲙⲁ
ϩⲛ ⲧⲃⲃⲟ ⲛⲓⲙ·
ⲉⲙⲛ ⲕⲱϩ· ⲉⲙ̄ⲛ̄
ⲙⲟⲥⲧⲉ· ⲉⲙ
ⲡⲟⲩⲉⲡⲓⲑⲩⲙⲉⲓ
ⲉⲙⲡⲟⲩⲥⲱϣ
ⲙⲡⲟⲩϩⲱⲧⲃ ⲙ
ⲡⲟⲩⲕⲁⲧⲁⲗⲁⲗⲉⲓ
ⲙⲡⲟⲩⲡⲁⲣⲁⲇⲓ

<column right>
ⲇⲟⲩ ⲛ̄ⲛⲉⲩⲉ̄ⲣⲏⲩ
ⲉⲡⲙⲟⲩ· ⲛⲁї
ⲙ̄ⲛ̄ ⲛⲉⲧⲉⲓⲛⲉ ⲛ̄
ⲛⲁї· ⲛⲉⲧϯ ⲟⲩ
ⲃⲉ ⲡⲛⲟⲙⲟⲥ· ⲁⲩⲱ
ⲉⲣⲉ ⲡⲛⲟⲙⲟⲥ ϯ
ⲟⲩⲃⲏⲩ :~
ⲛⲁїⲁⲧⲟⲩ ⲛⲛⲉⲧⲱϣ
ⲁⲩⲱ ⲉⲧⲛⲟї ϫⲉ
ⲡⲁї ⲡⲉ ⲡⲙⲁⲉⲓⲛ
ⲛⲧⲉⲥⲫⲣⲁⲅⲓⲥ·
ⲛⲁї ⲛⲉⲛⲧⲁ ⲡⲉϩⲓ
ⲉⲓⲃ ⲥⲫⲣⲁⲅⲓⲍⲉ
ⲙⲙⲟⲟⲩ·
ⲛⲁї ⲛⲉⲛⲧⲁ ⲡⲉ
ϩⲓⲉⲓⲃ ⲙⲡⲛⲟⲩ
ⲧⲉ ⲡⲱϩ ϣⲁⲣⲟⲟⲩ·
ⲛⲁїⲁⲧⲟⲩ ⲛⲛⲉ
ⲧⲱϣ· ⲙ̄ⲛ̄ ⲛⲉⲧ
ⲛⲟї· ϫⲉ ⲡⲁї ⲡⲉ
ⲡⲙⲁ ⲛⲑⲩⲡⲟⲙⲟ
ⲛⲏ :~ ⲛⲁїⲁⲧⲟⲩ
ⲛⲛⲉⲧⲱϣ ⲙⲛ ⲛⲉⲧ
ⲛⲟї ϫⲉ ⲡⲁї ⲡⲉ ⲡ
ⲥⲱⲧⲉ ⲛⲧⲁⲩⲥⲫ
ⲣⲁⲅⲓⲍⲉ ⲙⲙⲟⲛ
ⲛϩⲏⲧϥ· ⲁⲩⲱ
ⲛⲧⲛϣⲱⲡⲉ ⲉⲛ
ⲉⲓⲛⲉ ⲛ̄ⲛⲉⲛⲉ
ⲣⲏⲩ ϩ̄ⲛ̄ ⲑⲟⲧⲉ ⲙ
ⲡⲛⲟⲩⲧⲉ :~
ⲡⲉⲧⲟⲩⲱϣ ϭⲉ ⲉⲣ
ⲛⲟⲃⲉ· ⲙⲁⲣⲉϥⲉⲓ

<page 40>
<column left>
ⲙⲉ ⲉⲡⲁⲓ̈ ϫⲉ ⲁϥ
ⲟⲩⲉ ⲉⲃⲟⲗ ⲙⲡⲙⲁ
ⲉⲓⲛ ⲛⲧⲉⲥⲫⲣⲁ
ⲅⲓⲥ· ⲉⲧϩⲙ ⲡⲉⲭ̅ⲥ̅
ⲓ̅ⲥ̅ ⲡⲉⲛϫⲟⲉⲓⲥ·
Ⲛⲁⲓ̈ⲁⲧⲟⲩ ⲡⲉϫⲁϥ
ⲛⲛⲉⲧⲱϣ ⲁⲩⲱ
ⲉⲧⲛⲟⲓ̈· ϫⲉ ⲡⲉϩⲓ
ⲉⲓⲃ ⲛⲧⲟϥ ⲡⲉ ⲡ
ϩⲟⲙⲟⲟⲩⲥⲓⲟⲛ ⲙ
ⲡⲉⲓⲱⲧ· ⲛ̄ⲧⲟϥ
Ⲡⲉ ⲡϩⲟⲙⲟⲟⲩⲥⲓⲟⲛ
ⲛⲧⲁ ⲧⲡⲁⲣⲑⲉ
ⲛⲟⲥ ϫⲡⲟϥ· ⲡⲉⲧ
ⲧⲱⲱⲃⲉ ⲙⲡⲟⲩⲁ
ⲡⲟⲩⲁ· ϩⲓϫⲛ ⲧⲉϥ
ⲧⲉϩⲛⲉ ϩⲙ ⲡⲙⲁ ⲉ
ⲛⲧⲉⲥⲫⲣⲁⲅⲓⲥ·
Ⲛⲁⲓⲁⲧⲟⲩ ⲛⲛⲉ
ⲧⲱϣ· ⲁⲩⲱ ⲉⲧ
ⲛⲟⲓ̈ ϫⲉ ⲡⲉⲛⲧⲁϥ
ⲙⲉⲣⲉ ⲡⲱⲛϩ· ⲁⲩ
ⲧⲁⲁϥ ⲛⲁϥ· ⲡⲉⲛ
Ⲧⲁϥⲙⲉⲣⲉ ⲡⲙⲟⲩ
ⲁⲡⲛⲟⲩⲧⲉ ⲉⲓⲛⲉ
ⲙⲙⲟϥ ⲛⲁϥ· ⲛⲑⲉ
ⲉⲛⲉϥⲟⲩⲁϣϥ ⲙ
ⲙⲟⲥ· ⲡⲉⲛⲧⲁϥ
Ⲙⲟⲟⲛⲉ ⲅⲁⲣ ⲙⲙⲟⲟⲩ
ⲡⲉ ⲡⲣⲣⲟ ⲡⲙⲟⲩ
ⲡⲉⲧⲟⲩⲙⲟⲩⲧⲉ ⲉ
ⲣⲟϥ ⲛϩⲉⲃⲣⲁⲉⲓⲥⲧⲓ
ϫⲉ ⲁⲃⲃⲁⲧⲟⲛ :~

<column right>
†ⲥⲱⲧⲙ ⲟⲛ ⲉⲣⲟϥ
ⲙⲛⲛⲥⲁ ⲛⲁⲓ̈ ϫⲉ
ⲁⲡⲙⲉϩⲥⲟⲟⲩ ⲛⲁⲅ
ⲅⲉⲗⲟⲥ ⲥⲁⲗⲡⲓⲍⲉ
ⲁⲓ̈ⲥⲱⲧⲙ ⲉⲩⲥⲙⲏ
ⲉⲃⲟⲗ ϩⲛ̄ⲛ̄ⲧⲁⲡ ⲙ̄
ⲡⲉⲑⲏⲥⲓⲁⲥⲧⲏⲣⲓ
ⲟⲛ· ⲉⲧⲙⲡⲉⲙⲧⲟ
ⲉⲃⲟⲗ ⲙⲡⲛⲟⲩⲧⲉ
ⲉⲥϫⲱ ⲙⲙⲟⲥ ⲙ
ⲡⲙⲉϩⲥⲟⲟⲩ ⲛⲁⲅ
ⲅⲉⲗⲟⲥ· ⲡⲉⲧⲉⲣⲉ ⲧ
Ⲥⲁⲗⲡⲓⲅⲝ ⲛⲧⲟⲟⲧϥ
ϫⲉ ⲃⲱⲗ ⲉⲃⲟⲗ ⲙ
ⲡⲉϥⲧⲟⲟⲩ ⲛⲁⲅ
ⲅⲉⲗⲟⲥ· ⲉⲧⲙⲏⲣ
ⲉϫⲙ ⲡⲛⲟϭ ⲛⲓⲣ
ⲣⲟ ⲡⲉⲩⲫⲣⲁⲧⲏⲥ
ⲁⲩⲱ ⲁⲩⲃⲟⲗⲟⲩ ⲉ
ⲃⲟⲗ· ⲉⲣⲉ ⲟⲣⲅⲏ ⲛⲓⲙ
ⲥⲃⲧⲱⲧ ⲉⲉⲓ·
Ⲕⲁⲧⲁ ⲟⲩϫⲱⲛϥ
ⲏ ⲕⲁⲧⲁ ϩⲉⲛⲟⲩ
ⲟⲉⲓϣ· ⲡⲉⲓ ⲡⲉ
ⲑⲟⲟⲩ ⲡⲁⲓ̈ ⲛⲧⲟϥ
ⲉϥⲧⲏϣ ⲉⲓ· ⲛⲛⲁⲩ
ⲛⲓⲙ ⲙⲛ ⲟⲩⲛⲟⲩ
ⲛⲓⲙ· ⲛⲁⲓ̈ ⲡⲉ
Ϫⲁϥ ⲉⲩⲥⲃⲧⲱⲧ
ⲛⲧⲉⲩⲛⲟⲩ· ⲙⲛ
ⲛⲉϩⲟⲟⲩ· ⲙⲛ ⲛⲉ
ⲃⲟⲧ· ⲙⲛ ⲧⲉⲣⲟⲙ
ⲡⲉ· ⲉⲧⲉ ⲕⲉ ⲙⲡⲟⲩ

<page 41>
<column left>
ⲚϢⲞⲘⲚⲦ Ⲛ̄ⲚⲢⲰ
ⲘⲈ· ⲀⲨⲰ ⲠⲈ
ϪⲀϤ ϪⲈ ⲦⲎⲠⲈ Ⲛ
ⲚⲈⲚⲦⲀⲨⲦⲀⲔⲞ
ⲤⲈⲈⲒⲢⲈ ⲚⲞⲨⲦⲂⲀ
ⲚⲤⲈⲠ ⲤⲚⲀⲨ· ⲀⲢⲀ
ⲈⲢⲈ ⲚⲈⲒⲔⲞⲖⲀⲤⲒⲤ
ⲚⲎⲨ ⲚⲀⲨ ⲦⲎⲢⲞⲨ
ⲔⲀⲦⲀ ⲞⲨⲘⲎⲚⲈ
ⲚⲤⲈⲔⲦⲞⲞⲨ ⲈϨⲞⲨ̄
ⲈⲦⲘⲈⲦⲀⲚⲞⲒⲀ
ⲈⲢⲈ ⲠⲚⲞⲨⲦⲈ ⲄⲀⲢ
ⲈⲒⲚⲈ ⲚⲀⲚ ⲚⲦⲈⲒ
ⲪⲰⲚⲎ ⲚⲦⲈⲒⲘⲒ̈
ⲚⲈ· ϪⲈ ⲈⲒⲘⲈ ⲚⲎ
ⲦⲚ Ⲱ ⲚⲢⲰⲘⲈ
ϪⲈ ⲦⲞⲢⲄⲎ ⲤⲂⲦⲰⲦ
ⲘⲠⲈⲦⲚⲀⲢⲚⲀⲢ ⲚⲀⲂⲈ
ⲚⲞⲨϨⲞⲞⲨ ⲚⲞⲨⲰⲦ
ⲀⲚ ⲞⲨⲆⲈ ⲚⲞⲨⲈⲂⲞⲦ
ⲀⲚ· ⲞⲨⲆⲈ ⲚⲞⲨ
ⲢⲞⲘⲠⲈ ⲀⲚ· ⲀⲖⲖⲀ
ϨⲚ ⲞⲨⲞⲨⲚⲞⲨ ⲚⲞⲨ
ⲰⲦ ϢⲀⲢⲈ ⲠⲠⲈ
ⲐⲞⲞⲨ ⲈⲒ ϢⲀⲢⲞϤ
ⲀⲨⲰ ⲞⲚ ⲘⲈⲢⲈ ⲠⲚⲞⲨ
ⲦⲈ ⲔⲞⲖⲀⲌⲈ ⲚⲖⲀ
ⲀⲨ· ⲈⲒⲘⲎⲦⲈⲒ Ⲛ
ⲦⲈ ⲚⲈϤⲀⲚⲞⲘⲒⲀ
ϪⲒⲤⲈ ⲚⲤⲈⲠⲰⲦ
ⲚⲤⲰϤ ⲈⲠⲈⲒⲤⲀ
ⲘⲚ ⲠⲀⲒ̈· ⲚⲐⲈ Ⲛ
ϨⲈⲚϨⲦⲰⲰⲢ ⲈⲨ

<column right>
ⲤⲂⲦⲰⲦ ⲈⲠⲠⲞⲖⲈ
ⲘⲞⲤ· ⲀⲨⲰ ⲚⲤⲈ
ϪⲒⲎⲠⲈ ⲚⲚⲈϤⲚⲞⲂⲈ
Ⲛ̄ⲤⲈϪⲒ ⲘⲘⲞⲞⲨ Ⲉ
ⲢⲀⲦϤ ⲘⲠⲚⲞⲨⲦⲈ
ⲈⲨⲈⲒⲢⲈ ⲚⲞⲨⲦⲂⲀ
ⲚⲦⲂⲀ ⲚⲤⲈⲠ Ⲥ
ⲚⲀⲨ· ⲠⲢⲞⲤ ⲚⲈⲚ
ⲦⲀ ⲠⲚⲞϬ ⲒⲰϨⲀⲚ
ⲚⲎⲤ ⲌⲰⲄⲢⲀⲪⲈⲒ
ⲘⲘⲞⲞⲨ ⲚⲀⲚ ⲦⲈ
ⲚⲞⲨ ϨⲚ ⲦⲈϤⲀⲠⲞ
ⲔⲀⲖⲨⲘⲮⲒⲤ·
ⲚⲈⲦⲦⲀⲖⲎⲨ ⲈⲚⲈϨ
ⲦⲰⲰⲢ ⲠⲈϪⲀϤ
ⲈⲢⲈ ϨⲦⲞ ϨⲰⲔ Ⲙ
ⲘⲞⲞⲨ· ⲀⲨⲰ ⲞⲨ
ⲔⲰϨⲦ . . . . .
ⲐⲨ . . Ⲛ. ⲈⲦⲈ ⲚⲀⲒ
ⲚⲈ ⲚⲈⲚⲚⲞⲂⲈ ⲈⲨⲞ
ⲚⲞⲨⲀⲦⲈ ⲚⲤⲘⲞⲦ
ⲚⲀⲒ ⲚⲦⲀⲚⲈⲒⲘⲈ
ⲈⲢⲞⲞⲨ ϪⲈ ϨⲈⲚⲚⲞ
ⲂⲈ ⲚⲦⲀⲚϮ Ⲙ
ⲠⲈⲚⲞⲨⲞⲒ ⲈⲢⲞⲞⲨ
..ⲀⲨ :~
ⲀⲨⲰ ⲠⲈϪⲀϤ ϪⲈ Ⲉ
ⲢⲈ ⲚⲀⲠⲎⲨⲈ ⲚⲚⲈϨ
ⲦⲰⲰⲢ Ⲟ ⲚⲐⲈ Ⲛ
ⲚⲀ ⲚⲈⲒⲘⲞⲨ..
ⲀⲨⲰ ⲚⲈϤⲚⲎⲨ Ⲉ
ⲂⲞⲖ ⲚⲢⲰⲞⲨ ⲚϬⲒ
ⲞⲨⲔⲰϨⲦ ⲘⲚ ⲞⲨ

<page 42>
<column left>
ⲕⲁⲡⲛⲟⲥ ⲙ̄ⲛ̄ ⲟⲩ
ⲑⲏⲛ· ⲛⲉⲧⲛⲏⲩ
ⲅⲁⲣ ⲉⲃⲟⲗ ϩⲛ ⲧⲉⲛ
ⲧⲁⲡⲣⲟ· ⲡⲁⲛ
ⲧⲱⲥ· ⲧⲛⲛⲁϯ ⲗⲟ
ⲅⲟⲥ ϩⲁⲣⲟⲟⲩ ⲙⲡ̄ⲙ
ⲧⲟ ⲉⲃⲟⲗ ⲙⲡⲛⲟⲩ
ⲧⲉ· ϫⲉ ⲉⲣⲉ ⲧⲉⲩ
ⲉⲝⲟⲩⲥⲓⲁ ⲅⲁⲣ ϩ̄ⲛ̄
ⲣⲱⲟⲩ· ⲙ̄ⲛ̄ ⲛⲉⲩⲥⲁⲧ
ⲉⲣⲉ ⲛⲉⲩⲥⲁⲧ ⲅⲁⲣ
ⲟ ⲛⲑⲉ ⲛⲛⲁ ⲛⲓ
ϩⲟϥ· ⲉⲣⲉ ϩⲛⲁⲡⲏⲩⲉ
ⲙⲙⲟⲟⲩ· ⲁⲩⲱ ϩ
ⲣⲁï ⲛ̄ϩⲏⲧⲟⲩ ⲉⲩϫⲓ
ⲛϭⲟⲛⲥ ⲛⲛⲣⲱ
ⲙⲉ· ⲡⲕⲉⲥⲉⲉⲡⲉ
ⲇⲉ ⲡⲉϫⲁϥ ⲛ̄ⲛ̄ⲣⲱ
ⲙⲉ· ⲉⲧⲉ ⲙⲡⲟⲩⲙⲉ
ⲧⲁⲛⲟï ⲉⲃⲟⲗ ϩ̄ⲛ̄ ⲧⲉⲡ
ⲗⲩⲅⲏ· ⲉⲙⲡⲟⲩⲙⲉ
ⲧⲁⲛⲟï ⲉⲃⲟⲗ ϩⲛ
ⲛⲉⲩϩⲃⲏⲩⲉ· ⲉⲧ
ⲣⲉⲩⲗⲟ ⲉⲩⲟⲩⲱϣⲧ
ⲛ̄ⲛ̄ⲇⲁⲓⲙⲱⲛ ⲛ
ⲛⲟⲩⲃ ϩⲓ ϩⲁⲧ· ⲙ̄ⲛ̄
ⲛⲉⲛϣⲉ ⲙ̄ⲛ̄ ⲛⲱ
ⲛⲉ· ⲛⲁï ⲉⲧⲉ
ⲙ̄ⲛ̄ϭⲟⲙ ⲙⲙⲟⲟⲩ
ⲉⲛⲁⲩ ⲉⲃⲟⲗ· ⲟⲩ
ⲇⲉ ⲉⲥⲱⲧⲙ· ⲟⲩⲇⲉ
ⲉⲛⲟï· ⲟⲩⲇⲉ ⲉⲙⲟ
ⲟϣⲉ· ⲟⲩⲇⲉ ⲉϣⲁ

<column right>
ϫⲉ· ⲟⲩⲇⲉ ⲙ̄ⲡⲟⲩ
ⲙⲉⲧⲁⲛⲟï ⲉⲃⲟⲗ ϩ̄ⲛ̄
ⲛⲉⲩϩⲱⲧⲃ· ⲙ̄ⲛ̄
ⲛⲉⲩⲕⲁⲕⲓⲁ· ⲙ̄ⲛ̄
ⲛⲉⲩⲡⲟⲣⲛⲓⲁ :~
ⲁⲩⲱ ⲛⲉⲓⲛⲟⲃⲉ ⲉⲩ
ⲟⲩⲏϩ ⲛⲥⲁ ⲛⲉⲩⲉ
ⲣⲏⲩ· ⲉⲙⲡⲉⲛⲥⲁ
ⲁⲧ ⲟⲩⲁ· ⲙⲡⲉⲛϭⲛ
ⲟⲩⲁ· ϩⲓⲑⲏ ⲛⲟⲩⲁ
ⲛϩⲏⲧⲟⲩ :~
ⲁⲩⲱ ⲛⲁï ⲧⲏⲣⲟⲩ
ⲛⲧⲁ ⲡⲉⲡ̄ⲛ̄ⲁ̄ ⲉ
ⲧⲟⲩⲁⲁⲃ ⲧⲥⲁⲃⲉ
ⲡⲛⲟϭ ⲓⲱϩⲁⲛ
ⲛⲏⲥ ⲉⲣⲟⲟⲩ· ϫⲉ ⲉⲩⲉ
ⲉⲓⲙⲉ ⲛ̄ⲥⲉⲥⲁϩⲱⲟⲩ
ⲉⲃⲟⲗ ⲙⲡⲛⲟⲃⲉ
ⲁⲩⲱ ϩⲛ ⲛⲁï ⲧⲏ
ⲣⲟⲩ ⲙⲡⲟⲩⲙⲉⲧⲁ
ⲛⲟï· ϩⲙ ⲡⲛⲁⲩ
ⲇⲉ ⲉⲧⲙⲙⲁⲩ ⲛⲧⲁ
ⲡⲥⲁⲇⲁⲛⲁⲥ ⲡ
ϩⲟϥ ⲛⲁⲣⲭⲁⲓⲟⲥ
ϣⲟⲩϣⲟⲩ ⲙⲙⲟϥ
ⲉϫⲱϥ· ϫⲉ ⲉⲓⲥ
ϩⲏⲏⲧⲉ ⲁïϭⲙ ⲡⲉ
ϯϣⲓⲛⲉ ⲛⲥⲱϥ
ⲁïⲥⲉⲕ ⲟⲩⲟⲛ ⲛⲓⲙ
ϩⲁ ⲛⲁϩⲁϭⲉ· ⲁï
ϣⲟⲟϭⲟⲩ· ⲁⲩⲱ
ⲛⲉ ⲙ̄ⲛ̄ ⲡⲉⲧⲧⲱ
ϭⲉ ⲙⲙⲟⲟⲩ· ⲁï

<page 43>
<column left>
ⲧⲟⲣⲡⲟⲩ· ⲁⲩⲱ ⲛⲉ
ⲙⲛ ⲡⲉⲧⲛⲟⲩϩⲙ
ⲙⲙⲟⲟⲩ ⲉⲃⲟⲗ ϩ̄ⲛ
ⲛⲁϭⲓϫ :~
Ⲡⲛⲟⲩⲧⲉ ⲇⲉ ⲡ
ϣⲁⲛϩⲧⲏϥ· ⲁⲩⲱ
ⲛⲛⲁⲏⲧ· ⲛ̄ⲧⲉ
ⲣⲉϥⲛⲁⲩ ⲉⲧⲉⲛⲛⲟϭ
ⲙⲙⲛⲧⲉⲃⲓⲏⲛ
ⲁϥϣⲱⲡ ⲉⲣⲟϥ ⲙ
ⲡⲉⲛⲥⲟⲡⲥ· ⲁϥ
Ⲧⲣⲉ ⲡⲉⲛⲣⲙⲛⲁⲥ
ϣⲱⲡⲉ ⲛⲣⲙⲛ
ⲃⲣⲣⲉ· ⲁⲩⲱ ⲁϥ
ⲟⲩⲱϣ ⲉⲕⲧⲟ ⲉ
ⲣⲟϥ ⲛⲛⲧⲁⲩⲁⲓⲭ
ⲙⲁⲗⲱⲧⲓⲍⲉ ⲙ
ⲙⲟⲟⲩ· ϫⲉⲕⲁⲥ
ⲉⲩⲉⲙⲉⲧⲁⲛⲟⲓ̈ ⲛϥ
ⲥⲁⲕⲟⲩ ϣⲁⲣⲟϥ
ϩⲓⲧⲛ ⲛⲉϣⲛⲏⲩ
ⲛⲧⲉϥ ⲙ̄ⲛ̄ⲧⲙⲁⲓ
ⲣⲱⲙⲉ :~
Ⲉⲓⲧⲁ ⲡⲉϫⲁϥ ϫⲉ
ⲁⲓ̈ⲛⲁⲩ· ⲁⲩⲱ ⲉⲓⲥ
ⲕⲉ ⲁⲅⲅⲉⲗⲟⲥ ⲁϥ
ⲉⲓ ⲉⲃⲟⲗ ϩⲛ ⲧⲡⲉ·
ⲉⲣⲉ ⲟⲩⲛⲟϭ ⲛϭⲟⲙ
ϣⲟⲟⲡ ⲙⲙⲟϥ
ⲉⲣⲉ ⲟⲩⲕⲗⲟⲟⲗⲉ
ⲧⲟ ϩⲓⲱⲱϥ· ⲉⲣⲉ
ⲟⲩⲕⲗⲟⲙ ϩⲓϫⲛ ⲧⲉϥ

<column right>
ⲁⲡⲉ· ⲉⲣⲉ ⲡⲉϥϩⲟ
ⲟ ⲛⲑⲉ ⲙⲡⲣⲏ· ⲉⲣⲉ
ⲛⲉϥⲟⲩⲉⲣⲏⲧⲉ ⲉⲓ
ⲛⲉ ⲛϩⲉⲛⲥⲧⲩⲗ
ⲗⲟⲥ ⲛⲕⲱϩⲧ·
ⲁⲩⲱ ⲁⲓ̈ⲛⲁⲩ ⲉⲩ
ϫⲱⲱⲙⲉ ⲉϥⲡⲟ
ⲣϣ ⲉⲃⲟⲗ ϩⲛ ⲛⲉϥ
ϭⲓϫ· ⲁⲩⲱ ⲁϥ
Ⲕⲱ ⲛⲧⲉϥⲟⲩⲉⲣⲏ
ⲧⲉ ⲛⲟⲩⲛⲁⲙ ϩⲛ
ⲑⲁⲗⲁⲥⲥⲁ· ⲁⲩⲱ
ⲧⲕⲉ ϩⲃⲟⲩⲣ ϩⲓ ⲡⲉⲕ
ⲣⲟ· ⲁϥⲁϣⲕⲁⲕ
ⲉⲃⲟⲗ ϩⲛ ⲟⲩⲛⲟϭ
ⲛⲥⲙⲏ ⲛⲑⲉ ⲛⲟⲩ
ⲙⲟⲩⲓ̈· ⲛⲧⲉⲣⲉϥ
Ⲁϣⲕⲁⲕ ⲇⲉ ⲉⲃⲟⲗ
ⲁⲩϣⲁϫⲉ ⲛϭⲓ ⲧ
ⲥⲁϣϥⲉ ⲛϩⲣⲟⲩⲃ
ⲃⲁⲓ̈ ϩⲛ ⲧⲉⲩⲁⲥⲡⲉ·
Ⲛⲧⲁⲩϣⲁϫⲉ ⲟⲛ
ⲁⲩϫⲟⲟⲥ ϫⲉ ⲟⲩ·
ⲛⲧⲁⲩϫⲟⲟⲥ ϫⲉ
ⲛⲉⲛⲧⲁⲩⲣ̄ⲛⲟⲃⲉ
ⲉⲡϣⲏⲣⲉ ⲙⲡⲛⲟⲩ
ⲧⲉ· ⲙⲁⲣⲟⲩⲉⲓⲙⲉ
ⲛⲁⲩ ϫⲉ ⲥⲉⲛⲁⲧⲁ
ⲕⲟ· ⲁⲩⲱ ⲡⲃⲛⲧ
Ⲡⲉⲧⲛⲁⲕⲗⲏⲣⲟ
ⲛⲟⲙⲉⲓ ⲙⲙⲟⲟⲩ·
ⲁⲩⲱ ⲡⲕⲱϩⲧ ⲛⲧ

<page 44>
<column left>
ⲄⲈϨⲈⲚⲚⲀ ⲠⲈⲦⲚⲀ
ⲔⲖⲎⲢⲞⲚⲞⲘⲈⲒ Ⲙ
ⲘⲞⲞⲨ· ⲪⲎⲖⲎ
ⲚⲒⲘ ⲚⲦⲀⲨⲢ ⲠⲈⲐⲞ
ⲞⲨ ⲈⲠϢⲎⲢⲈ ⲘⲠ
ⲚⲞⲨⲦⲈ· ⲘⲀⲢⲞⲨⲈⲒ
ⲚⲤⲈⲚⲈϨⲠⲈ ⲈϪⲰⲞⲨ
ⲘⲘⲒⲚⲘⲘⲞⲞⲨ· Ⲛ
ⲤⲈⲚⲀⲨ ⲈⲢⲞϤ ϨⲰⲰϤ
ⲈϤⲚⲎⲨ ⲈⲠⲈⲤⲎⲦ
ⲈⲢⲈ ⲠⲞⲨⲞⲈⲒⲚ ⲚⲦⲈϤ
ⲘⲚⲦⲚⲞⲨⲦⲈ Ⲛ̅Ⲙ̅
ⲘⲀϤ· ⲈⲢⲈ ⲠⲈϤϨⲞ
ⲢⲞⲨⲞⲈⲒⲚ ⲠⲀⲢⲀ Ⲡ
ⲢⲎ· ⲘⲘⲎⲦⲚϢⲈ
Ⲛ̅ⲔⲰⲂ ⲚⲤⲞⲠ :~
ⲘⲀⲢⲞⲨⲈⲒ ⲚϬⲒ ⲚⲈⲚ
ⲦⲀⲨⲤϮⲞⲨ ⲘⲘⲞϤ
ⲚⲤⲈⲈⲒⲘⲈ ⲚⲀⲨ ϪⲈ
ⲠⲀⲒ̈ ⲠⲈ ⲠⲢⲢⲞ ⲚⲚ̅Ⲣ̅
ⲢⲰⲞⲨ ⲈⲢⲈ ⲦⲈϤⲆⲒ
ⲀⲐⲎⲔⲎ ⲚⲦⲞⲞⲦϤ
ϤⲚⲀⲈⲒⲢⲈ ⲠⲢⲞⲤ Ⲛ̅Ⲛ̅
ⲦⲀϤϪⲞⲞⲨ ⲚⲚ̅Ⲙ̅
ⲠⲀⲦⲢⲒⲀⲢⲬⲎⲤ·
ⲀⲨⲰ ϤⲚⲀⲚⲀ ⲚⲚⲈⲦ
ϤⲚⲀⲚⲀ· ⲚⲀⲨ :~
ⲀⲨⲰ ϤⲚⲀϢⲀⲚϨ
ⲦⲎϤ ϨⲀ ⲚⲈⲦϤⲚⲀ
ϢⲀⲚϨⲦⲎϤ ϨⲀⲢⲞⲞⲨ
ⲚϤⲈⲒⲢⲈ ⲚⲞⲨⲚⲞϬ
ⲚϬⲞⲘ ⲘⲚ ⲚⲈⲚ

<column right>
ⲦⲀⲨϨⲈⲖⲠⲒⲤⲈ ⲈⲠⲈϤ
ⲢⲀⲚ ⲈⲦⲞⲨⲀⲀⲂ· ϨⲒ
ⲦⲘ ⲠⲈϤⲚⲞϬ ⲚϬ
ⲂⲞⲒ̈ ⲚⲢⲈϤⲚⲞⲨϨⲘ
ⲦⲤⲀϢϤⲈ ⲄⲀⲢ ⲚⲈⲔ
ⲔⲖⲎⲤⲒⲀ ⲚⲦⲤⲀϢϤⲈ
ⲘⲠⲞⲖⲒⲤ· ⲚⲦⲀⲚ
ⲤⲰⲦⲘ ⲈⲦⲂⲎⲎⲦⲞⲨ
ϪⲈ ⲀⲨϢⲰⲠ ⲈⲢⲞⲞⲨ
ⲚⲦϮ· Ⲏ̅ ⲦⲤⲀϢϤⲈ
ⲚⲈⲔⲔⲖⲎⲤⲒⲀ
ϨⲰⲤⲦⲈ ⲈⲦⲢⲈ ⲠⲈ
Ⲡ̅Ⲛ̅Ⲁ̅ ⲈⲦⲞⲨⲀⲀⲂ ⲈⲒ
ⲈϪⲚ ⲚⲀⲠⲞⲤⲦⲞⲖⲞⲤ
ⲘⲠⲈⲚϪⲞⲈⲒⲤ Ⲓ̅Ⲥ̅
ⲠⲈⲬ̅Ⲥ̅· ⲚⲀⲒ̈ ⲞⲚ ⲚⲈ
ⲦⲈϤⲈⲒⲚⲈ ⲘⲘⲞⲞⲨ
ⲈϪⲚ ⲦⲘⲚⲦⲤⲚⲞⲞⲨ
ⲤⲈ ⲘⲪⲨⲖⲎ ⲚⲚϢⲎ
ⲢⲈ ⲘⲠⲒ̅Ⲏ̅Ⲗ̅· ⲚⲀⲒ̈
Ⲛ̅ⲦⲀ ⲠⲈⲦⲢⲀ ⲤⲚⲀⲨ
Ⲣ̅ ϨⲒϨⲎ ⲘⲘⲞⲞⲨ· Ⲙ̅Ⲛ̅
ⲠⲈϤⲦⲞⲞⲨ Ⲛ̅ϢⲞ
ⲈⲀⲚⲔⲰ ⲈϨⲢⲀⲒ̈ Ⲙ
ⲠⲈϤⲦⲞⲞⲨ ⲚϢⲞ
Ⲙ̅Ⲛ̅ ⲠϮⲞⲨ ⲚϢⲞ
ⲈⲀⲨⲤⲒ ⲈⲂⲞⲖ ϨⲘ
ⲠⲦⲒⲞⲨ ⲚⲞⲈⲒⲔ
ⲀⲨⲰ ⲚⲦⲈ ⲠⲈⲒⲔⲈ
ⲮⲒⲤ ⲚϢⲞ ϪⲈⲔ
ⲠⲈⲨⲀⲢⲒⲐⲘⲞⲤ Ⲉ
ⲂⲞⲖ· ϨⲘ ⲠⲒⲔⲈⲦ

<page 45>

<column left>

ⲂⲀ ⲤⲚⲀⲨ· ⲀⲨⲰ Ⲛ
ⲦⲈ ⲠⲤⲞⲞⲨⲚ ⲚⲦⲈ
ⲬⲀⲢⲒⲤ ⲀϢⲀⲒ ⲚⲀⲨ
ⲈⲂⲞⲖ ⲚϨⲎⲦⲞⲨ· Ⲛ
ⲦⲚⲤⲞⲨⲚ ⲠⲦⲨⲠⲞⲤ
ⲘⲠϢⲀϪⲚⲈ ⲈⲦ
ⲦⲎϢ· ϪⲈ ⲈⲢⲈ ⲚⲒ
ϢⲞ ⲘⲚ ⲚⲒⲦⲂⲀ ⲚⲀ
ⲈⲒ ⲈⲦⲞⲨⲈ ⲚⲚⲈⲨⲈ
ⲢⲎⲨ· ⲚⲤⲈⲤⲘⲒⲚⲈ
ⲘⲠⲈⲒⲦⲰϢ ⲚⲞⲨ
ⲰⲦ· ⲚⲤⲈⲠⲢⲞⲤ
ⲔⲨⲚⲈⲒ ⲘⲠⲈⲒⲚⲞⲨ
ⲦⲈ· ⲚⲞⲨⲰⲦ· Ⲓ̅Ⲥ̅
ⲠⲈⲬ̅Ⲥ̅ ⲠⲈⲚⲦⲀϤ
ⲦⲀⲘⲒⲞ ⲦⲠⲈ ⲘⲚ Ⲡ
ⲔⲀϨ· ⲚⲦⲈ ⲠⲒⲀⲢⲒⲐ
ⲘⲞⲤ ⲚⲞⲨⲰⲦ ⲈⲒ Ⲉ
ⲂⲞⲖ ϨⲘ ⲠⲈⲒⲀⲢⲒⲐⲘⲞⲤ
ⲚⲞⲨⲰⲦ· ⲈⲂⲞⲖ ϨⲚ
ϨⲒⲈⲢⲒⲬⲰ· ⲚⲀÏ ⲞⲚ
ⲚⲦⲀ ⲠⲈⲨⲤⲰⲞⲨϨ Ⲉ
ϨⲞⲨⲚ ϢⲰⲠⲈ ⲈϤⲞⲨ
ⲞϪ ϨⲒⲦⲚ ⲞⲨⲤϨⲒⲘⲈ·
ⲈⲨϮⲘⲀⲈⲒⲚ ⲚⲀⲚ
ⲈⲠⲦⲨⲠⲞⲤ ⲈⲦⲤⲞⲦⲠ
ⲀⲒⲤⲰⲦⲘ ⲠⲈϪⲀϤ
ⲈⲨⲤⲘⲎ ⲈⲤϪⲰ Ⲙ
ⲘⲞⲤ ⲚⲀÏ· ϪⲈ ⲦⲰ
ⲰⲂⲈ ⲈⲢⲚ ⲚⲈⲚⲦⲀ Ⲧ
ⲤⲀϢϤⲈ ⲚϨⲢⲞⲨⲂⲀⲒ
ϪⲞⲞⲨ ⲚⲄⲦⲘⲤ<sic>

<column right>

ⲤϨⲀÏⲤⲞⲨ·
Ⲱ ⲠⲈⲠ̅Ⲛ̅Ⲁ ⲈⲦⲞⲨ
ⲀⲀⲂ ⲈⲔⲞⲨⲰϢ
ⲈⲦⲰⲰⲂⲈ ⲈⲢ̅Ⲛ̅
ⲚⲒϢⲀϪⲈ ϢⲀ ⲀϢ
ⲚⲞⲨⲞⲈⲒϢ· ϢⲀⲚ
ⲦⲈ ⲚⲈⲦⲘⲞⲤⲦⲈ Ⲛ
ⲐⲒⲔⲰⲚ ⲘⲠⲚⲞⲨ
ⲦⲈ ϪⲒ ϢⲒⲠⲈ ⲚⲤⲈ
ⲔⲞⲦⲞⲨ ⲈⲠⲀϨⲞⲨ·
ⲚⲦⲈ ⲠⲞⲨⲞⲈⲒⲚ
ⲚⲚⲈϤⲠⲈⲦⲞⲨⲀ
ⲀⲂ· ⲞⲨⲰⲚϨ ⲈⲂⲞⲖ
ⲀⲨⲰ Ⲛ̄ⲤⲈⲈⲨⲀⲄⲄⲈ
ⲖⲒⲌⲈ ⲚⲦⲈϤϬⲞⲘ
Ⲛ̄ⲤⲈϪⲞⲞⲤ ϪⲈ ⲀⲚ
ⲤⲞⲨⲚ ⲠⲘⲀ ⲚⲦⲀ
ⲄⲀⲠⲎ· ⲘⲚ ⲐⲨⲠⲞ
ⲘⲞⲚⲎ· ⲀⲨⲰ ⲀⲚ
ⲈⲒⲘⲈ ϪⲈ ⲠϪⲞⲈⲒⲤ
ⲤⲰⲦⲘ ⲚⲚⲈϤⲠⲈ
ⲦⲞⲨⲀⲀⲂ· ⲀⲨⲰ
ϤⲞⲨⲰϢ ⲈϮ ⲚⲀⲨ
ⲚⲞⲨⲘⲈⲢⲒⲦ ⲘⲚ
ⲞⲨⲔⲖⲎⲢⲞⲤ ⲚϢⲀ
ⲈⲚⲈϨ· ϪⲈ ⲚⲚⲈⲨ
ⲤⲰⲂⲈ ⲚⲤⲰⲞⲨ Ⲛ
ϬⲒ ⲚⲈⲦⲈ ⲞⲨⲚⲦⲀⲨ
ⲘⲘⲀⲨ· ⲘⲠⲘⲀⲈⲒⲚ
ⲘⲠⲤⲀⲆⲀⲚⲀⲤ·
ⲘⲚ ⲚⲈⲦⲤⲞⲞⲨⲚ
ⲘⲘⲞϤ· ⲘⲚ ⲚⲈϤ

<page 46>
<column left>
ⲡⲉⲑⲟⲟⲩ :~
ⲁⲩⲱ ⲡⲁⲅⲅⲉⲗⲟⲥ
ⲡⲉϫⲁϥ ⲛⲧⲁïⲛⲁⲩ
ⲉⲣⲟϥ· ϩⲓϫⲛ̄ ⲑⲁⲗⲁⲥ
ⲥⲁ· ⲁϥϥⲓ ⲛⲧⲉϥ
ϭⲓϫ ⲉϩⲣⲁï ⲉⲧⲡⲉ
ⲁϥⲱⲣⲕ ⲙⲡⲉⲧⲟ
ⲛϩ ϣⲁⲛⲓⲉⲛⲉϩ
ⲛⲉⲛⲉϩ· ⲡⲉⲛⲧⲁϥ
ⲥⲱⲛⲧ ⲛⲧⲡⲉ
ⲙⲛ ⲛⲉⲧⲛϩⲏⲧⲥ
ⲁⲩⲱ ⲡⲕⲁϩ ⲙⲛ
ⲛⲉⲧⲛϩⲏⲧϥ·
ϫⲉ ⲙⲛϭⲉ ⲟⲩⲟⲉⲓϣ
ϭⲉ ⲛⲁϣⲱⲡⲉ·
ⲁⲗⲗⲁ ϩⲣⲁï ϩⲛ ⲧⲉⲥ
ⲙⲏ ⲙⲡⲙⲉϩⲥⲁϣϥ
ⲛⲁⲅⲅⲉⲗⲟⲥ· ⲉϥ
ϣⲁⲛⲥⲁⲗⲡⲓⲍⲉ
ϥⲛⲁϫⲱⲕ ⲉⲃⲟⲗ
ⲙⲡⲙⲏⲥⲧⲏⲣⲓⲟⲛ
ⲙⲛⲟⲩⲧⲉ· ⲛ̄ⲑⲉ
ⲛⲧⲁϥⲉⲩⲁⲅⲅⲉⲗⲓ
ⲍⲉ ⲛⲛⲉϥϩⲙϩⲁⲗ
ⲛⲉⲡⲣⲟⲫⲏⲧⲏⲥ·
ⲁϣ ϭⲉ ⲡⲉ ⲡⲙⲏⲥ
ⲧⲏⲣⲓⲟⲛ· ⲛⲑⲉ
ⲛⲧⲁϥⲉⲩⲁⲅⲅⲉ
ⲗⲓⲍⲉ ⲛⲛⲉϥϩⲙ
ϩⲁⲗ ⲛⲉⲡⲣⲟⲫⲏ
ⲧⲏⲥ ⲙⲙⲟⲥ· ⲉⲓ
ⲙⲏⲧⲉⲓ ⲉⲡⲙⲏⲥ

<column right>
ⲧⲏⲣⲓⲟⲛ· ⲉⲧⲟ ⲛ
ϣⲟⲙⲛⲧ ⲙⲙⲏⲥ
ⲧⲏⲣⲓⲟⲛ· ⲛⲁï ⲛ̄
ⲧⲁϥϩⲟⲧⲣⲟⲩ· ⲙ̄ⲛ̄
ⲛⲉⲩⲉⲣⲏⲩ· ⲁⲩⲱ
ⲁϥⲡⲁⲣϩⲓⲥⲧⲁ ⲙ
ⲙⲟⲟⲩ ⲛⲁⲛ ϩⲓⲟⲩ
ⲥⲟⲡ· ⲉⲧⲉ ⲛⲁï ⲛⲉ
ⲡϣⲟⲙⲛⲧ ⲛⲧⲁⲅ
ⲙⲁ ⲛⲧⲉⲕⲕⲗⲏ
ⲥⲓⲁ ⲙⲡⲉⲭ̄ⲥ̄· ⲉ
ⲧⲉ ⲡⲙⲏⲥⲧⲏⲣⲓⲟ̄
ⲡⲉ ⲛⲧⲟⲓⲕⲟⲛⲟ
ⲙⲓⲁ ⲙⲡⲃⲁⲡⲧⲓⲥ
ⲙⲁ ⲉⲧⲟⲩⲁⲁⲃ·
ⲁⲩⲱ ⲧⲡⲁⲣⲣⲟⲩⲥⲓⲁ
ⲙⲡⲃⲁⲡⲧⲓⲥⲙⲁ
ⲉⲧⲟⲩⲁⲁⲃ· ⲙ̄ⲛ̄
ⲧⲁⲛⲁⲥⲧⲁⲥⲓⲥ ⲛ̄
ⲣⲉϥϯⲱⲛϩ· ⲟⲩⲱ
ⲛϩ ⲅⲁⲣ ⲧⲉ ⲁⲗⲏⲑⲱⲥ
ⲛⲥⲁⲥⲁ ⲛⲓⲙ :~
ⲁⲩⲱ ⲟⲛ ⲧⲕⲉⲡⲁⲣ
ⲣⲟⲩⲥⲓⲁ· ⲙⲡⲥⲱⲙⲁ
ⲙⲛ ⲡⲉⲥⲛⲟϥ ⲙ
ⲡⲉⲭ̄ⲥ̄· ⲛⲁï ⲛⲉ ⲛⲉ
ϣⲁϫⲉ ⲙⲡⲧⲟⲩⲉⲓⲟ
ⲛ̄ⲛ̄ⲧⲁⲩⲕⲁⲁⲩ
ⲛⲁⲛ ⲉϩⲣⲁï ⲉⲧⲣⲉⲛ
ⲙⲟϣⲧⲟⲩ :~
ⲁⲩⲱ ⲟⲛ ⲡⲉϫⲁϥ ϫⲉ
ⲧⲉⲥⲙⲏ ⲛⲧⲁïⲥⲱ

<page 47>
<column left>
ⲧⲙ ⲉⲣⲟⲥ ⲉⲥϣⲁ
ϫⲉ ⲛⲙⲙⲁⲓ̈ ⲉⲃⲟⲗ
ϩⲛ ⲧⲡⲉ ⲛⲉⲥϫⲱ
Ⲙⲙⲟⲥ ⲛⲁⲓ̈· ϫⲉ ⲃⲱⲕ
ⲛ̄ⲅ̄ϫⲓ ⲙⲡϫⲱⲱ
ⲙⲉ ⲉⲃⲟⲗ ϩⲛ ⲧϭⲓϫ
ⲙⲡⲁⲅⲅⲉⲗⲟⲥ
ⲡⲁⲓ̈ ⲉⲧⲡⲟⲣϣ ⲉ
ⲃⲟⲗ· ⲟⲩⲙⲏⲥⲧⲏ
Ⲣⲓⲟⲛ ⲉϥⲟⲩⲁⲧⲃ ⲉ
ⲙⲏⲥⲧⲏⲣⲓⲟⲛ· ⲉⲩ
ⲧⲥⲁⲃⲟ· ⲙⲡⲙⲉⲥ
ⲧⲁⲅⲟⲅⲟⲥ ⲓⲱϩⲁⲛ
ⲛⲏⲥ ⲉⲣⲟϥ· ⲟⲩ
Ⲡⲣⲟⲥⲟⲡⲟⲛ ⲛⲟⲩ
ⲟⲉⲓⲛ ⲡⲉ ⲡⲉⲧⲛⲁ
ⲉⲓⲱⲣϩ ⲕⲁⲗⲱⲥ
ⲛ̄ⲛⲉⲅⲣⲁⲫⲏ ⲛ̄
ⲛⲓⲃⲉ ⲛ̄ⲧⲉ ⲡⲛⲟⲩ
ⲧⲉ· ⲟⲩⲛ ϫⲱⲱ
ⲙⲉ ⲅⲁⲣ ⲛⲧⲟⲩⲉⲓⲟ
ⲙⲙⲁⲩ· ⲟⲩⲛ ϫⲱⲱ
ⲙⲉ ⲛⲁⲝⲓⲱⲙⲁ ⲙ
ⲙⲁⲩ ⲟⲛ· ⲡⲉⲓϫⲱⲱ
Ⲙⲉ ⲇⲉ ⲡⲁⲓ̈· ⲙⲛϣ
ϭⲟⲙ ⲛⲗⲁⲁⲩ ⲉϫⲓ
ⲧϥ· ⲏ ⲉⲙⲁϣⲧϥ·
ⲉⲓⲙⲏⲧⲉⲓ ⲡⲉⲧⲛⲁ
ⲧⲃⲃⲟ ⲙⲡⲉϥ ⲥⲱ
ⲙⲁ· ⲛ̄ϥϣⲱⲡⲉ
ⲛⲥⲫⲣⲁⲅⲓⲥ· ⲛⲑⲉ
ⲛⲓⲱϩⲁⲛⲛⲏⲥ ⲡⲉ
ⲧⲉⲣⲉ ⲓ̅ⲥ̅ ⲙⲉ ⲙⲙⲟϥ

<column right>
ⲉⲧⲃⲉ ⲡⲉϥⲧⲃⲃⲟ
Ⲡⲁⲓ̈ ⲅⲁⲣ ⲡⲉⲛⲧⲁ
ⲧⲉϥⲑⲉⲛⲓⲁ ϭⲁⲓⲟ
ⲛ̄ⲛⲉⲡ̅ⲛ̅ⲁⲧⲓⲕⲟ̅
ⲛⲧⲡⲟⲛⲏⲣⲓⲁ
ⲉⲧϩⲁ ⲙⲡⲏⲩⲉ·
Ⲛⲉⲧⲟⲩⲱϣ ⲟⲩⲛ
ⲉϫⲓ ⲙⲡϫⲱⲱ
ⲙⲉ ⲉⲃⲟⲗ ϩⲛ ⲧϭⲓϫ
ⲙⲡⲁⲅⲅⲉⲗⲟⲥ
Ⲙⲁⲣⲟⲩⲉⲓⲙⲉ ⲉⲡⲁⲓ̈
ϫⲉ ⲉⲓⲙⲏⲧⲉⲓ ⲛⲥⲉ
ⲧⲃⲃⲟ· ⲛⲥⲉⲟⲩⲟⲙϥ
ⲛⲥⲉⲛⲁⲉⲓⲙⲉ ⲁⲛ
ⲉⲡⲉϥϩⲗⲟϭ· ⲙ̄ⲛ̄
ⲡⲉϥⲥⲓϣⲉ· ⲛⲥⲉ
ⲡⲉⲣϫ ⲡⲁⲓ̈ ⲉⲃⲟⲗ
ⲙⲡⲁⲓ̈· ⲛ̄ⲥⲉⲉⲓⲙⲉ
ⲛⲉⲧⲉϣϣⲉ· ⲛ̄
ⲥⲉⲉⲓⲛⲉ ⲙⲡⲥⲓϣⲉ
ⲉϫⲙ ⲡⲙⲟⲩ ⲛⲧ
ⲥⲁⲣⲝ· ⲁⲩⲱ ⲡⲱ
Ⲛϩ ⲉϫⲙ ⲡⲱⲛϩ
ⲛⲧⲉ ⲯⲩⲭⲏ
Ⲁⲩⲱ ⲟⲛ ⲡⲉϫⲁϥ
ϫⲉ ⲁⲩϯ ⲛⲁⲓ̈ ⲛⲟⲩ
ⲕⲁϣ ⲉϥⲉⲓⲛⲉ ⲛⲟⲩ
ϭⲉⲣⲱⲃ· ⲉϥϫⲱ
ⲙⲙⲟⲥ ϫⲉ ⲧⲱ
ⲟⲩⲛ ⲛ̄ⲅ̄ϣⲓ ⲙⲡⲣ̄
ⲡⲉ ⲙⲡⲛⲟⲩⲧⲉ·
ⲙⲛ ⲡⲉⲑⲏⲥⲓⲁⲥⲧⲏ
ⲣⲓⲟⲛ· ⲉⲩⲡⲣⲟⲥⲟ

<page 48>
<column left>
ⲡⲟⲛ ⲛⲟⲩⲱⲧ ⲡⲉ
ⲡⲉⲩϣⲙϣⲉ ϩⲓⲟⲩ
ⲥⲟⲡ· ⲁⲩⲱ ⲟⲩ
Ⲛⲟⲩⲧⲉ ⲛⲟⲩⲱⲧ
ⲡⲉⲧⲟⲩⲡⲣⲟⲥⲕⲩ
ⲛⲉⲓ ⲛⲁϥ· ⲡⲛⲟ
ⲙⲟⲥ· ⲅⲁⲣ· ⲁⲩⲱ ⲡ
ⲣⲉϥⲥⲙⲛⲛⲟⲙⲟⲥ
ⲉⲩⲛⲏⲩ ⲉⲃⲟⲗ ϩ̄ⲙ
ⲡⲣⲡⲉ ⲙⲡϫⲟⲉⲓⲥ·
ⲙⲛ ⲡⲉⲑⲏⲥⲓⲁⲥ
ⲧⲏⲣⲓⲟⲛ· ⲁⲩⲱ
Ⲟⲩⲡ̄ⲛ̄ⲁ̄ ⲛⲟⲩⲱⲧ
ⲡⲉⲧⲙⲙⲁⲩ ⲧⲏ
ⲣⲟⲩ ϩⲓⲟⲩⲥⲟⲡ·
ⲡⲟⲩⲏⲏⲃ ⲇⲉ· ⲁⲩⲱ
ⲡⲗⲉⲩⲉⲓⲧⲏⲥ·
ⲁⲩⲱ ⲧⲉⲑⲩⲥⲓⲁ·
ⲁⲩⲱ ⲡⲉⲑⲏⲥⲓⲁⲥ
ⲧⲏⲣⲓⲟⲛ· ϩⲛⲉⲃⲟⲗ
ϩⲙ ⲡⲉⲓⲛⲟⲩⲧⲉ
ⲛⲟⲩⲱⲧ ⲧⲏⲣⲟⲩ
ⲛⲉ· ⲁⲩⲱ ⲉⲩⲛⲁ
Ⲃⲱⲕ ⲉⲣⲁⲧϥ· ϩⲟ
ⲧⲁⲛ ⲉⲩϣⲁⲛϭⲙ
ⲡϣⲓⲛⲉ ⲛⲧⲉⲑⲩ
ⲥⲓⲁ ⲙⲛ ⲧⲉⲡⲣⲟⲥ
ⲫⲟⲣⲁ· ⲛⲁⲓ̈ ⲛⲧⲁϥ
ⲡⲁⲣⲓⲥⲧⲁ ⲙⲙⲟⲟⲩ
ϫⲉ ⲉⲩⲛⲁⲥⲱⲧⲙ
ⲉⲣⲟⲟⲩ· ⲛ̄ϭⲓ ⲛⲉ
ⲛⲧⲁ ⲡⲉⲡ̄ⲛ̄ⲁ̄ ⲉ
ⲧⲟⲩⲁⲁⲃ ϫⲟⲟⲥ

<column right>
ϩⲛ ⲧⲧⲁⲡⲣⲟ ⲛ
ⲇ̄ⲁ̄ⲇ̄· ϫⲉ ⲙⲁⲣⲉ
ⲛⲉⲛϣⲗⲏⲗ ϣⲱ
ⲡⲉ ⲛⲁϥ ⲉⲩⲕⲓⲱⲟⲩ
ⲇ̄ⲓ̄ⲁ̄ⲯ̄ⲁ̄ⲗ̄ⲙ̄ⲁ̄· ⲁⲩⲱ
ⲧⲁⲩⲗⲏ ⲉⲧϩⲓⲃⲟⲗ
ⲙⲡⲉⲣⲡⲉ· ⲕⲁⲁⲥ
ⲉⲃⲟⲗ ⲉⲡⲁϩⲟⲩ ⲛⲅ
ⲧⲙϣⲓⲧⲥ· ϫⲉ ⲛ̄
ⲧⲁⲩⲧⲁⲁⲥ ⲛⲛϩⲉⲑ
ⲛⲟⲥ· ⲁϣ ϭⲉ ⲛⲉ ⲛ
ϩⲉⲃⲣⲁⲓⲟⲥ ⲛⲥⲁ ⲛⲉϯ
ⲣⲉ ⲙⲡⲟⲩⲱϣ
ⲙⲡϫⲟⲉⲓⲥ· ⲕⲁ
ⲧⲁⲑⲉ ⲛⲧⲁϥϫⲟ
ⲟⲥ· ϫⲉ ϩⲉⲛⲉⲑ
ⲛⲟⲥ ⲛⲓⲙ· ⲉⲧⲉⲓⲣⲉ
ⲛⲧⲇⲓⲕⲁⲓⲟⲥⲩ
ⲛⲏ· ϥϣⲏⲡ ⲛⲁϩ
ⲣⲁϥ :~ ⲁⲩⲱ ⲛ
Ⲧⲟϥ ⲟⲛ ⲡⲉⲛⲧⲁϥ
ϫⲟⲟⲥ ϫⲉ ⲟⲩⲛ ϩⲁϩ
ⲙⲙⲁⲛϣⲱⲡⲉ
ϩⲙ ⲡⲏⲓ̈ ⲙⲡⲁⲉⲓ
ⲱⲧ· ⲛⲁⲓ̈ ⲅⲁⲣ
Ⲛⲉ ⲛⲉⲙⲁⲛϣⲱ
ⲡⲉ ⲛⲉⲡⲟⲩⲣⲁⲛⲓ
ⲟⲛ· ⲉⲧⲙⲉϩ ϩⲙ ⲡⲉ
ⲟⲟⲩ ⲙⲡⲛⲟⲩⲧⲉ·
ⲁⲩⲱ ⲥⲉⲛⲁϩⲱⲙ
ⲡⲉϫⲁϥ ⲛⲧⲡⲟⲗⲓⲥ
ⲉⲧⲟⲩⲁⲁⲃ ⲛϩⲙⲉ
ⲥⲛⲟⲟⲩⲥ ⲛⲉⲃⲟⲧ·

<page 49>
<column left>
ⲁϣ ⲟⲛ ⲧⲉ ⲧⲡⲟⲗⲓⲥ
ⲉⲧⲟⲩⲁⲁⲃ· ⲏ̄
ⲁϣ ⲡⲉ ⲡⲓϩⲙⲉ
ⲥⲛⲟⲟⲩⲥ ⲛⲉⲃⲟⲧ
ⲧⲡⲟⲗⲓⲥ ⲥⲓⲱⲛ
ⲧⲟⲩⲛⲉⲥ ⲧⲟⲩϭⲟⲙ
ⲉϩⲣⲁï· ⲉⲓⲥ ⲡⲟⲩⲣ̄
ⲣⲟ ⲛⲏⲩ ⲛⲏ· ⲁⲩⲱ
ⲁϥⲉⲓ· ⲡⲉⲧⲁⲣⲭⲉⲓ
ⲉⲛⲁⲣⲓⲑⲙⲟⲥ ϣⲁϥ
ⲱⲡ ⲛ̄ⲛⲉⲃⲟⲧⲉ
ⲁⲩⲱ ⲛ̄ϥⲛⲧⲟⲩ
ⲉⲃⲟⲗ ⲉⲡⲧⲟⲩⲛ
ⲙⲡϯⲟⲩ ⲛϣⲉ ⲛ
ⲥⲁⲃⲃⲁⲧⲟⲛ·
ⲁⲩⲱ ⲡⲉⲩⲱⲡ ⲉⲣ̄ⲛ
ⲧⲥⲁϣϥⲉ ⲛϩⲉⲃ
ⲇⲱⲙⲁⲥ· ⲁⲩⲱ ⲧ
ⲡⲁϣⲉ ⲛⲑⲉⲃⲇⲱ
ⲙⲁⲥ· ⲛⲁï ⲛⲉϣⲁⲩ
ⲉⲓⲛⲉ ⲉⲃⲟⲗ ⲙⲡⲉⲩ
ⲱⲡ· ⲕⲁⲧⲁ ⲡⲙⲛⲧ
ⲥⲛⲟⲟⲩⲥ ⲛϣⲉ ⲛ
ϩⲟⲟⲩ ⲙ̄ⲛ ⲡⲥⲉ·
ⲛⲁï ⲉⲩⲕⲉⲃ ⲙⲡⲥⲉⲡ
ⲥⲛⲁⲩ· ⲉⲩⲛⲏⲩ ⲉⲡ
ⲥⲟⲟⲩ ⲛϣⲉ ⲙⲁⲁⲃ
ⲛⲁï ⲉϣⲁⲩⲉⲓⲛⲉ
ⲉⲃⲟⲗ ⲙⲡⲉⲩⲁⲣⲓⲑ
ⲙⲟⲥ· ⲡⲣⲟⲥ ⲧⲉⲣⲟⲙ
ⲡⲉ ⲥⲛⲧⲉ· ⲁⲩⲱ
ⲧϣⲟⲙⲧⲉ ⲛϩⲉⲃ
ⲇⲱⲙⲁⲥ· ⲛⲧⲛ

<column right>
ⲕⲁ ⲕⲉ ϩⲉⲃⲇⲱ
ⲙⲁⲥ ⲉⲡⲡⲁⲥⲭⲁ
ⲉⲧⲟⲩⲁⲁⲃ· ⲁⲩⲱ
ⲛⲧ̄ⲛ̄ⲉⲓⲛⲉ ⲉⲣⲟⲟⲩ
ⲛⲧⲉⲅⲛⲱⲙⲏ ⲛⲧ
ⲫⲏⲥⲓⲥ ⲛⲛⲉⲛ
ⲧⲁⲩϣⲣⲡⲟⲛⲟ
ⲙⲁϫⲉ ⲙⲙⲟⲟⲩ
ϩⲁⲑⲏ ⲛⲟⲩⲕⲟⲩï
ⲁⲩⲱ ⲛⲉⲧⲛⲁϥⲓ
ⲱⲡ ⲛⲛⲁï· ⲥⲉⲣ
ⲭⲣⲓⲁ ⲛϯ ϩⲓⲱⲟⲩ
ⲛϩⲉⲛⲕⲉ ϭⲟⲟⲩ
ⲛⲉ· ⲛⲥⲉⲡⲣⲟⲫⲏ
ⲧⲉⲩⲉ ⲛⲥⲉⲛⲟï ⲛ̄
ⲛⲉⲧⲉϣϣⲉ·
ⲡⲉⲧⲛⲁϯ ϩⲓⲱⲱϥ
ⲛⲟⲩϭⲟⲟⲩⲛⲉ
ⲉϥϣⲓⲛⲉ ⲛⲥⲁ ⲙⲉ
ⲧⲁⲛⲟï ϩⲁ ⲛⲉϥ
ⲛⲟⲃⲉ· ⲡⲉⲧϣⲓ
ⲛⲉ ⲛⲥⲁ ⲙⲉⲧⲁ
ⲛⲟï ⲉϥϣⲓⲛⲉ ⲛ
ⲥⲁ ⲣⲁⲛⲁϥ ⲙⲡ
ⲛⲟⲩⲧⲉ· ⲡⲉⲧ
ⲛⲁϣⲓⲛⲉ ⲛⲥⲁ ⲣⲁ
ⲛⲁϥ ⲙⲡⲛⲟⲩⲧⲉ
ⲉϥϣⲓⲛⲉ ⲛⲥⲁ ⲣ
ⲁⲛⲁϥ ⲙⲡⲛⲟⲩⲧⲉ
ⲟⲛ ⲛϥⲟⲃⲟⲗ<sic> ⲉⲛ
ⲕⲟⲗⲁⲥⲓⲥ·
ⲡⲁï ⲅⲁⲣ ⲉⲛⲉⲓⲙⲉ
ⲉⲣⲟϥ ϫⲉ ⲡⲟⲣⲛⲟⲥ

<page 50>
<column left>
ⲏ ⲛⲟⲉⲓⲕ· ⲙⲛ ⲛⲉ
ⲧⲉⲓⲣⲉ ⲛⲛⲉϩⲃⲏⲩⲉ
ⲉⲑⲟⲟⲩ· ⲛⲥⲉⲛⲁ
ϣ ⲟⲩϫⲁⲓ̈ ⲁⲛ ⲉⲛ
ⲕⲟⲗⲁⲥⲓⲥ· ⲛⲁⲓ̈ ⲛ̄
ⲧⲁ ⲡⲛⲟⲩⲧⲉ ⲕⲁ_
ⲁⲩ ⲉⲩϯ_ϩⲟⲧⲉ ⲛ̄ⲛ̄
ϣⲏⲣⲉ ⲛ̄ⲛ̄ⲣⲱⲙⲉ
Ⲡⲉⲧⲛⲁⲟⲩⲱϣ
ⲅⲁⲣ ⲉⲕⲗⲏⲣⲟⲛⲟ
ⲙⲉⲓ ⲛⲛⲁⲓ̈· ⲛⲥⲉⲧⲱ
ⲣⲡ̄ ⲙⲙⲟⲟⲩ ⲛⲧⲟ
ⲟⲧϥ ⲁⲛ· ⲛⲁⲓ̈ ⲛⲉ
ⲛⲉⲥⲁⲧⲉ ⲙⲡⲡⲟ
ⲛⲏⲣⲟⲥ· ⲉⲧⲉⲣⲉ ⲡⲉ
Ⲡⲣⲟⲫⲏⲧⲏⲥ ⲡⲁ
ⲣⲁⲅⲅⲓⲗⲉ ⲛⲁⲛ ⲉⲧ
ⲃⲏⲏⲧⲟⲩ ϫⲉⲕⲁⲥ
ⲛⲛⲉⲩϫⲉⲧ ⲛⲛ
ⲥⲱⲙⲁ· ⲁⲩⲱ ⲛⲥⲉ
ⲣ ⲧⲉⲛⲯⲩⲭⲏ ⲉⲛ
ϣⲙⲙⲟ ⲉⲡⲛⲟⲩⲧⲉ·
Ⲁⲩⲱ ⲛⲁⲓ̈ ⲟⲛ ⲛⲉ
ϣⲁⲩⲧⲟⲣⲡⲉⲛ
ⲉⲃⲟⲗ ϩⲓⲧⲟⲟⲧⲟⲩ
ⲁⲗⲗⲁ ⲉⲛϣⲓⲛⲉ
Ⲛⲥⲁ ⲡⲛⲟⲏⲙⲁ ⲛ
ⲛⲉⲛⲧⲁ ⲡⲛⲟⲩⲥ
ϣⲱⲡⲉ ⲛⲁⲩ ⲛⲥⲟ
ⲟⲩⲛ ϩⲓ ⲥⲃⲱ· ⲛⲉ
ⲡⲣⲟⲫⲏⲧⲏⲥ ⲟⲛ
ⲉⲧⲙⲙⲁⲩ ⲙⲟⲩ
ϣⲧ ⲙⲡⲍⲏⲧⲏ

<column right>
ⲙⲁ· ⲛⲧⲉⲣⲛⲛⲁⲩ
ϫⲉ ⲡⲉⲡ̄ⲛ̄ⲁ̄ ⲉⲧⲟⲩ
ⲁⲁⲃ· ⲧⲁⲙⲟ ⲙⲙⲟ
ⲟⲩ· ⲁⲩⲱ ⲟⲛ ϥϯ
ⲙⲟ<sic>· ⲙⲙⲟⲟⲩ ⲛⲁϣ
ⲛⲥⲙⲟⲧ· ⲡⲉⲧⲟⲩ
Ⲱϣ ⲇⲉ ⲉϫⲓⲧⲟⲩ ⲛ̄
ϭⲟⲛⲥ ⲡⲉϫⲁϥ· ⲟⲩ
ⲕⲱϩⲧ ⲡⲉⲧⲛⲏⲩ
ⲉⲃⲟⲗ ϩⲛ ⲧⲉⲩⲧⲁⲡ
ⲣⲟ ⲛϥⲟⲩⲱⲙ ⲛ̄
ⲛⲉⲩϫⲁϫⲉ·
Ⲡⲉⲧⲛⲁⲟⲩⲱϣ ⲇⲉ
ⲉϫⲓⲧⲟⲩ ⲛϭⲟⲛ̄ⲥ̄
ⲧⲁⲓ̈ ⲧⲉ ⲑⲉ ⲉⲧⲟⲩ
ⲛⲁⲙⲟⲟⲩⲧϥ· ⲛⲁⲓ̈
ⲉⲧⲉ ⲟⲩⲛⲧⲟⲩ ⲉ
ⲝⲟⲩⲥⲓⲁ ⲙⲙⲁⲩ·
ϫⲉ ⲛⲛⲉⲥϩⲱⲟⲩ
ⲉϩⲣⲁⲓ̈ ⲉϫⲙ ⲡⲕⲁϩ
ⲛⲛⲉϩⲟⲟⲩ ⲧⲏⲣⲟⲩ
ⲛⲧⲉⲩⲡⲣⲟⲫⲏⲧⲓⲁ
Ⲛⲓⲙ ⲡⲉⲧⲛ̄ϥ̄ⲛⲁⲣ̄
ϣⲡⲏⲣⲉ ⲁⲛ ⲛⲟⲩ
ⲧⲁⲡⲣⲟ ⲛϣⲏⲣⲉ
ⲛⲣⲱⲙⲉ· ⲉϥϣⲁ
ϫⲉ· ⲉⲣⲉ ⲡⲉⲥⲧⲉⲣⲉ
ⲱⲙⲁ ⲧⲏⲣϥ ⲛⲧ
ⲡⲉ ⲥⲱⲧ̄ⲙ̄· ⲁⲩⲱ
Ⲟⲩⲛⲧⲁⲩ ⲧⲉⲝⲟⲩⲥⲓⲁ
ⲙⲙⲁⲩ· ⲉⲕⲧⲟ ⲛ
ⲛⲙⲙⲟⲟⲩ· ⲉⲩⲥ
ⲛⲟϥ· ⲁⲩⲱ ⲟⲛ

<page 51>
<column left>
ⲉⲡⲗⲩⲅⲉ ⲙⲡⲕⲁϩ
ϩⲙ ⲡⲗⲩⲅⲏ ⲛⲓⲙ
ⲉⲧⲟⲩⲁϣⲥ· ⲉⲩ
ϣⲁⲛϫⲱⲕ ⲇⲉ ⲉ
ⲃⲟⲗ ⲛ̄ⲧⲉⲩⲙⲛ̄ⲧ
ⲙⲛⲧⲣⲉ· ⲧⲟⲧⲉ
ⲡⲉⲑⲏⲣⲓⲟⲛ ⲉⲧ
ⲛⲏⲩ ⲉϩⲣⲁï ϩⲙ ⲡ
ⲛⲟⲩⲛ· ϥⲛⲁⲙⲓϣⲉ
ⲛⲙⲙⲁⲩ· ⲁϣ ϭⲉ
ⲡⲉ ⲡⲉⲑⲏⲣⲓⲟⲛ ⲉⲧⲙ
ⲙⲁⲩ· ⲛⲥⲁ ⲡⲉⲛ
ⲧⲁⲡⲛⲟⲩⲧⲉ ⲡⲁ
ⲧⲁⲥⲥⲉ· ⲙⲙⲟϥ
ⲁϥⲕⲱ ⲙⲙⲟϥ ϩⲙ
ⲡⲛⲟⲩⲛ ⲛϩⲁⲉ
ⲙⲛ ⲛⲉⲧⲛⲙⲙⲁϥ
ⲡⲁï ⲉϥⲛⲁϯ ⲡⲉϥ
ⲟⲩⲟï ⲉⲩⲙⲏⲏϣⲉ
ϫⲉ ⲉⲩⲉϯⲧⲱⲛ ⲙⲛ
ⲛⲉϩⲙϩⲁⲗ ⲙⲡϫⲟ
ⲉⲓⲥ· ⲁⲩⲱ ⲉϯⲟⲩⲃⲏⲩ
ⲛⲥⲉⲡⲱϩⲧ ⲉⲃⲟⲗ
ⲙⲡⲉⲩⲥⲛⲟϥ ⲙⲡ
ⲕⲱⲧⲉ ⲛⲧⲛⲟϭ ⲙ
ⲡⲟⲗⲓⲥ ⲑⲓⲗⲏⲙ·
ⲙⲛⲛⲥⲱⲥ ⲟⲛ ⲛⲧⲉ
ⲡⲛⲟⲩⲧⲉ ϯϭⲟⲙ
ⲙⲡⲉϥⲗⲁⲟⲥ ⲛⲥⲉ
ⲡⲁⲣⲣⲏⲥⲓⲁⲍⲉ ⲙ
ⲙⲟⲟⲩ ϩⲛ ⲧⲛⲟϭ
ⲛϭⲟⲙ ⲙⲡϫⲟⲉⲓⲥ
ⲁⲩⲱ ⲛⲥⲉⲡⲱⲧ ⲛ

<column right>
ⲥⲁ ⲛⲁⲛⲟⲙⲟⲥ ⲛⲥⲉ
ⲑⲙⲕⲟⲟⲩ· ⲛⲧⲉ ⲟⲩⲁ
ⲡⲱⲧ ⲛⲥⲁ ⲟⲩϣⲟ
ⲛⲧⲉ ⲥⲛⲁⲩ ϯⲧⲱ̄
ⲙⲛ ⲟⲩⲧⲃⲁ· ⲛ̄
ⲧⲉ ϫⲟⲩⲧϣⲙⲏ
ⲛⲉ ⲛϩⲉⲃⲇⲱⲙⲁⲥ
ⲡⲁⲧⲁⲥⲥⲉ ⲙⲡⲁⲛ
ⲧⲓⲕⲓⲙⲉⲛⲟⲥ· ⲛⲧⲉ
ϣⲉ ⲙⲛ ϣⲟⲙⲛⲧ
ⲛϩⲟⲟⲩ· ⲟⲩⲉⲓⲛⲉ
ⲉϫⲱϥ ⲙⲡⲁⲧⲉϥ
ⲛⲁⲩ ⲉⲡⲟⲩⲟⲉⲓⲛ
ⲛⲧⲉ ⲧⲕⲉ ϯ ⲛ
ϩⲉⲃⲇⲱⲙⲁⲥ ⲛ
ϣⲟⲣⲡ· ⲧⲟⲩⲛⲓⲁ
ⲧⲟⲩ ⲉⲃⲟⲗ ϩⲁ ⲛⲉⲛ
ⲧⲁⲩⲁⲁⲩ :~
ⲡⲗⲏⲛ ⲡⲉϫⲁϥ ϫⲉ
ⲡⲉⲑⲏⲣⲓⲟⲛ ⲛⲁϫ
ⲣⲟ ⲉⲣⲟⲟⲩ· ⲛϥⲙⲟ
ⲟⲩⲧⲟⲩ ϩⲛ ⲧⲁⲛⲟⲭⲏ
ⲙⲡⲛⲟⲩⲧⲉ· ⲛⲧⲉ
ⲛⲉⲩⲥⲱⲙⲁ ϭⲱ ⲉⲩ
ⲛⲏϫ ⲉⲃⲟⲗ ϩⲛ ⲛⲉ
ⲡⲗⲁⲧⲓⲁ ⲛⲧⲛⲟϭ
ⲙⲡⲟⲗⲓⲥ ⲥⲟⲇⲟⲙⲁ
ⲉⲡⲉⲥⲣⲁⲛ ⲡⲉ ⲡⲁï
ⲡⲛⲓⲕⲟⲥ· ⲁⲩⲱ
ⲕⲏⲙⲉ· ⲡⲙⲁ ⲛ
ⲧⲁⲩⲥϯⲟⲩ ⲙⲡ
ϫⲟⲉⲓⲥ ⲛϩⲏⲧϥ
ⲁⲩⲱ ⲉⲃⲟⲗ ϩⲛ ⲛ

<page 52>
<column left>
ⲗⲁⲟⲥ ⲧⲏⲣⲟⲩ· ⲙ̅ⲛ̅
ⲛⲉⲫⲩⲗⲏ· ⲁⲩⲱ
ⲛⲁⲥⲡⲉ· ⲙ̅ⲛ̅ ⲛϩⲉⲑ
ⲛⲟⲥ· ⲥⲉⲛⲁⲩ ⲉⲛ
ϩⲱⲧⲃ ⲛϣⲟⲙⲛⲧ
ⲛϩⲟⲟⲩ ⲟⲩϭⲟⲥ· ⲛ
ⲧⲉⲧⲙⲗⲁⲁⲩ ⲧⲙ
ⲙⲟ ⲛⲛⲉⲩⲥⲱⲙⲁ
ϩⲛ ⲛⲉⲛⲧⲁⲫⲟⲥ·
ⲁⲩⲱ ⲛⲉⲧⲟⲩⲏϩ ϩⲓ
ϫⲙ ⲡⲕⲁϩ· ⲥⲉⲛⲁ
ⲛⲁⲩ ⲛⲥⲉⲣⲁϣⲉ ⲛ
ⲥⲉⲟⲩⲛⲟϥ ⲛⲥⲉ
ϫⲟⲟⲩ ⲛϩⲉⲛⲇⲱ
ⲣⲟⲛ ⲉⲛⲉⲩⲉⲣⲏⲩ
ϫⲉ ⲡⲉⲡⲣⲟⲫⲏⲧⲏⲥ
ⲥⲛⲁⲩ ⲁⲩϩⲟⲧⲃⲟⲩ
ⲛⲉⲧⲃⲁⲥⲁⲛⲓⲍⲉ
ⲛⲛⲉⲧⲟⲩⲏϩ ϩⲓϫⲙ
ⲡⲕⲁϩ :~
ⲁⲧⲉⲧⲛⲛⲁⲩ ⲱ ⲛⲁ
ⲙⲉⲣⲁⲧⲉ ϫⲉ ϣⲁⲣⲉ
ⲡⲛⲟⲩⲧⲉ ⲉⲓⲛⲉ ⲛ
ⲧⲉϥⲁⲛⲟⲭⲏ ⲡⲣⲟⲥ
ϩⲉⲛⲟⲩⲟⲉⲓϣ· ⲁⲩⲱ
ⲟⲛ ϣⲁϥⲧⲟⲩⲛⲉⲥ
ⲧⲉϥⲉⲛⲉⲣⲅⲓⲁ ϩⲛ
ϩⲉⲛϩⲟⲟⲩ· ⲛϥⲧ
ⲣⲉ ⲟⲩⲟⲛ ⲛⲓⲙ ⲉⲓ
ⲙⲉ ϫⲉ ⲛⲧⲟϥ ⲡⲉ
ⲡⲛⲟⲩⲧⲉ ⲙⲙⲉ
ⲙⲁⲩⲁⲁϥ· ⲙⲛ
ⲡⲉⲧⲉⲓⲛⲉ ⲙⲙⲟϥ

<column right>
ⲉϥⲉⲛⲉⲣⲅⲉⲓ ⲛⲛⲉϥ
ϭⲟⲙ ⲙⲛ ⲛⲉϥϣ
ⲡⲏⲣⲉ· ϣⲁⲣⲟⲛ ⲕⲁ
ⲧⲁ ⲕⲁⲓⲣⲟⲥ· ⲁⲩⲱ
ⲟⲛ ϫⲉ ⲛⲛⲉ ⲛⲓ̈ⲁⲛ
ⲧⲓⲭⲣⲏⲥⲧⲟⲥ ⲙⲉ
ⲉⲩⲉ ⲉⲕⲉⲥⲱϣ· ⲏ
ⲕⲉ ⲙⲓⲛⲉ :~
ⲥⲱⲧⲙ ⲉⲡⲛⲟϭ ⲓⲱ
ϩⲁⲛⲛⲏⲥ ⲉϥϫⲱ
ⲙⲙⲟⲥ· ϫⲉ ⲙⲛⲛ
ⲥⲁ ⲡϣⲟⲙⲛⲧ ⲟⲩ
ϭⲟⲥ ⲛϩⲟⲟⲩ ⲁⲡⲉ
ⲡ̅ⲛ̅ⲁ̅ ⲛⲱⲛϩ ⲉⲓ ⲉ
ⲃⲟⲗ ⲁϥⲃⲱⲕ ⲉϩⲟⲩ̅
ⲉⲣⲟⲟⲩ· ⲁⲩⲱ ⲁⲩ
ⲛⲟϭ ⲛϩⲟⲧⲉ ϩⲉ ⲉϫⲱ
ⲟⲩ ⲛⲉⲛⲧⲁⲩⲛⲁⲩ
ⲇⲉ ⲉⲣⲟⲟⲩ ⲁⲩⲣϩⲟⲧⲉ·
ⲁⲩⲱ ⲁϣ ⲧⲉ ⲧⲕⲉ ϩⲟⲧⲉ
ⲏ ⲁϣ ⲧⲉ ⲡⲕⲉⲥⲧⲱⲧ
ⲛⲑⲉ ⲉⲧⲣⲉ ⲛⲣⲱⲙⲉ
ⲧⲱⲟⲩⲛ ⲙⲛⲛⲥⲁ ⲧ
ⲣⲉⲩⲙⲟⲩ· ⲛⲥⲉⲉⲓ
ϣⲁ ⲛⲉⲧⲉⲛⲟⲩⲟⲩ
ⲛⲉ· ⲛⲥⲉⲡⲁⲣⲣⲏ
ⲥⲓⲁⲍⲉ ⲙⲙⲟⲟⲩ ⲛ
ⲛⲁϩⲣⲛ ⲛⲉⲧⲛⲁⲩ
ⲉⲣⲟⲟⲩ· ⲱ ϣⲡⲏ
ⲣⲉ ⲛⲧⲉ ⲡⲛⲟⲩⲧⲉ
ⲉⲧⲟⲛϩ· ⲱ ⲡⲥⲟ
ⲟⲩⲛ ⲛⲧⲉ ⲡⲛⲟⲩ
ⲧⲉ ⲙⲙⲉ· ⲛⲓⲙ

<page 53>
<column left>
ⲞⲨⲚ ⲠⲈ ⲠⲚⲞⲨⲦⲈ
ⲈⲦⲈ ⲞⲨⲚϬⲞⲘ ⲘⲘⲞϤ
ⲈⲢ ⲠⲀЇ· ⲘⲀⲢⲞⲨ
ϪⲒϢⲒⲠⲈ ⲦⲈⲚⲞⲨ
ⲚϬⲒ ⲚⲈⲦⲆⲒⲤⲆⲀ
ⲌⲈ ⲈⲦⲀⲚⲀⲤⲦⲀⲤⲒⲤ
ⲘⲠⲤⲰⲦⲎⲢ· Ⲁ
ⲚⲞⲚ ⲆⲈ ⲦⲚϨⲞⲘⲞ
ⲖⲞⲄⲈⲒ ⲘⲘⲞⲤ· ϪⲈ Ⲓ̅Ⲥ̅
ⲠⲈⲬ̅Ⲥ̅ ⲀⲨⲤ⳨ⲞⲨ Ⲙ
ⲘⲞϤ· ⲀⲨⲰ ⲀϤⲘⲞⲨ
ϨⲀ ⲚⲈⲚⲚⲞⲂⲈ·
ⲀⲨⲰ ⲀϤⲦⲰⲞⲨⲚ
ⲈⲂⲞⲖ ϨⲚ ⲚⲈⲦⲘⲞ
ⲞⲨⲦ ⲘⲠⲘⲈϨϢⲞ
ⲘⲚⲦ ⲚϨⲞⲞⲨ· ⲀϤ
ⲂⲰⲔ ⲈϨⲢⲀⲒ ⲈⲘⲠⲎⲨⲈ
ⲀϤϨⲘⲞⲞⲤ Ⲛ̄ⲤⲀ ⲞⲨ
ⲚⲀⲘ ⲘⲠⲈϤⲈⲒⲰⲦ
ⲀⲨⲰ ⲦⲀЇ ⲦⲈ ⲐⲈ ⲈⲦϤ
ⲚⲎⲨ ⲘⲘⲞⲤ ⲈⲔⲢⲒ
ⲚⲈ ⲚⲚⲈⲦⲞⲚϨ· ⲘⲚ
ⲚⲈⲦⲘⲞⲞⲨⲦ· ⲀⲨⲰ
ⲈⲔⲢⲒⲚⲈ ⲘⲠⲞⲨⲀⲠⲞⲨⲀ
ⲠⲢⲞⲤ ⲚⲈⲚⲦⲀϤⲀⲀⲨ
ⲈⲒⲦⲈ ⲀⲄⲀⲐⲞⲚ ⲈⲒⲦⲈ
ⲠⲈⲐⲞⲞⲨ· ϢⲀⲚⲦⲈ
ⲚⲖⲀⲞⲤ ⲦⲎⲢⲞⲨ· ⲘⲚ
ⲚⲈⲪⲨⲖⲎ· ⲘⲚ ⲚⲀⲤ
ⲠⲈ ⲚⲒⲘ ⲈⲒⲘⲈ ϪⲈ
ⲠⲀЇ ⲠⲈⲚⲦⲀⲨⲤ⳨ⲞⲨ
ⲘⲘⲞϤ· ϨⲀⲐⲎ Ⲛ
ⲚⲈⲨⲞⲈⲒϢ·

<column right>
ⲈⲒⲦⲀ ⲞⲚ ⲠⲈϪⲀϤ
ⲚϬⲒ ⲠⲐⲈⲞⲖⲞⲄⲞⲤ
ⲒⲰϨⲀⲚⲚⲎⲤ· ϪⲈ
ⲀⲨⲰ ⲀⲨⲂⲰⲔ ⲈϨ
ⲢⲀЇ ⲈⲦⲠⲈ ⲈⲨϬⲰϢⲦ
ⲚⲤⲰⲞⲨ ⲚϬⲒ ⲚⲈⲨ
ϪⲀϪⲈ· Ⲱ ⲈⲚⲰⲬ
ⲘⲚ ϨⲎⲖⲒⲀⲤ· ⲞⲨⲔ
ⲖⲞⲞⲖⲈ ⲚⲞⲨⲞⲈⲒⲚ
ⲠⲈⲦⲈ ⲚⲈⲤⲦⲰⲞⲨⲚ
ϨⲀ ⲠⲈⲦⲚⲈⲞⲞⲨ·
ⲀⲖⲖⲀ ⲘⲀⲢⲈⲚⲚⲀⲨ
ϪⲈ ⲞⲨ ⲠⲈⲚⲦⲀϤ
ϢⲰⲠⲈ ⲘⲠⲈ
ϨⲞⲞⲨ ⲈⲦⲘⲘⲀⲨ·
ⲞⲨⲚⲞϬ ⲚⲔⲘⲦⲞ
ⲀϤϢⲰⲠⲈ· ⲀⲨⲰ
ⲀⲨϨⲈ ⲀⲨⲘⲞⲨ ⲚϬⲒ
ⲤⲀϢϤ ⲚϢⲞ Ⲛ
ⲢⲰⲘⲈ· ⲀⲦⲈⲦⲚ
ⲚⲀⲨ ϪⲈ ⲠⲚⲞⲨⲦⲈ
ϪⲒⲔⲂⲀ ⲚⲞⲨⲎⲢ
ⲈⲦⲂⲈ ⲚⲈϤⲠⲈⲦⲞⲨ
ⲀⲀⲂ· ⲚⲀⲒ ⲚⲦⲀⲨ
ⲢⲀⲚⲀϤ ⲘⲠⲚⲞⲨ
ⲦⲈ· ⲘⲠⲈϨⲞⲞⲨ
ⲘⲚ ⲦⲈⲨϢⲎ·
ⲞⲨⲚⲞϬ ⲘⲠⲞⲖⲒⲤ ⲈⲤ
ⲦⲀϪⲢⲎⲨ· ⲀⲤ
ⲂⲰⲖ ⲈⲂⲞⲖ ⲚⲐⲈ
ⲚⲞⲨⲘⲞⲨⲖϨ· ϪⲈ Ϩ
ⲢⲀЇ ⲚϨⲎⲦⲤ ⲚⲦⲀⲨ
ⲠⲒⲢⲀⲌⲈ Ⲛ̄ⲚⲈⲦ

<page 54>
<column left>
ⲥⲱⲧⲙ· ⲁⲩⲱ ⲛⲉⲧ̅
ϣⲙϣⲉ ⲛⲁϥ· ϣⲁ̅
ⲧⲉ ⲛⲉⲓⲙⲏⲏϣⲉ
ⲧⲏⲣⲟⲩ ⲥⲟⲩⲛ ⲡⲛⲟⲩ
ⲧⲉ· ⲁⲩⲱ ⲛⲧⲉ ⲡⲉ
ⲡⲣⲟⲫⲏⲧⲏⲥ ⲇ̅ⲁ̅ⲇ̅
ⲉⲓ ⲉⲧⲙⲏⲧⲉ ⲙ̅ⲛ̅
ⲧⲉϥⲕⲓⲑⲁⲣⲁ· ⲛ̅ϥ
ϫⲟⲟⲥ ϫⲉ ⲛⲓⲙ ⲡⲉ
ⲡⲛⲟⲩⲧⲉ ⲛⲑⲉ ⲙ
ⲡⲉⲛⲛⲟⲩⲧⲉ· ⲁⲩⲱ
ⲛⲓⲙ ⲡⲉ ⲡϫⲟⲉⲓⲥ
ⲛⲃⲗ ⲡⲉⲛϫⲟⲉⲓⲥ
ⲡⲕⲉⲥⲉⲉⲡⲉ ⲇⲉ ⲛ
ⲛⲉⲧⲙ̅ⲡⲟⲩⲙⲟⲩ
ⲁⲩⲣ̅ϩⲟⲧⲉ· ⲁⲩϯ ⲉⲟⲟⲩ
ⲙⲡⲛⲟⲩⲧⲉ ⲛⲧ
ⲡⲉ· ⲛⲛⲟⲩⲧⲉ
ⲅⲁⲣ ⲉⲧⲙⲡⲟⲩⲧⲁ
ⲙⲓⲉ ⲧⲡⲉ ⲙⲛ ⲡ
ⲕⲁϩ· ⲙⲁⲣⲟⲩⲧⲁ
ⲕⲟ ⲉⲃⲟⲗ ϩⲓϫⲙ ⲡ
ⲕⲁϩ· ϫⲉ ⲛϩⲉⲛ
ⲛⲟⲩⲧⲉ ⲁⲛ ⲛⲉ·
ⲁⲩⲱ ⲟⲛ ϣⲁⲣⲉ ⲡ
ⲙⲉϩⲥⲛⲁⲩ ⲛⲟⲩⲟï
ⲟⲩⲱ ⲙ̅ⲡⲉⲓⲙⲁ
ⲕⲁⲧⲁⲑⲉ ⲛⲧⲁ ⲡⲉ
ⲡ̅ⲛ̅ⲁ̅ ⲉⲧⲟⲩⲁⲁⲃ
ⲧⲁⲙⲉ ⲡⲉⲛⲉⲓⲱⲧ
ⲓⲱϩⲁⲛⲛⲏⲥ·
ϩⲣⲁï ⲅⲁⲣ ϩⲙ ⲡⲥⲉ
ⲉⲡⲉ ⲛⲛⲉⲡⲗⲩⲅⲏ

<column right>
ϣⲁⲣⲉ ⲛⲉⲣⲱⲙⲉ
ⲛⲁⲛⲟⲙⲟⲥ ϣⲱ
ⲡⲉ ⲉⲩⲑⲉⲱⲣⲉⲓ ⲛ
ⲑⲟⲧⲉ· ⲙⲛ ⲡⲉⲥⲧⲱⲧ
ⲉⲧⲛⲁϣⲱⲡⲉ ⲙⲛ
ⲛⲥⲁ ⲛⲁⲓ· ϣⲁⲛ
ⲧⲉ ⲧⲛⲟϭ ⲙⲡⲟⲗⲓⲥ
ⲧⲁⲓ ⲉⲧⲙⲉϩ· ⲙⲙⲛⲧ
ⲉϣⲱⲧ ⲛⲓⲙ ⲛ̅ⲧⲉ
ⲡⲕⲁϩ ⲣ ϫⲁïⲉ·
ⲁⲩⲱ ⲛⲧⲉ ⲛⲉⲧ<sic>
ϫⲁϫⲉ ⲙⲡⲛⲟⲩ
ⲧⲉ ⲧⲁⲕⲟ ⲉⲃⲟⲗ
ϩⲓⲧⲟⲟⲧⲟⲩ ⲙ
ⲙⲓⲛⲙⲙⲟⲟⲩ· ⲛ
ⲧⲟⲟⲩ· ⲙⲛ ⲛⲉⲩⲕⲉ
ϣⲏⲣⲉ· ⲙⲛ ⲛⲉ
ϣⲏⲣⲉ ⲛⲛⲉⲩϣⲏⲣⲉ
ϫⲉ ⲧⲉⲩϩⲁⲏ̅ ⲡⲉ ⲡ
ⲧⲁⲕⲟ· ⲉⲩⲛⲏⲩ ⲉ
ⲃⲟⲗ ϩⲛ ⲟⲩⲣⲓⲙⲉ· ⲛ
ⲥⲉⲃⲱⲕ ⲉϩⲟⲩⲛ ⲉ
ⲕⲉ ⲣⲓⲙⲉ· ⲉϥϩⲟⲟⲩ
ⲉⲡⲁⲓ· ⲁⲩⲱ ⲉϥ
ⲙⲁⲕϩ· ⲛϥⲓ ϩⲁⲣⲟϥ·
ⲙ<sic> ⲡⲉϫⲁϥ ⲟⲛ ⲙⲛ
ⲛⲥⲁ ⲛⲁⲓ ϫⲉ ⲁⲩⲱ
ⲡ<added: ⲙⲉϩ>ⲥⲁϣϥ ⲛⲁⲅⲅⲉ
ⲗⲟⲥ· ⲁϥⲥⲁⲗⲡⲓⲍⲉ
ⲁⲩⲱ ⲁⲩϣⲱⲡⲉ
ⲛϭⲓ ϩⲉⲛⲛⲟϭ ⲛⲥ
ⲙⲏ ⲉⲩϫ̅ⲱ̅ ⲙⲙⲟⲥ
ϫⲉ ⲁⲧⲙ̅ⲛ̅ⲧ̅ⲉⲣⲟ

<page 55>
<column left>
ⲙⲡⲕⲟⲥⲙⲟⲥ ⲣ̄ ⲧⲁ
ⲡϫⲟⲉⲓⲥ· ⲙⲛ ⲡⲉϥ
ⲭ̄ⲣ̄ⲥ̄· ⲁⲩⲱ ϥⲛⲁⲣ ⲣ
ⲣⲟ ϣⲁ ⲉⲛⲉϩ ⲛⲉⲛⲉϩ·
ⲱ ⲡⲥⲟⲫⲟⲥ ⲛⲛⲁ
ⲡⲛⲟⲩⲧⲉ· ⲓⲱϩⲁⲛ
ⲛⲏⲥ· ⲉⲓⲉ ⲛⲧⲁ ⲧ
ⲙⲛⲧⲉⲣⲟ ⲙⲡⲛⲟⲩ
ⲧⲉ ⲉⲣ ⲧⲁ ⲡⲛⲟⲩⲧⲉ
ⲙⲡⲉϩⲟⲟⲩ ⲉⲧⲙ
ⲙⲁⲩ· ⲙⲙⲁⲧⲉ·
ⲙⲡⲁⲧⲉ ⲧⲡⲉ ⲅⲁⲣ
ϣⲱⲡⲉ ⲙⲛ ⲡⲕⲁϩ
ⲛⲉⲧⲛⲧⲡⲉ ⲛⲛⲉⲙ
ⲡⲏⲩⲉ· ⲙⲛ ⲛⲉⲧ
ⲥⲁⲡⲉⲥⲏⲧ ⲙⲡ
ⲕⲁϩ ⲙⲡⲁⲧⲟⲩ
ϣⲱⲡⲉ ⲛ̄ⲧⲟϥ ϥ
ϣⲟⲟⲡ ⲛⲛⲟⲩⲧⲉ·
ⲁⲩⲱ ⲛⲣⲣⲟ· ⲁⲩⲱ
ⲛⲥⲱⲧⲏⲣ· ⲙⲛ ⲡⲉϥ
ⲙⲟⲛⲟⲅⲉⲛⲏⲥ ⲛ̄
ϣⲏⲣⲉ ⲓ̄ⲥ̄ ⲡⲉⲭ̄ⲥ̄·
ⲡⲉⲛϫⲟⲉⲓⲥ ⲙ̄ⲛ̄
ⲡⲉϥⲡ̄ⲛ̄ⲁ̄ ⲉⲧⲟⲩⲁⲁⲃ
ϯⲥⲟⲟⲩⲛ ϩⲱ ⲡⲉϫⲁϥ
ⲁⲩⲱ ⲁⲛⲟⲕ ⲡⲉⲛ
ⲧⲁⲓⲧⲁⲙⲱⲧⲛ ⲉⲧⲙⲉ
ⲛⲛⲁⲓ̈ ⲧⲏⲣⲟⲩ·
ⲁⲗⲗⲁ ϩⲙ ⲡⲧⲣⲉ ⲡ
ⲛⲟⲩⲧⲉ ⲥⲩⲛⲭⲱ
ⲣⲉⲓ ⲉⲧⲣⲉ ⲡϫⲁϫⲉ

<column right>
ⲡⲁⲣⲣⲏⲥⲓⲁⲍⲉ ⲙ
ⲙⲟϥ· ϫⲉⲕⲁⲥ ⲉⲣⲉ
ⲛⲉϥⲥⲱⲧⲡ ⲛⲁⲟⲩ
ⲱⲛϩ ⲉⲃⲟⲗ· ⲁϥⲕⲁ
ⲡⲙⲁ ⲙⲡϫⲁϫⲉ
ⲙⲛ ⲛⲉⲧⲉ ⲛⲟⲩϥ
ⲛⲉ· ϣⲁⲛⲧⲟⲩⲉⲓⲣⲉ
ⲙⲡⲉⲧⲣⲁⲛⲁⲩ·
ⲥⲭⲉⲇⲟⲛ ⲛⲉ ⲡⲣⲟ
ⲫⲏⲧⲏⲥ ⲁⲩⲙⲟⲟⲩ
ⲧⲟⲩ· ⲛⲛⲟⲙⲟⲑⲉⲧⲏⲥ
ⲛⲥⲉⲕⲁ ⲱⲛⲉ ⲉⲣⲟⲟⲩ
ⲡⲕⲉⲛⲟϭ ⲛⲣⲁⲛ
ⲛⲧⲉ ⲡⲛⲟⲩⲧⲉ ⲛ
ⲥⲉⲉⲡⲓⲃⲟⲩⲗⲉⲩⲉ
ⲉⲣⲟϥ· ϩⲱⲥⲧⲉ ⲛ
ⲧⲉ ⲟⲩⲙⲏⲏϣⲉ ϫⲟ
ⲟⲥ ϩⲛ ⲧⲉⲩⲙⲛⲧ
ⲁⲑⲏⲧ· ϫⲉ ⲁⲧⲙⲛ
ⲧⲉⲣⲟ ⲙⲡⲛⲟⲩⲧⲉ
ⲣ ⲧⲁ ⲡⲉⲑⲏⲣⲓⲟⲛ
ϣⲁⲉⲛⲉϩ·
ⲙⲛⲛⲥⲁ ⲛⲁⲓ̈ ⲇⲉ ⲟⲛ
ϩⲙ ⲡⲧⲣⲉ ⲡⲛⲟⲩ
ⲧⲉ ⲑⲃⲃⲓⲉ· ⲡⲁⲥⲉ
ⲃⲏⲥ· ⲁⲩⲱ ϩⲙ ⲡ
ⲧⲣⲉϥⲁⲓⲥⲑⲁⲛⲉ ⲛ̄
ⲧⲉ ⲡⲉϥⲣ̄ⲡⲙⲉⲉⲩⲉ
ϣⲱⲡⲉ ⲙⲡⲟⲛⲏ
ⲣⲟⲛ· ⲛⲁϩⲣⲛ ⲟⲩ
ⲟⲛ ⲛⲓⲙ· ⲛⲧⲉ ⲛⲉⲛ
ⲧⲁⲩⲧⲟϭⲟⲩ ⲉⲡϫⲁ

<page 56>
<column left>
ϫⲉ ⲣ̄ϩⲧⲏⲩ ϫⲉ ⲁⲩ
ⲙⲟⲟϣⲉ ϩⲛ ⲧⲉϥ
ⲟⲧϩⲉ· ⲧⲟⲧⲉ ⲛⲥⲉ
ⲛⲁⲩ ⲉⲛϩⲙϩⲁⲗ ⲉⲡ
ⲛⲟⲩⲧⲉ ⲉⲩϫⲓ ⲉⲟⲟⲩ
ⲁⲩⲱ ⲛϩⲙϩⲁⲗ ⲙ
ⲡϫⲁϫⲉ ⲉⲩϫⲓ ϣⲓ
ⲡⲉ· ⲧⲟⲧⲉ ⲥⲉⲛⲁ
ⲱϣ ⲉⲃⲟⲗ ⲛϭⲓ ⲟⲩ
ⲟⲛ ⲛⲓⲙ ϫⲉ ⲁⲧ
ⲙⲛⲧⲉⲣⲟ ⲙⲡⲕⲟⲥ
ⲙⲟⲥ ⲣ̄ ⲧⲁ ⲡϫⲟⲉⲓⲥ
ⲙⲛ ⲡⲉϥⲭⲣⲏⲥⲧⲟⲥ
ϣⲁⲉⲛⲉϩ ⲛⲉⲛⲉϩ
Ⲁⲡⲛⲟⲩⲧⲉ ⲥⲙⲛ
ⲟⲩⲑⲣⲟⲛⲟⲥ ⲛⲉⲟⲟⲩ
ⲛⲛⲉϥⲥⲱⲧⲡ :~
Ⲁⲡⲛⲟⲩⲧⲉ ⲧⲣⲉ ⲛⲉϥ
ϩⲙϩⲁⲗ ⲡⲁⲣⲣⲏⲥⲓ
ⲁⲍⲉ ⲙⲙⲟⲟⲩ· ⲁⲩⲱ
ⲛⲉⲧⲥⲟⲟⲩⲛ ⲙⲡ
ⲛⲁ· ⲁϥϣⲟⲡⲟⲩ ⲉ
ⲣⲟϥ ϩⲛ ⲟⲩⲉⲓⲣⲏⲛⲏ
Ⲛⲉⲛⲧⲁⲩⲙⲟⲟϣⲉ
ⲙⲛ ⲡⲡⲟⲛⲏⲣⲟⲥ
ⲁⲧⲉⲩϭⲟⲙ ⲱϫⲛ
ⲛⲧⲟⲟⲧⲟⲩ ϩⲙ ⲡ
ⲥⲱⲙⲁ· ⲟⲩⲡ̄ⲛ̄ⲁ̄
ⲛϩⲙϩⲁⲗ ⲡⲉⲛⲧⲁⲩ
ϩⲉⲗⲡⲓⲍⲉ ⲉⲣⲟϥ·
Ⲟⲩⲡ̄ⲛ̄ⲁ̄ ⲙⲡⲟⲛⲏ
ⲣⲟⲛ· ⲡⲉⲧϣⲉⲉⲓ

<column right>
ϩⲛ ⲧⲉⲩⲧⲁⲡⲣⲟ·
Ⲁⲩⲱ ⲛⲥⲉⲕⲧⲟⲟⲩ ⲛ
ⲥⲉⲉⲓⲙⲉ ⲉⲡⲉⲩⲧⲁⲕⲟ
ⲁⲩⲱ ⲥⲉⲛⲁⲕⲟⲧⲟⲩ
ⲛⲥⲉⲙⲟⲩⲧⲉ ⲉⲣⲟⲟⲩ
ⲙⲡⲣⲁⲛ ⲙⲡϫⲟ
ⲉⲓⲥ· ⲁⲩⲱ ⲙⲡⲉ ⲡ
ϫⲟⲉⲓⲥ ⲥⲱⲧⲙ ⲉⲣⲟⲟⲩ
Ⲁⲗⲗⲁ ⲥⲉⲛⲁⲥⲱⲧⲙ
ⲉⲧⲉⲥⲙⲏ ⲉⲧϩⲁ ϩⲟ
ⲧⲉ ⲉⲧⲙⲙⲁⲩ ϫⲉ
ⲡⲉⲧⲟ ⲛⲁⲧⲥⲟⲟⲩ̄
ⲥⲉⲟ ⲛⲁⲧⲥⲟⲟⲩⲛ
ⲉⲣⲟϥ· ⲟⲩⲟⲓ̈
Ⲅⲁⲣ ⲛⲁⲩ ϫⲉ ⲛⲥⲉ
ⲧⲟⲟⲃⲉ ⲁⲛ ⲉϫⲛ
ⲧⲉⲩⲁⲡⲉ ϩⲛ ⲧⲉⲥⲫⲣ
ⲁⲅⲓⲥ ⲧⲁⲓ ⲁⲛⲟⲛ ⲛⲧⲁ
ⲡϩⲓⲉⲓⲃ ⲭⲁⲣⲓⲍⲉ
ⲙⲙⲟⲥ ⲛⲁⲛ· ⲛⲁ
Ⲛⲟⲛ ⲅⲁⲣ ⲡⲉⲛ
ⲧⲁ ⲛⲉⲛⲁⲣⲉⲧⲏ ⲭⲁ
ⲣⲓⲍⲉ ⲙⲙⲟⲥ ⲛⲁⲛ
ⲁⲗⲗⲁ ⲧⲉϥⲁⲅⲁⲡⲏ
ⲧⲉ ⲉⲧⲛⲁϣⲱⲥ·
Ⲡⲁⲗⲓⲛ ⲟⲛ ⲙⲛⲛⲥⲁ
ⲛⲁⲓ̈· ⲁⲩⲱ ⲙⲛⲛ
ⲥⲁ ⲧⲉⲡⲣⲟⲥⲕⲩⲛⲏ
ⲥⲓⲥ ⲙⲛ ⲧϩⲟⲙⲟ
ⲗⲟⲅⲏⲥⲓⲥ ⲛⲛⲉ
ⲡⲣⲉⲥⲃⲩⲧⲉⲣⲟⲥ· ⲁⲩⲱ

<page 57>
<column left>
ⲘⲚⲚⲤⲀ ⲦⲢⲈⲨϢⲰ
ⲠⲈ ⲚϬⲒ ⲚⲈⲤⲘⲎ
ⲘⲚ ⲚⲈϨⲢⲞⲨⲂⲀⲒ̈
ⲘⲚ ⲚⲈⲘⲔⲞ· ⲘⲚ
ⲚⲚⲞϬ ⲚⲀⲖⲘⲠⲈ·
ⲘⲚ ⲞⲨⲚⲞϬ ⲘⲘⲀ
ⲈⲒⲚ ⲈⲀϤⲞⲨⲰⲚϨ
ⲈⲂⲞⲖ ϨⲚ ⲦⲠⲈ·
ⲘⲚⲚⲤⲀ ⲚⲀⲒ̈ ⲘⲀⲢⲈ̄
ⲚⲀⲨ ϪⲈ ⲞⲨ ⲠⲈ Ⲡ
ⲘⲀⲈⲒⲚ ⲚⲦⲀϤϢⲰ
ⲠⲈ· ⲞⲨⲤϨⲒⲘⲈ ⲈⲤ
ϬⲞⲞⲖⲈ ⲘⲠⲢⲎ ⲈⲢⲈ
ⲠⲞⲞϨ ϨⲀⲠⲈⲤⲎⲦ
ⲚⲚⲈⲤⲞⲨⲈⲢⲎⲦⲈ
ⲈⲢⲈ ⲘⲚⲦⲤⲚⲞⲞⲨⲤ
ⲚⲤⲒⲞⲨ Ⲟ ⲚⲞⲨⲔⲖⲞⲘ
ϨⲒϪⲚ ⲦⲈⲤⲀⲠⲈ·
ⲈⲤⲈⲈⲦ ⲈⲤϮⲚⲀⲀⲔⲈ
ⲈⲤⲀϢⲔⲀⲔ ϨⲚ ⲞⲨ
ⲀϢⲔⲀⲔ ⲈⲘⲒⲤⲈ
ⲀϢ ϬⲈ ⲦⲈ ⲦⲈⲤϨⲒⲘⲈ
ⲈⲦⲘⲘⲀⲀⲨ· ⲚⲤⲀ
ⲦⲈⲦ·ⲞⲨⲚⲞⲘⲀⲌⲈ
ⲘⲠⲈⲤⲢⲀⲚ ϨⲀⲐⲎ
ⲚⲞⲨⲔⲞⲨⲒ· ⲚⲦⲞⲤ
ⲄⲀⲢ ⲦⲈ ⲚⲦⲀⲤⲤⲞⲨⲚ
ⲚⲈⲦⲈ ⲚⲞⲨⲚ ⲚⲈ Ⲉ
ⲂⲞⲖ ϨⲚ ϨⲎⲦⲤ·
ⲚⲦⲞⲤ ⲞⲚ ⲦⲈⲚⲦⲀⲤ
ⲔⲀⲐⲀⲢⲒⲌⲈ ⲚⲚⲈ
ⲦⲘⲠⲈⲚⲔⲰⲦⲈ

<column right>
ⲈⲀⲤⲞⲨⲰⲚϨ ⲈⲂⲞⲖ
ⲈϪⲒⲚ̄ⲦⲘⲎⲦⲈ· Ⲉ
ⲦⲞⲨⲦⲰⲚ· ⲘⲚ Ⲡ
ϪⲞⲈⲒⲤ ⲘⲠⲦⲎⲢϤ
ⲈⲀⲦⲞⲒⲔⲞⲨⲘⲈⲚⲎ
ⲦⲎⲢⲤ ϪⲒ ⲞⲨⲞⲈⲒⲚ
ⲈⲂⲞⲖ ⲚϨⲎⲦϤ· ⲔⲀ
ⲦⲀ ⲦⲘⲚⲦⲘⲚⲦ
ⲢⲈ ⲘⲠⲘⲚⲦⲤⲚⲞ
ⲞⲨⲤ ⲚⲤⲒⲞⲨ· ⲚⲀⲒ̈
ⲈⲦⲈⲢⲈ ⲠⲢⲎ ⲘⲚ̄
ⲠⲞⲞϨ· ⲘⲚ ⲚⲈⲤⲒⲞⲨ
ⲘⲚ ⲦⲈⲨⲈⲚⲈⲢ
ⲄⲒⲀ ⲚⲘⲘⲀⲨ· ⲈⲠ
ⲘⲎⲤⲦⲎⲢⲒⲞⲚ Ⲛ
ⲦⲀϤⲞⲨⲰⲚϨ ⲈⲂⲞⲖ
ⲚⲀⲒ ⲞⲚ ⲚⲦⲀ ⲦⲈⲨ
ⲪⲰⲚⲎ ⲈⲒ ⲈⲂⲞⲖ
ⲈⲤϢⲎϢ ⲘⲚ ⲚⲈⲤ
ⲈⲢⲎⲨ· ⲚⲐⲈ ⲘⲠ
ⲔⲈⲤⲈⲈⲠⲈ ⲚⲚⲈⲪⲰⲤ
ⲦⲎⲢ· ⲈⲒⲘⲞⲨ
ⲦⲈ ⲄⲀⲢ ⲈⲚⲀⲠⲞⲤⲦⲞ
ⲖⲞⲤ ϪⲈ ⲪⲰⲤⲦⲎⲢ
ⲚϨⲪⲰⲤⲦⲎⲢ ⲄⲀⲢ
ⲚⲈ ⲀⲖⲎⲐⲰⲤ· Ⲉ
ⲀⲠⲈⲨⲞⲨⲞⲈⲒⲚ ⲠⲰ
ⲢϢ ⲈⲂⲞⲖ ⲈϪⲚ ⲦⲞⲒ
ⲔⲞⲨⲘⲈⲚⲎ ⲦⲎⲢⲤ
ⲘⲀⲢⲈⲚⲚⲞⲒ ϬⲈ ⲦⲈ
ⲚⲞⲨ ⲚⲦⲒⲤϨⲒⲘⲈ· Ⲛ
ⲤⲈⲢⲬⲢⲒⲀ ⲄⲀⲢ ⲀⲚ Ⲉ

<page 58>

<column left>

ϯⲥⲁ ⲉⲣⲟⲥ ϩⲛ ⲧⲉⲛ
ⲧⲁⲡⲣⲟ· ⲟⲩⲟⲛ
ⲅⲁⲣ ⲛⲓⲙ ⲥⲟⲟⲩⲛ ⲙ
ⲙⲟⲥ· ⲁⲩⲱ ⲉⲩⲛⲏⲩ̄
ⲉⲃⲟⲗ ϩⲏⲧⲥ ⲛϭⲓ ⲣⲁ̄
ⲛⲓⲙ· ⲉⲛ̄ⲧⲛⲛⲁϣ
ⲙⲉⲉⲩⲉ ⲉⲣⲟϥ ⲁⲛ·
ⲏ̄ ⲡⲟⲗⲓⲥ· ⲏ̄ ⲡⲣⲟⲑⲉⲥ
ⲙⲓⲁ· ⲏ̄ ⲡⲁⲣⲑⲉⲛⲟⲥ
ⲏ̄ ⲙⲏⲥⲉ· ⲏ̄ ⲙⲉⲥⲓⲱ·
ⲏ ⲙⲁⲁⲩ· ⲏ ⲙⲟⲛⲏ·
ⲏ ⲙⲁⲛⲉⲙⲧⲟⲛ·
ⲏ ⲙⲁⲛⲟⲩⲟⲉⲓⲛ
ⲏ ⲙⲁⲛⲁⲃⲟⲛ· ⲏ ⲙⲁ
ⲁⲩ ⲛⲭ̄ⲣ̄ⲥ̄· ⲏ ⲛⲁϩⲟ
ⲉϥⲧⲃⲃⲏⲩ· ⲛⲧⲟⲥ
ⲅⲁⲣ ⲧⲉ ⲧⲉⲑⲉⲟⲇⲟ
ⲕⲟⲥ· ⲉⲧⲟⲩⲁⲁⲃ ⲙⲁ
ⲣⲓⲁ· ⲧⲉⲛⲧⲁⲥϫⲡⲟ
ⲙⲡⲛⲟϭ ⲛⲟⲩⲟⲉⲓⲛ
ⲛⲧⲟⲓⲕⲟⲩⲙⲉⲛⲏ
ⲧⲏⲣⲥ· ⲡⲉⲛϫⲟⲉⲓⲥ
ⲓ̄ⲥ̄ ⲡⲉⲭ̄ⲥ̄· ⲁⲩⲱ
ⲡⲉⲛⲛⲟⲩⲧⲉ ⲡⲉⲛ
ⲥⲱⲧⲏⲣ :~
ⲁⲩⲱ ⲟⲛ ⲡⲉϫⲁϥ ϫⲉ
ⲁϥⲟⲩⲱⲛϩ ⲉⲃⲟⲗ
ϩⲛ ⲧⲡⲉ ⲛϭⲓ ⲕⲉ
ⲛⲟϭ ⲙⲙⲁⲉⲓⲛ
ⲟⲩⲛⲟϭ ⲛⲇⲣⲁ
ⲕⲱⲛ· ⲉϥⲧⲣⲉϣ
ⲣⲱϣ ⲉⲣⲉ ⲥⲁϣϥⲉ

<column right>

ⲛⲁⲡⲉ ⲙⲙⲟϥ· ⲙⲛ
ⲙⲏⲧ ⲛⲧⲁⲡ· ⲁⲩⲱ
ⲛⲉⲣⲉ ⲥⲁϣϥⲉ ⲛϭⲣⲏ
ⲡⲉ ϩⲓϫⲛ ⲛⲉϥⲧⲁⲡ
ⲁⲩⲱ ⲟⲛ ⲡⲉϫⲁϥ ϫⲉ
ⲁϥⲥⲱⲕ ⲙⲡⲙⲛⲧ
ⲥⲛⲟⲟⲩⲥ ⲛⲥⲓⲟⲩ ⲉ
ⲡⲉⲥⲏⲧ ⲙⲡⲉϥⲣⲁⲧ
ⲁϥⲛⲟϫⲟⲩ ϩⲓϫⲙ ⲡ
ⲕⲁϩ· ⲁⲩⲱ ⲁⲡⲉⲇ
ⲣⲁⲕⲱⲛ ⲁϩⲉⲣⲁⲧϥ
ⲉⲧⲉⲥϩⲓⲙⲉ· ϫⲉⲕⲁⲥ
ⲉϥϣⲁⲛⲛⲁⲩ ⲉⲣⲟⲥ
ⲉⲁⲥϫⲡⲟ ⲙⲡⲉⲥ
ϣⲏⲣⲉ ⲉϥⲉⲟⲩⲟⲙϥ
ⲁⲩⲱ ⲁⲥϫⲡⲟ ⲛⲟⲩ
ϣⲏⲣⲉ ⲛⲛϩⲟⲟⲩⲧ
ⲡ̄ⲁⲓ̈ ⲉⲧⲛⲁⲙⲟⲟⲛⲉ
ⲛ̄ⲛ̄ϩⲉⲑⲛⲟⲥ ⲧⲏⲣⲟⲩ
ϩⲛ ⲟⲩϭⲉⲣⲱⲃ ⲙⲡⲉ
ⲛⲓⲡⲉ· ⲁⲗⲗⲁ ⲙ
ⲡⲉϥϯⲟⲉ ⲙⲡⲁⲓ̈ ϫⲉ
ⲙⲡⲁⲧⲉ ⲡⲉϥⲟⲩⲟⲉⲓϣ
ⲉⲓ ⲉⲧⲣⲉϥⲁⲗⲉ ⲉⲡⲉ
ⲥϯⲟⲥ ⲛⲥⲉⲥϯⲟⲩ ⲙ
ⲙⲟϥ ϩⲁ ⲡⲉⲛⲅⲉⲛⲟⲥ
ϫⲉ ⲉⲛⲉⲡⲁⲣⲣⲏⲥⲓⲁ
ⲍⲉ ⲙⲙⲟⲛ· ⲛⲥⲉⲣ
ϣⲡⲏⲣⲉ ⲙⲙⲟⲛ ⲛ
ϭⲓ ⲛⲉⲛϩⲉⲑⲛⲟⲥ
ⲛⲧⲟϥ ⲟⲛ ⲡⲉⲛⲧⲁϥ
ⲉⲡⲓⲃⲟⲩⲗⲉⲩⲉ ⲉⲡⲉⲛ

<page 59>
<column left>
ⲄⲈⲚⲞⲤ· ϨⲒⲦⲚ ⲞⲨ
ⲘⲎⲎϢⲈ ⲈⲀϤⲀⲀⲨ
ⲚⲞⲢⲄⲀⲚⲞⲚ ⲚⲀϤ
ⲚⲦⲈⲢⲞⲨⲈⲒⲘⲈ ⲆⲈ
ϪⲈ ⲘⲚϬⲞⲘ ⲚⲖⲀⲀⲨ
ⲈⲢⲠⲈⲐⲞⲞⲨ ⲚⲀϤ·
ⲀⲨⲞⲨⲀϨⲞⲨ ⲚⲤⲰϤ
ⲚϬⲒ ⲚϨⲈⲐⲚⲞⲤ ⲦⲎ
ⲢⲞⲨ· ⲀϤⲘⲞⲞⲚⲈ
ⲘⲘⲞⲞⲨ ϨⲚ ⲞⲨϬⲈ
ⲢⲰⲂ ⲘⲠⲈⲚⲒⲠⲈ
ⲀⲨⲰ ⲘⲚ ⲠⲈⲐⲞⲞⲨ
ⲚⲀϢⲰⲠⲈ ⲘⲘⲞϤ
ⲈⲠⲒⲆⲎ ⲚⲦⲞϤ ⲠⲈ
ⲠϢⲎⲢⲈ ⲘⲠⲚⲞⲨⲦⲈ
ⲈⲦⲂⲈ ⲠⲀЇ ⲢⲰ ⲚⲦⲀⲨ
ⲦⲞⲢⲠϤ ϢⲀ ⲠⲚⲞⲨ
ⲦⲈ· ⲈⲠⲒⲆⲎ ⲚⲦⲞϤ
ⲞⲨⲈⲂⲞⲖ ϨⲘ ⲠⲚⲞⲨ
ⲦⲈ ⲠⲈ· ⲀⲨⲰ ⲞⲨⲘⲞ
ⲚⲞⲄⲈⲚⲎⲤ ⲚⲀϤ ⲠⲈ·
ⲀⲨⲰ ⲞⲚ ⲠⲈϪⲀϤ
ϪⲈ ϢⲀ ⲠⲈϤⲐⲢⲞⲚⲞⲤ
ⲦⲈⲤϨⲒⲘⲈ ⲆⲈ ϨⲰⲰⲤ
ⲀⲤⲂⲰⲔ ⲈⲦⲈⲢⲎⲘⲞⲤ
ⲈⲨⲘⲀ ⲈⲀⲨⲤⲂⲦⲰⲦϤ
ⲚⲀⲤ ⲈⲂⲞⲖ ϨⲒⲦⲘ Ⲡ
ⲚⲞⲨⲦⲈ· ϪⲈ ⲈⲨⲤⲀ
ⲚⲞⲨϢⲤ ⲚϨⲎⲦϤ Ⲙ
ⲘⲚⲦⲤⲚⲞⲞⲨⲤ Ⲛ
ϢⲈ· ⲘⲚ ⲤⲈ Ⲛ̄ϨⲞⲞⲨⲦ
ⲈⲢⲈ ⲠⲈⲒⲘⲚⲦⲤⲚⲞ
ⲞⲨⲤ ϬⲈ ⲚϢⲈ· ⲘⲚ̄

<column right>
ⲠⲈⲒⲤⲈ ⲚϨⲞⲞⲨ· ⲈⲒ
ⲚⲈ ⲚⲦⲘⲀϤ ϢⲞⲘ
ⲦⲈ ⲚϨⲈⲂⲆⲰⲘⲀⲤ
ⲚϢⲞⲢⲠ· ⲈϤⲤⲨⲚ
ϨⲒⲤⲦⲀ ⲘⲘⲞⲞⲨ· ⲘⲚ
ⲚⲈⲨⲈⲢⲎⲨ· ⲈϤⲈⲒ
ⲚⲈ ⲘⲘⲞⲞⲨ ⲈⲂⲞⲖ
ⲞⲨⲆⲈ ⲚⲈⲦⲂⲀ ⲚⲐ
ⲢⲞⲚⲞⲤ· ϨⲒ ⲀⲢⲒⲐⲘⲞⲤ
ⲀⲨⲰ ⲠⲘⲀ ⲚⲦⲀ ⲦⲒ
ⲠⲀⲢⲐⲈⲚⲞⲤ ⲠⲰⲦ
ⲈⲢⲞϤ· ⲘⲚ ⲢⲘⲚⲤⲀ
ⲢϮ ⲤⲞⲞⲨⲚ ⲘⲘⲞϤ
ϢⲀⲦⲈⲚⲞⲨ
ⲈⲒⲦⲀ ⲞⲚ ⲠⲈϪⲀϤ ϪⲈ
ⲀϤϢⲰⲠⲈ ⲚϬⲒ ⲞⲨ
ⲠⲞⲖⲈⲘⲞⲤ ⲈⲂⲞⲖ Ϩ̄Ⲛ
ⲦⲠⲈ· ⲘⲒⲬⲀⲎⲖ ⲘⲚ̄
ⲚⲈϤⲀⲄⲄⲈⲖⲞⲤ ⲈⲨ
ⲘⲒϢⲈ· ⲘⲚ ⲠⲆⲒⲀ
ⲂⲞⲖⲞⲤ· ⲀⲨⲰ ⲠⲈⲆ
ⲢⲀⲔⲰⲚ ⲠⲈ ⲠⲤⲀ
ⲆⲀⲚⲀⲤ· ⲀⲨⲰ ⲚⲈϤ
ⲀⲄⲄⲈⲖⲞⲤ Ⲛ̄ⲚⲆⲀⲒ
ⲘⲞⲚⲒⲞⲚ· ⲚⲀЇ Ⲛ
ⲦⲀⲨⲚⲞϪⲞⲨ ⲈⲂⲞⲖ
ϨⲚ ⲦⲠⲈ ϨⲚ ⲞⲨϢⲒ
ⲠⲈ· ⲈⲀⲨⲀⲤⲬⲎⲘⲞ
ⲚⲈⲒ· ⲘⲚ̄ ⲠⲈⲨⲈⲒⲰⲦ
ⲠⲆⲒⲀⲂⲞⲖⲞⲤ· Ⲙ
ⲠⲞⲨⲈϢ ϬⲘϬⲞⲘ ⲄⲀⲢ
ⲞⲨⲆⲈ ⲘⲠⲞⲨϬⲘ ⲘⲀ
ⲚⲀⲨ ϨⲚ ⲦⲠⲈ· ⲚⲦⲞϤ

<page 60>
<column left>
Ⲟⲛ ⲡⲉ ⲡϩⲟϥ ⲛⲁⲣ
ⲭⲁⲓⲟⲥ· ⲡⲁⲣⲭⲉⲟⲥ
ϩⲛ ⲧⲕⲁⲕⲓⲁ ⲙⲛ
ⲧⲡⲟⲛⲏⲣⲓⲁ ⲉⲑⲟⲟⲩ
ⲡⲁⲣⲭⲁⲓⲟⲥ ϩⲙ ⲡ
ⲧⲁⲕⲟ ⲡⲉⲧⲉⲣⲉ ⲡⲉ
Ⲑⲟⲟⲩ ⲛⲓⲙ ⲛⲏⲩ ⲉⲃⲟⲗ
ⲙⲙⲟϥ· ⲡⲉⲛⲧⲁ ⲡⲉ
ⲑⲟⲟⲩ ⲛⲓⲙ ϣⲱⲡⲉ
ⲉⲃⲟⲗ ϩⲓⲧⲟⲟⲧϥ· ⲡⲉⲛ
ⲧⲁϥⲉⲓ ⲉⲡⲉⲥⲏⲧ ⲉ
ϫⲙ ⲡⲕⲁϩ·
Ⲙⲛⲛⲥⲱⲥ ⲡⲉϫⲁϥ
ϫⲉ ⲁϊⲥⲱⲧⲙ ⲉⲩⲛⲟϭ
ⲛⲥⲙⲏ ⲉⲃⲟⲗ ϩⲛ ⲧⲡⲉ
ⲉⲥϫⲱ ⲙⲙⲟⲥ ⲛⲁⲓ
ϫⲉ ⲁⲛⲁⲩ ⲉⲛⲉⲛⲧⲁⲩ
ϣⲱⲡⲉ· ⲧⲉⲛⲟⲩ ⲅⲁⲣ
Ⲁϥϣⲱⲡⲉ ⲛϭⲓ ⲡⲟⲩ
ϫⲁⲓ· ⲙⲛ ⲧϭⲟⲙ
ⲙⲛ ⲧⲙⲛⲧⲉⲣⲟ ⲙⲡ
ⲛⲟⲩⲧⲉ· ⲉⲓⲥ ⲙⲓⲭⲁ
ⲏⲗ ⲉϥⲙⲓϣⲉ ⲉϥϫ
ⲣⲁⲉⲓⲧ· ⲙⲏ ⲛⲧⲁ ⲟⲩ
ⲡⲟⲗⲉⲙⲟⲥ ⲧⲱⲟⲩⲛ
ⲉϫⲙ ⲡⲁⲣⲭⲁⲅⲅⲉⲗⲟⲥ
ⲏ̄ <sic> ⲧⲁϥⲣ̄ ⲭⲣⲓⲁ ⲛⲧⲟⲩ
ⲛⲉⲥ ⲉⲙⲗⲁϩ· ⲙⲙⲟ̄
ⲛ̄ⲛⲉⲥϣⲱⲡⲉ·
Ⲁⲗⲗⲁ ϩⲙ ⲡⲧⲣⲉϥⲁ
ⲧⲁⲕⲧⲓ ⲛϭⲓ ⲡⲁⲛⲧ<lege ϯ>
ⲕⲓⲙⲉⲛⲟⲥ· ⲛⲧⲁϥ
ⲟⲩⲱϣ ⲉⲱⲙⲕ ⲙⲡ

<column right>
ⲅⲉⲛⲟⲥ ⲧⲏⲣϥ ⲛⲛⲣⲱ
ⲙⲉ· ⲛⲧⲉⲩⲛⲟⲩ· ⲁ
ⲙⲓⲭⲁⲏⲗ ϯⲧⲱⲛ ⲛⲙ̄
ⲙⲁϥ· ⲛⲟⲩⲟⲉⲓϣ ⲅⲁⲣ
Ⲛⲓⲙ ⲉⲣⲉ ⲙⲓⲭⲁⲏⲗ
ⲡⲁⲣⲭⲁⲅⲅⲉⲗⲟⲥ ⲙⲓ
ϣⲉ ⲉϩⲣⲁⲓ ⲉϫⲙ ⲡ
ⲅⲉⲛⲟⲥ ⲧⲏⲣϥ ⲛⲧ
ⲙⲛⲧⲣⲱⲙⲉ· ⲉϥ
ⲃⲟⲏⲑⲓⲁ ⲉⲣⲟⲟⲩ ⲉϥ
ϣⲟⲟⲡ ⲛⲁⲩ ⲙⲡⲣⲟⲥ
ⲧⲁⲧⲏⲥ· ⲛⲁϩⲣⲙ ⲡ
ⲛⲟⲩⲧⲉ ⲛⲧⲁϥⲧⲁ
ⲙⲓⲟⲛ· ⲉⲧⲃⲉ ⲡⲁⲓ
Ⲛⲁⲓⲁⲧϥ ⲙⲡⲉⲧⲛⲁ
ⲙⲟⲩ ⲉϥⲟⲩⲁⲁⲃ ⲉ
ⲧⲁⲡⲓⲗⲏ ⲙⲡⲉⲇ
ⲣⲁⲕⲱⲛ ⲉⲧⲙⲙⲁⲩ·
Ⲟⲩⲛⲟϭ ⲙⲡⲉⲑⲟⲟⲩ
ⲁϥϣⲱⲡⲉ ⲛⲁⲛ
ⲱ ⲛⲁⲙⲉⲣⲁⲧⲉ ϫⲉ
ⲁⲩⲛⲟⲩϫⲉ ⲉⲡⲉⲥⲏⲧ
ϣⲁⲣⲟⲛ ⲙⲡⲁⲛⲧⲓ
ⲕⲓⲙⲉⲛⲟⲥ ⲉⲑⲟⲟⲩ
Ⲡϫⲁϫⲉ ⲛⲧⲙⲉ
ⲙⲁⲣⲉⲛⲛⲟⲩϫⲉ ⲛ
ⲥⲁⲃⲟⲗ ⲙⲙⲟⲛ ⲛ
ⲛⲉϥϩⲃⲏⲩⲉ ⲉⲑⲟⲟⲩ
ϫⲉ ⲛⲛⲉϥⲥⲟⲕⲛ
ⲉⲡⲉⲥⲏⲧ ⲉⲡⲧⲁ
ⲕⲟ ⲛⲙⲙⲁϥ
Ⲙⲁⲣⲉⲛⲛⲁⲩ ϫⲉ ⲟⲩ
ⲡⲉⲛⲧⲁⲩϫⲟⲟϥ ⲛϭⲓ

<page 61>
<column left>
ⲚⲀ ⲘⲠⲎⲨⲈ· ⲚⲦⲈ
ⲢⲞⲨⲚⲞⲨϪⲈ ⲈⲠⲈⲤⲎⲦ
ⲈⲠⲠⲞⲚⲎⲢⲞⲤ· ⲠⲈ
ϪⲀⲨ ⲄⲀⲢ ϪⲈ ⲀⲨⲚⲞⲨϪ
ⲈⲠⲈⲤⲎⲦ ⲈⲠⲈⲤⲎⲦ
ⲈⲠⲔⲀⲦⲎⲄⲞⲢⲞⲤ Ⲛ
ⲚⲈⲤⲚⲎⲨ· ⲠⲈⲦⲔⲀ
ⲦⲎⲄⲞⲢⲈⲒ ⲚⲚⲈⲤⲚⲎⲨ
ⲘⲠⲈⲘⲦⲞ ⲈⲂⲞⲖ ⲘⲠ
ⲚⲞⲨⲦⲈ· ⲈϢϪⲈ
ϤⲔⲀⲦⲎⲄⲞⲢⲈⲒ ⲚⲚⲒ̈
ⲀⲤⲰⲘⲀⲦⲒⲞⲤ· ⲚⲀⲒ̈
Ⲉ<N?>ⲤⲈϨⲨⲠⲞⲄⲒⲤⲐⲈ ⲀⲚ
ⲈⲠⲦⲎⲢϤ̄· ⲠⲞ
ⲤⲰ ⲘⲀⲖⲖⲞⲚ· ⲞⲨⲎⲢ
ⲦⲈ ⲦⲔⲀⲦⲎⲄⲞⲢⲒⲀⲤ<ⲈⲦ?>
ⲈϤⲚⲀⲀⲀⲤ ⲔⲀⲦⲀ
ⲢⲞⲚ· ⲀⲚⲞⲚ ⲠⲈⲦⲈ
ⲢⲈ ⲚϢⲰⲚⲈ ⲚⲒⲘ Ⲙ
ⲠⲀⲐⲞⲤ ϢⲞⲞⲠ Ⲙ
ⲠⲔⲰⲦⲈ ⲚⲦⲚⲮⲨ
ⲬⲎ· ⲘⲚ ⲠⲈⲚⲤⲰⲘⲀ
ⲚⲚⲈⲤϢⲰⲠⲈ ⲘⲘⲞ̄
ⲚⲦⲈ ⲚⲈϤⲠⲖⲨⲄⲎ
ⲠⲖⲨⲄⲎ ⲘⲘⲞⲚ·
ⲀⲨⲰ ⲚⲤⲈⲦⲀⲨⲞⲚ
ⲈⲠⲈⲤⲎⲦ· ⲀⲨⲰ
ⲠⲈϪⲀⲨ ⲚϬⲒ ϨⲞⲒ̈ⲚⲈ
ⲚϨⲎⲦⲦⲎⲨⲦⲚ
ϪⲈ ⲈⲦⲂⲈⲞⲨ ⲢⲰ ⲀⲠ
ⲚⲞⲨⲦⲈ ⲔⲀ ⲠⲠⲞⲚⲎ
ⲢⲞⲤ ⲈⲠⲒⲢⲀⲌⲈ ⲘⲘⲞⲚ
ⲘⲠⲀⲢⲀ ⲦⲈⲚϬⲞⲘ·

<column right>
ⲀⲚⲞⲔ ϨⲰ ϯⲚⲀϪⲞ
ⲞⲤ ⲚⲀⲨ ϪⲈ Ⲛ̄ⲚⲈ ⲠⲈ
ⲠⲚⲞⲨⲦⲈ ⲔⲀ ⲠⲠⲞ
ⲚⲎⲢⲞⲤ ⲚⲦⲈⲒϨⲈ ⲈϤ
ⲈⲠⲒⲂⲞⲨⲖⲈⲨⲈ Ⲉ
ⲢⲞⲚ· ⲈⲢⲈ ⲚⲆⲒⲔⲀⲒ
ⲞⲤ ⲚⲀϪⲒ Ⲛ̄ⲚⲈϤⲢⲀ
ⲂⲒⲞⲚ ⲚⲀϢ ⲚϨⲈ
Ⲏ ϨⲚ ⲀϢ ⲚⲤⲘⲞⲦ
ⲀⲨⲰ ⲞⲚ ⲈⲨⲚⲀⲔⲞ
ⲖⲀⲌⲈ ⲘⲠⲆⲒⲀⲂⲞ
ⲖⲞⲤ ⲚⲀϢⲚϨⲈ·
ⲘⲚ ⲚⲈⲚⲦⲀⲨⲘⲞ
ⲞϢⲈ ϨⲚ ⲚⲈϤⲂⲎⲨⲈ<sic>
ⲈⲐⲞⲞⲨ· ⲀⲨⲰ ⲞⲚ
ⲈⲚⲈ ⲘⲚ ⲆⲒⲔⲀⲒⲞⲤ
ⲚⲀⲞⲨⲰⲚϨ ⲈⲂⲞⲖ
ⲞⲨⲆⲈ ⲈⲢⲈϤⲢ̄ ⲚⲞⲂⲈ
ⲈⲢⲈ ⲠⲚⲞⲨⲦⲈ ⲚⲀ
ⲔⲢⲒⲚⲈ ⲚⲚⲒⲘ ⲠⲈ
ⲘⲠⲈϨⲞⲞⲨ ⲘⲠϨⲀⲠ
ⲘⲘⲈ· ⲀⲨⲰ Ⲉ
ⲢⲈ ⲦⲀⲚⲀⲤⲦⲀⲤⲒⲤ
ⲚⲀϢⲰⲠⲈ ⲚⲀϢ
ⲚϨⲈ· ⲈⲢⲈ ⲚⲒⲘ
ⲖⲞⲒⲠⲞⲚ ⲚⲀϢ ϪⲞ
ⲞⲤ ϪⲈ ⲚϨⲈⲚϨⲀⲠ
ⲘⲘⲈ ⲀⲚ· ⲚⲈ ⲚⲈ
ϨⲀⲠ ⲘⲠⲚⲞⲨⲦⲈ
ⲠⲚⲞⲨⲦⲈ ⲄⲀⲢ ⲞⲨ
ⲞⲈⲒⲚ ⲠⲈ· ⲀⲨⲰ ϨⲚ
ⲞⲨⲞⲈⲒⲚ ⲚⲈ ⲚⲈϨ
ⲂⲎⲨⲈ ⲦⲎⲢⲞⲨ ⲘⲠ

<page 62>
<column left>
ⲘⲠ<sic>ⲚⲞⲨⲦⲈ· ⲈⲦ
ⲂⲈ ⲠⲀЇ ϨⲰⲰϤ ⲀϤ
ⲦⲤⲀⲂⲞⲚ· ⲈⲦⲈϤ
ϬⲒⲚⲢⲞⲨⲞⲈⲒⲚ Ⲙ
ⲘⲀⲔⲀⲢⲒⲞⲚ
ⲚⲦⲈⲢⲈϤⲚⲀⲨ ⲚϬⲒ
ⲠⲈⲦⲢⲀⲔⲰⲚ ϪⲈ
ⲀⲨⲚⲞϪϤ ⲈⲠⲈⲤⲎⲦ
ⲈϪⲘ ⲠⲔⲀϨ· ⲀϤⲠⲰⲦ
ⲚⲤⲀ ⲦⲈⲤϨⲒⲘⲈ ⲚⲦⲀⲤ
ⲘⲒⲤⲈ ⲘⲠϢⲢⲠϨⲞ
ⲞⲨⲦ· ⲀⲨⲰ ⲦⲈⲤϨⲒ
ⲘⲈ· ⲀⲨϮ ⲚⲀⲤ Ⲛ
ⲦⲚϨ ⲤⲚⲀⲨ ⲚⲀⲈⲦⲞⲤ·
ⲀϢ ϬⲈ ⲦⲈ ⲦⲈⲤϨⲒⲘⲈ
ⲚⲤⲀ ⲦⲠⲀⲢⲐⲈⲚⲞⲤ
ⲈⲦⲞⲨⲀⲀⲂ· ⲘⲀⲢⲒⲀ
ⲦⲈⲚⲦⲀⲤⲘⲒⲤⲈ ⲘⲠ
ⲘⲞⲚⲞⲄⲈⲚⲎⲤ Ⲙ
ⲠⲈⲒⲰⲦ· ⲀϢ ⲠⲈ
ⲠⲈⲒⲦⲚϨ ⲤⲚⲀⲨ Ⲛ
ⲤⲀ ⲦⲔⲨⲚⲎ· ⲘⲚ Ⲧ
ⲠⲀⲖⲀⲒⲀ· ⲀϢ ⲠⲈ
ⲠⲠⲀⲢⲀⲔⲖⲎⲦⲞⲤ
ⲚⲤⲀ ⲠⲈⲠ̅Ⲛ̅Ⲁ̅ ⲈⲦⲞⲨ
ⲀⲀⲂ ⲈϤⲚⲀ ⲈϤⲚⲎⲨ
ϨⲒϪⲚ ⲚⲈⲘⲞⲨⲚ
ⲈⲒⲞⲞⲨⲈ· ϪⲈⲔⲀⲤ
ⲈⲤⲚⲀϨⲰⲖ ⲈⲂⲞⲖ Ⲉ
ⲦⲎⲢⲎⲘⲞⲤ· ⲠⲘⲀ
ⲈⲦⲞⲨⲚⲀⲤⲀⲚⲞⲨϢⲤ
ⲚϨⲎⲦϤ· ⲚⲞⲨⲞⲈⲒϢ
ⲘⲚ ϨⲈⲚⲞⲨⲞⲈⲒϢ·

<column right>
ⲘⲚ ⲦⲠⲀϢⲈ ⲚⲞⲨ
ⲞⲈⲒϢ· ⲀϢ ⲞⲚ ⲦⲈ
ⲦⲈⲢⲎⲘⲞⲤ ⲚⲤⲀ Ⲡ
ⲘⲀ ⲚⲦⲀⲨⲤϮⲞⲨ Ⲙ
ⲠϢⲎⲢⲈ ⲘⲠⲚⲞⲨ
ⲦⲈ ⲚϨⲎⲦ̅Ϥ̅· ⲀⲦⲈ
ⲬⲀⲢⲒⲤ· Ⲙ̅Ⲛ̅ ⲦⲠⲀⲢⲐⲈ
ⲚⲒⲀ ⲠⲰⲰⲚⲈ ⲈⲂⲞⲖ
ϨⲚ ⲦⲤⲨⲚⲀⲄⲰⲄⲎ
ⲚⲚⲒⲞⲨⲆⲀЇ· ⲀⲤⲈⲒ
ⲈϨⲞⲨⲚ ϢⲀⲢⲞⲚ Ⲉ
ⲦⲈⲔⲔⲖⲎⲤⲒⲀ ⲈⲦⲞⲨ
ⲀⲀⲂ· ⲀⲤϢⲰⲠ ⲈⲢⲞⲤ
ⲚⲚⲈⲐⲨⲤⲒⲀ ⲚⲚⲘ
ⲘⲀⲔⲀⲢⲒⲞⲤ ⲚⲈⲠЇⲤ
ⲔⲞⲠⲞⲤ· ⲘⲚ ⲚⲈⲨ
ϢⲖⲎⲖ· ⲘⲚ ⲚⲈⲨⲠ
ⲢⲞⲤⲪⲞⲢⲀ· ⲀⲤⲤⲀⲚϢ
ⲈⲂⲞⲖ ⲚϨⲎⲦⲞⲨ· ⲀⲨⲰ
ⲠⲈⲤϮⲚⲞⲨⲂⲈ ⲘⲠⲈ
ⲐⲎⲤⲒⲀⲤⲦⲎⲢⲒⲞⲚ
ⲀⲨⲰ ⲚϨⲨⲘⲚⲞⲤ Ⲛ̄
ⲚⲈⲦⲞⲨⲀⲀⲂ· ϢⲀⲚ
ⲦⲈ ⲠⲈⲨⲞⲨⲞⲈⲒϢ ⲞⲨ
ⲈⲒⲚⲈ· ⲘⲚⲚⲤⲰⲤ
ⲞⲚ ⲚⲦⲈ ⲘⲘⲀⲢⲦⲨ
ⲢⲞⲤ † ⲘⲠⲈⲨⲤⲰⲘⲀ
ⲈⲠⲔⲰϨⲦ· Ⲙ̅Ⲛ̅
ϨⲈⲚⲔⲈ ⲘⲎⲎϢⲈ
ⲚⲂⲀⲤⲀⲚⲞⲤ· ϢⲀ̅
ⲦⲈ ⲚⲈⲨⲤⲰⲘⲀ
ⲘⲈϨ ⲦⲞⲒⲔⲞⲨⲘⲈⲚⲎ
ⲦⲎⲢⲤ· ϢⲀⲚⲦⲈ ⲔⲈ

<page 63>
<column left>
ⲟⲩⲟⲉⲓϣ· ⲟⲩⲉⲓⲛⲉ
Ⲙⲛⲛⲥⲱⲥ ⲟⲛ ⲛⲧⲉ
ⲙⲙⲁⲣⲧⲩⲣⲟⲥ ϯ
ⲙⲡⲉⲩⲟⲩⲟⲓ̈ ⲉⲡⲛⲟⲩⲧⲉ·
Ⲁⲩⲱ ⲙ̄ⲛ̄ⲛ̄ⲥⲱⲥ ϯⲣⲏ
ⲛⲏ ⲛⲛⲟⲩϫ ⲛⲁⲁⲣ
ⲭⲉⲓ ⲛϣⲱⲡⲉ ⲛ̄ⲧ
ⲡⲁϣⲉ ⲙⲡⲉⲩⲟⲉⲓϣ
ϣⲁⲛⲧⲉ ⲟⲩⲟⲛ ⲛⲓⲙ
ϫⲟⲟⲥ ϫⲉ ⲡⲁⲓ ⲡⲉ
ⲡⲉⲩⲟⲉⲓϣ ⲛϯⲣⲏ
ⲛⲏ· ⲙⲛⲛⲥⲱⲥ ϥ<sic>
ⲧⲁⲕⲟ ⲛⲏⲩ ϩⲛ ⲟⲩϭⲉ
ⲡⲏ· ϣⲁⲛⲧⲉ ⲡ
ⲙⲛⲧⲥⲛⲟⲟⲩⲥ ⲛ̄
ϣⲉ· ⲙⲛ ⲥⲉ ⲛϩⲟⲟⲩ
ⲉⲓ ⲉϩⲟⲩⲛ ϣⲁ ⲡⲁ
ⲣⲓⲑⲙⲟⲥ ⲛⲧⲙⲛⲧⲁϥ
ⲧⲉ ⲛϩⲉⲃⲇⲱⲙⲁⲥ
ⲙⲛ ⲧⲕⲉ ϣⲟⲙⲧⲉ ⲉⲧ
ϩⲛ̄ ⲧϯ· ⲛⲁⲓ̈ ϥⲛⲁ
Ⲉⲓⲙ<ⲛ?>ⲉ ⲉⲣⲟⲟⲩ· ⲧⲥⲛⲧⲉ
ⲁⲩⲱ ⲡϣⲟⲙⲛⲧ ⲟⲩ
ϭⲟⲥ ⲛϩⲟⲟⲩ· ⲉⲩⲛⲏⲩ
ϩⲙ ⲡⲉⲩⲁⲣⲓⲑⲙⲟⲥ·
ⲉϫⲙ ⲡϫⲱⲕ ⲉⲃⲟⲗ
ⲛⲛⲉⲟⲩⲟⲉⲓϣ· ⲛⲁⲓ̈
ⲉⲧϫⲓ ⲉϩⲟⲩⲛ ⲉⲛϣⲁ
ϫⲉ ⲛⲧⲁ ⲧⲥⲁϣϥⲉ
ⲛϩⲣⲟⲩⲃⲁⲓ̈ ϫⲟⲟⲩ
Ⲛⲁⲓ̈ ⲛⲧⲁⲩϫⲟⲟⲥ ⲙ
ⲡⲉⲛⲉⲓⲱⲧ ⲓⲱ
ϩⲁⲛⲛⲏⲥ ϫⲉ ⲧⲱ

<column right>
. . . .
. . . .
. . . .
. . . .
. . . .
ⲗ . . . .
ⲡⲉ . . . . . .
ϩⲟϥ ⲛⲁⲣⲭ[ⲁⲓⲟⲥ ..
ϫⲉ ⲉⲃⲟⲗ ϩⲛ ⲣⲱϥ
ⲛⲟⲩⲙⲟⲟⲩ ⲛⲑⲉ ⲛⲟⲩ
ⲉⲓⲉⲣⲟ ϩⲓⲡⲁϩⲟⲩ ⲛ̄
ⲧⲉⲥϩⲓⲙⲉ ϫⲉⲕⲁⲥ
ⲉϥⲉⲧⲣⲉⲥⲱⲙⲥ·
Ⲑⲉⲱⲣⲉⲓ ⲛⲁⲕ ⲛⲧ
ⲛⲟϭ ⲛϭⲟⲙ ⲙⲡ
ⲛⲟⲩⲧⲉ· ϫⲉ ⲛⲧ
ϭⲟⲙ ⲁⲛ ⲧⲉ ⲙⲡⲉⲇ
ⲣⲁⲕⲱⲛ ⲉϯ ⲛⲙⲙⲁϥ
Ⲟⲩⲇⲉ ⲛⲛⲉϥⲥⲁⲧⲉ
ⲛⲁϣ ϫⲱⲧⲉ ⲁⲛ
ⲛⲛⲉⲧϩⲉⲗⲡⲓⲍⲉ
ⲉⲡⲉϥⲣⲁⲛ :~
Ⲁⲗⲗⲁ ⲁⲡⲕⲁϩ ⲱⲙⲕ
ⲙⲡⲙⲟⲟⲩ· ⲡⲉϫⲁϥ
ⲉⲧⲛⲏⲩ ⲉⲃⲟⲗ ϩ̄ⲛ
ⲣⲱϥ ⲙ̄ⲡⲉⲇⲣⲁ
ⲕⲱⲛ ⲉⲧⲙⲙⲁⲩ
Ⲡⲉⲇⲣⲁⲕⲱⲛ ⲇⲉ
ⲁϥϭⲱⲛⲧ ⲉⲧⲉⲥϩⲓ
ⲙⲉ· ⲁϥⲃⲱⲕ ⲁϥ
ⲉⲓⲣⲉ ⲛⲟⲩⲡⲟⲗⲉⲙⲟⲥ
ⲙⲛ ⲡⲥⲉⲉⲡⲉ ⲙⲡⲉⲥ
ⲥⲡⲉⲣⲙⲁ· ⲛⲁⲓ̈ ⲉⲧ

<page 64>
<column left>
. . . .
. . . .
. . . .
. . . .
. . . .
. . . .
. . . . Ⲙ
. . . . ⲀⲨⲰ Ⲛ
. . . _ⲎⲤ ⲈⲦⲘⲚⲦⲘⲚⲦ
ⲢⲈ ⲚⲒ̅Ⲥ̅ ⲠⲈⲬ̅Ⲥ̅ ⲠⲈⲚ
ϪⲞⲈⲒⲤ· ϢⲀⲚⲦⲈⲚ
ⲠⲀⲢⲀⲄⲈ _ⲘⲠⲈⲒⲂⲒⲞⲤ
ⲈⲦⲘⲈϨ Ⲙ̅ⲠⲞⲚⲎ
ⲢⲒⲀ ⲚⲒⲘ· ϮⲚⲀⲨ
ⲄⲀⲢ ⲈⲠⲈⲚϨⲞⲨⲞ
ⲈⲨϬⲚ ⲀⲢⲒⲔⲈ ⲈⲦⲀ
ⲘⲚⲦⲈⲂⲒⲎⲚ· ϪⲈ
ⲈⲒⲤ ⲠⲚⲀⲨ· ⲀϤⲠⲢⲞ
ⲔⲞⲠⲦⲈⲒ ⲚⲦⲞⲞⲦ̅Ⲛ̅
ⲈⲠⲈϨⲞⲨⲞ· ⲚⲄϮ ⲚⲀ̅
ⲚϮⲢⲎⲚⲎ ϪⲈⲚⲈ
ⲂⲰⲔ ⲈⲚⲈⲘⲀ ⲈⲦ
ⲦⲎϢ ⲚⲀⲚ· ⲔⲀⲒ
ⲄⲀⲢ ⲀⲚⲀⲔⲈⲒ<sic> ϨⲚ ⲦⲈ
ⲦⲚⲘⲎⲦⲈ ⲚⲐⲈ
ⲚⲞⲨϢⲂⲎⲢ· Ⲏ ⲞⲨ
ⲤⲞⲚ· ϮⲠⲀⲢⲀⲔⲀ
ⲖⲈⲒ ϬⲈ ⲘⲘⲰⲦⲚ
ϪⲈⲦⲈⲦⲚϢⲀⲚⲈⲒ
ⲘⲈ ϪⲈ ⲀⲠⲚⲞⲨⲦⲈ
Ϯ ⲚⲀⲚ ⲚⲞⲨⲞⲈⲒϢ
ⲈϤϬⲚⲞⲚ· ⲀⲘⲎⲒ
ⲦⲚ ⲚⲦⲈⲦⲚⲈⲒⲘⲈ
.. ⲈⲚⲈⲦⲚⲀⲈⲒ ⲘⲚ

<column right>
ⲚⲤⲀ ⲚⲀⲒ̈· ⲚⲦⲈⲦⲚ
ⲈⲒⲘⲈ ⲞⲚ ϪⲈ ⲀϢ
ⲠⲈ ⲠⲈⲐⲎⲢⲒⲞⲚ Ⲛ̅
ⲦⲀϤⲚⲀⲨ ⲈⲢⲞϤ ⲈϤ
ⲚⲎⲨ ⲈϨⲢⲀⲒ̈ ϨⲚ ⲐⲀ
ⲖⲀⲤⲤⲀ· ⲈⲢⲈ ⲘⲎⲦ
Ⲛ̅ⲦⲀⲠ ⲘⲘⲞϤ· ⲀⲨⲰ
ⲤⲀϢϤⲈ ⲚⲀⲠⲈ· ⲈⲢⲈ
ⲞⲨⲢⲀⲚ ⲚϪⲒⲞⲨⲀ ⲤⲎϨ
ⲈϪⲚ ⲚⲈϤⲀⲠⲎⲨⲈ·
ⲈϤⲞ ⲚⲐⲈ ⲚⲞⲨⲠⲀⲢ
ⲆⲀⲖⲒⲤ :~
ⲀⲨⲰ ⲞⲚ ⲈⲦⲂⲈ ⲠⲈⲐⲎ
ⲢⲒⲞⲚ ⲈϤⲈⲒⲚⲈ ⲘⲠ
ϢⲞⲢⲠ ⲚⲐⲎⲢⲒⲞⲚ
ⲈⲢⲈ ⲦⲀⲠ ⲤⲚⲀⲨ Ⲙ
ⲘⲞϤ· ⲈⲢⲈ ⲠⲘⲀⲈⲒⲚ
ⲚⲦⲤⲞⲪⲒⲀ ϨⲚ ⲚⲀⲒ̈
ⲀⲨⲰ ⲞⲚ ⲈⲦⲂⲈ ⲠⲈϨⲒ
ⲈⲒⲂ ⲈⲦⲀϨⲈⲢⲀⲦϤ ϨⲒ
ϪⲘ ⲠⲦⲞⲞⲨ ⲚⲤⲒ
ⲰⲚ :~
ⲀⲨⲰ ⲈⲦⲂⲈ ⲦⲈⲤⲘⲎ
ⲚⲦⲀϤⲤⲰⲦⲘ ⲈⲢⲞⲤ
ⲈⲤⲰ ⲚⲐⲈ ⲚⲞⲨⲔⲒ
ⲐⲀⲢⲀ· ⲈϤϪⲰ ⲚⲞⲨ
ϪⲰ ⲚⲂⲢⲢⲈ ⲘⲠⲘ
ⲦⲞ ⲈⲂⲞⲖ ⲘⲠⲈⲐⲢⲞ
ⲚⲞⲤ ⲘⲠⲚⲞⲨⲦⲈ
ⲘⲚ ⲠⲈϤⲦⲞⲞⲨ Ⲛ
ⲌⲰⲞⲚ :~
ⲀⲨⲰ ⲈⲦⲂⲈ ⲠⲈⲨⲀⲄ
ⲄⲈⲖⲒⲞⲚ ⲈⲦⲚⲦⲞⲞⲦϤ

<page 65>
<column left>
ⲘⲠⲀⲄⲄⲈⲖⲞⲤ· ⲈϤ
ⲈⲨⲀⲄⲄⲈⲖⲒⲌⲈ ⲚⲞⲨ
ⲈⲒⲢⲎⲚⲎ ⲚϢⲀⲈⲚⲈϨ
ϪⲈ ⲀⲢⲒ ϨⲞⲦⲈ ϨⲎⲦϤ
ⲘⲠϪⲞⲈⲒⲤ ⲠⲚⲞⲨⲦⲈ
ϪⲈ ⲀⲤⲈⲒ ⲚϬⲒ ⲦⲈⲨ
ⲚⲞⲨ ⲚⲦⲈϤⲔⲢⲒⲤⲒⲤ·
ⲀⲨⲰ ⲞⲚ ⲈⲦⲂⲈ ⲠⲔⲈ
ⲀⲄⲄⲈⲖⲞⲤ ⲈⲦⲞ ⲘⲘⲈϨ
ⲤⲚⲀⲨ ⲈϤϪⲰ Ⲙ
ⲘⲞⲤ ϪⲈ ⲀⲤϨⲈ· ⲀⲤ
ϨⲈ· ⲚϬⲒ ⲦⲂⲀⲂⲨⲖⲞ̅
ⲦⲚⲞϬ :~
ⲀⲨⲰ ⲈⲦⲂⲈ ⲠⲔⲈ ⲀⲄ
ⲄⲈⲖⲞⲤ ⲈⲦⲠⲀⲢⲀⲄ
ⲄⲒⲖⲈ ⲈⲦⲘⲞⲨⲰϢⲦ
ⲘⲠⲈⲐⲎⲢⲒⲞⲚ Ⲏ
ⲦⲈϤϨⲒⲔⲰⲚ·
ⲀⲨⲰ ⲈⲦⲂⲈ ⲚⲈⲦϪⲰ
ⲘⲘⲞⲤ ϪⲈ ⲚⲀⲒ̈Ⲁ
ⲦⲞⲨ ⲚⲚⲈⲦⲚⲀ
ⲘⲞⲨ ϪⲒⲚ ⲦⲈⲚⲞⲨ
ϨⲘ ⲠⲢⲀⲚ ⲘⲠϪⲞⲈⲒⲤ·
ⲀⲨⲰ ⲈⲦⲂⲈ ⲦⲈⲔⲖⲞ
ⲞⲖⲈ ⲚⲞⲨⲰⲂϢ Ⲛ
ⲦⲀϤⲚⲀⲨ ⲈⲢⲞⲤ· Ⲉ
ⲢⲈ ⲠⲢⲰⲘⲈ ⲚⲞⲨⲞ
ⲈⲒⲚ ϨⲒϪⲰϤ :~
ⲀⲨⲰ ⲈⲦⲂⲈ ⲠⲔⲈ ⲀⲄ
ⲄⲈⲖⲞⲤ ⲚⲦⲀϤⲈⲒ Ⲉ
ⲂⲞⲖ ϨⲘ ⲠⲈⲢⲠⲈ Ⲙ
ⲠϪⲞⲈⲒⲤ :~
ⲀⲨⲰ ⲈⲦⲂⲈ ⲠⲈⲚⲦⲀϤ

<column right>
ⲈⲒ ⲈⲂⲞⲖ ϨⲘⲠⲢⲠⲈ
ⲈⲦⲚⲦⲘⲎⲦⲈ·
ⲀⲨⲰ ⲈⲦⲂⲈ ⲠⲈⲚ
ⲦⲀϤⲈⲒ ⲈⲂⲞⲖ ϨⲘ
ⲠⲈⲐⲎⲤⲒⲀⲤⲦⲎⲢⲒⲞ̅·
ⲀⲨⲰ ⲈⲦⲂⲈ ⲠⲦⲰϢ
ⲚⲦⲈⲐⲀⲖⲀⲤⲤⲀ ⲚⲀ
ⲂⲒϬⲀⲈⲒⲚ·
ⲦⲞⲦⲈ ⲖⲞⲒⲠⲞⲚ ⲈⲨ
ϢⲀⲚⲈⲒⲘⲈ ⲈⲠⲦⲰϢ
ⲘⲠⲈⲒⲔⲈ ⲘⲚⲦ
ϢⲞⲘⲦⲈ ⲚⲌⲎⲦⲎⲘⲀ·
ⲠⲈⲠ̅Ⲛ̅Ⲁ̅ ⲞⲨⲚ ⲘⲠ
ⲚⲞⲨⲦⲈ ⲚⲀϮ ⲚⲀⲚ
ⲚⲞⲨⲤⲨⲄⲔⲚⲰⲘⲎ
ⲈⲦⲢⲈⲚⲀⲚⲀⲬⲰⲢⲒ̈ Ⲉ
ⲚⲈⲚⲎⲒ· ⲀⲨⲰ ⲚϤ
Ϯ ⲚⲀⲚ ⲚⲞⲨⲠⲢⲞⲐⲈⲤ
ⲘⲒⲀ· Ⲛ̅ϤⲦⲀⲘⲞⲚ
ⲈⲠⲔⲈⲤⲈⲈⲠⲈ· ϨⲒⲦⲚ
ⲦⲈⲬⲀⲢⲒⲤ ⲘⲠⲈⲚ
ϪⲞⲈⲒⲤ Ⲓ̅Ⲥ̅ ⲠⲈⲬ̅Ⲥ̅
ⲠⲀⲒ̈ ⲈⲢⲈ ⲈⲞⲞⲨ ⲚⲒⲘ
ⲠⲢⲈⲠⲈⲒ ⲚⲀϤ ⲘⲚ
ⲠⲈϤⲈⲒⲰⲦ ⲚⲀⲄⲀ
ⲐⲞⲤ· ⲘⲚ ⲠⲈⲠ̅Ⲛ̅Ⲁ̅
ⲈⲦⲞⲨⲀⲀⲂ· ⲚⲢⲈϤ
ⲦⲀⲚϨⲞ· ⲀⲨⲰ ⲚϨⲞ
ⲘⲞⲞⲨⲤⲒⲞⲤ· ⲦⲈ
ⲚⲞⲨ· ⲀⲨⲰ ⲚⲞⲨⲞ
ⲈⲒϢ ⲚⲒⲘ· ϢⲀ
ⲚⲀⲒⲰⲚ ⲦⲎⲢⲞⲨ
ⲚⲀⲒⲰⲚ ϨⲀⲘⲎⲚ :~
= = = = = = = =

Appendices

Appendix 1

Creed of the Council of Chalcedon

Throughout this book I referred to the Council of Chalcedon, held in 451, which asserted that Christ is one person with two natures. Although it is upheld and considered the Fourth Ecumenical Council by Eastern Orthodox, Roman Catholic, Lutheran, Anglican, and Reformed communions, it was rejected by many Christians in the East including many Egyptian Christians. Therefore, I thought it would be helpful for our readers to include the creed from that council.

"Following the holy fathers, we all teach with one accord one and the same Son, our Lord Jesus Christ perfect in Godhead and perfect also in humanity, truly God and also truly man, being of a reasonable soul and body, of one being with the Father as touching his Godhead, and also of one being with us as touching his humanity, being like unto us in all things except sin, begotten of the Father before all times according to his Godhead, and also in the last days born for our sake and for our salvation, of the virgin Mary, the bearer of God, according to his humanity, one and the same Christ, the Son, Lord, only begotten of two natures, without confusion, without conversion, without division, and without separation; the differences of natures not being removed by their union, but rather the propriety of each being preserved and concurring in one *prosopon* and in one *hypostasis* so that he is not divided or separated into two *prosopa* but in one and the same only begotten Son, God the Word, Lord Jesus Christ, even as the prophets of old and Jesus Christ himself taught us concerning him, and the creed of our fathers that has been handed down to us."[1]

1 Quoted from Douglas F. Kelly, *Systematic Theology*, Vol. 2 (Ross-shire, Scotland: Christian Focus Publications, Ltd., 2014), 200. Italics mine.

Appendix 2

Other Sixth-Century Commentaries on the Apocalypse

Four major commentaries on the Book of Revelation have survived from the sixth century: those of Caesarius of Arles, Apringius of Beja, Primasius of Hadrumetum, and Oecumenius.

About 510 Caesarius of Arles wrote nineteen Latin homilies, or more precisely notes for homilies, on the Book of Revelation. Relying on Victorinus and Tyconius, but preferring Tyconius, Caesarius focused on ecclesiology, or how the passages of Revelation relate to contemporary life in the church.[1]

In the 530s or 540s Apringius of Beja (in modern Portugal) wrote a Latin *Tractate on the Apocalypse*. His commentary did not enjoy wide circulation in the Middle Ages, and consequently only its sections on Chapters 1-5 and 18-22 of Revelation are extant.[2] Its interpretations are centered on Jesus Christ and the Trinity. One of its unique features is its independence from the earlier exegesis of Tyconius. Apringius did not rely on Tyconius, as other Latin commentators of the sixth century did, in particular Caesarius and Primasius.[3]

1 Caesarius of Arles, *Exposition on the Apocalypse*. Translated in Weinrich, *Latin Commentaries on Revelation*. On Caesarius's sources and exegesis of the Apocalypse, Kevin Poole, "The Western Apocalypse Commentary Tradition of the Early Middle Ages," in Michael A. Ryan, ed., *A Companion to the Premodern Apocalypse* (Leiden: Brill, 2016), 103-143 at 122-130; Gryson, "Les commentaires patristiques latins de l'Apocalypse," *Revue théologique de Louvain* 28 (1997):305-337 at 317-322; Joël Courreau, "L'Exégèse allégorique de Saint Césaire d'Arles," *Bulletin de littérature ecclésiastique* 4 (1977):181-206.

2 Apringius of Beja, *Tractate on the Apocalypse*. Translated in Weinrich, *Latin Commentaries on Revelation*.

3 Poole, "The Western Apocalypse Commentary Tradition," 118-122.

About 540 Primasius of Hadrumetum in North Africa wrote a lengthy Latin commentary on the Apocalypse.[4] He relied heavily on Tyconius for his exegetical method, and fashioned Tyconius's comments, some of which had Donatist sympathies, in a way that was congruent with Catholic "orthodoxy." Primasius's commentary was extremely popular and influential on the tradition of exegesis of the Book of Revelation in the eighth century.[5] Of these commentaries from the sixth century, that of Primasius is the only one still not available in English translation, but Colin McAllister of the University of Colorado and I are presently working on a translation of it to be published in the Brepols Library of Christian Sources series.

In the early sixth century Oecumenius, a non-Chalcedonian, wrote a Greek *Commentary on the Apocalypse*; and two different English translations of it have been published recently.[6] The commentary gives figurative meanings for various words, phrases, and statements in Revelation. Unique in the exegetical tradition of the Apocalypse is Oecumenius's interpretation of the thousand years of Rev 20 as the time of Christ's Incarnation.

Besides these commentaries on the Book of Revelation from the sixth century, a host of other shorter texts related to the visions of Revelation were written in a variety of literary genres. These include: brief summaries of the contents of the Book of Revelation by Cassiodorus and pseudo-Athanasius; treatises on just one topic of the Book of Revelation such as *On the Seven Seals* and *On the Two Witnesses*; collections of brief comments on the Apocalypse by others, represented by *Scholia on the Apocalypse* and *Testimonies of Gregory the Great on the Apocalypse*; and prologues to the Apocalypse.

4 A. W. Adams, ed., *Primasivs episcopvs Hadrvmetvm. Commentarivs in Apocalypsin* [hereafter: Primasius, *Commentary on the Apocalypse*]. CCSL 92 (Turnhout: Brepols, 1985).

5 On Primasius's commentary and its influence, Poole, "The Western Apocalypse Commentary Tradition," 110-114; Gryson, "Les commentaires patristiques," 327-331; Matter, "The Apocalypse in Early Medieval Exegesis," 42-45.

6 Weinrich, *Greek Commentaries on Revelation* (Downers Grove, IL: InterVarsity, 2011); John N. Suggit, trans., *Oecumenius. Commentary on the Apocalypse.* FC112 (Washington, D.C.: The Catholic University of America Press, 2006).

Residing in Italy about the year 580, Cassiodorus wrote in Latin *Complexiones in Apocalypsin* or *Brief Explanations of the Apocalypse*. This text summaries, chapter by chapter, the contents of the Book of Revelation.[7] In the sixth or seventh century a Greek authored a "Synopsis of the Apocalypse of John," which has been incorrectly attributed to Athanasius. He too briefly summarized the contents of the Book of Revelation. A translation of it is provided in Appendix 3 of this book.

From Spain in the late sixth or early seventh century came *On the Seven Seals*, a brief Latin text that interpreted the seven seals of Rev 5-8 as events in the life of Christ, such as his nativity, baptism, crucifixion, etc.[8] *On the Two Witnesses* was produced in Italy about the year 500, give or take a decade or two, by an anonymous author who wrote in Latin. It identifies the two witnesses of Rev 11 as Enoch and Elijah and briefly narrates an end-time scenario which expressed the eschatology of the author and/or the community from which it arose.

In the early sixth century, a person edited a Greek collection of 39 *Scholia on the Apocalypse*. They consist of excerpts on Rev 1:1-14:5 taken from Irenaeus, Clement of Alexandria, and other writers who most likely include Origen and Didymus of Alexandria. Patristic scholar Panayiotis Tzamalikos believes that the collection was compiled by an abbot named Cassian (d. 548) of the monastery at St Sabas located near Jerusalem, but other scholars have been hesitant to accept the attribution to Cassian.[9] During the lifetime of Gregory the Great, a notary of Gregory named Paterius compiled testimonies from Gregory's various writings on each book of the Bible, including the Book of Revelation. This Latin

7 In Roger Gryson, ed., *Commentaria minora in Apocalypsin Johannis*. CCSL 107 (Turnhout: Brepols, 2003). An English translation by me is forthcoming in Vol 144 of Fathers of the Church, scheduled for publication by The Catholic University of America Press in the spring of 2022.

8 Critical edition in E. Ann Matter, "The Pseudo-Alcuinian 'De Septem Sigillis': An Early Latin Apocalypse Exegesis," *Traditio* 36 (1980):111-137. Translation in Gumerlock, *The Seven Seals of the Apocalypse: Medieval Texts in Translation* (Kalamazoo, MI: Medieval Institute Publications, 2009), 30-32.

9 Critical edition and English translation of the 39 scholia are in Panayiotis Tzamalikos, *An Ancient Commentary on the Book of Revelation: A Critical Edition of the Scholia in Apocalypsin* (New York: Cambridge University Press, 2013). A new translation of the scholia with updated introduction and discussion of its sources was prepared by T. C. Schmidt and is scheduled for publication in Vol 144 of Fathers of the Church to be published by The Catholic University of America Press in the spring of 2022.

compilation from Gregory's writings was used with frequency by early medieval authors, but sometime after the eighth century a large portion of Paterius's *Testimonies* was lost. Consequently, in the twelfth century an anonymous author sought to reproduce what had been lost, including the testimonies from Gregory on the Book of Revelation. His 55 excerpts from Gregory's writings are printed in PL 79:1107-1122.[10]

A Latin preface to the Book of Revelation which circulated in the name of Jerome but has been associated with a mid-sixth century bishop of Capua named Victor was found in a codex at Fulda. It mainly discusses the apostle John's life and his worthiness to write the Book of Revelation.[11] From the second half of the sixth century a Latin pseudo-Isidore prologue to the Apocalypse was written.[12] Most likely a prologue for a glossed Apocalypse which has not been identified, it explains the time, place, and author of the Book of Revelation.

What accounts for the many texts written on the Book of Revelation in the sixth century? What motivated them to write on it and what were their intentions in doing so? Sometimes the author was fulfilling a request by another person to write a commentary, as was the case with Primasius. Each specific author obviously had his own purpose for composing a text, but sixth-century commentators used the Book of Revelation to support tenets of Christian eschatology, to move the Book of Revelation away from being a text strictly about the end times, to augment the canonicity of the Book of Revelation, to offer "catholic" interpretations of this scriptural book, and to solve its enigmas and mysteries.

In the sixth century, authors used the Book of Revelation to expand in greater detail on certain tenets of eschatology. For example, Primasius

10 An English translation by Mark DelGogliano of the 55 *Testimonies of Gregory the Great on the Apocalypse* by pseudo-Paterius is scheduled for publication in the spring of 2022 in Vol. 144 of Fathers of the Church by The Catholic University of America Press.

11 The preface is edited in Donatien de Bruyne, *Préfaces de la Bible Latine* (Namur: Auguste Godenne, 1920), 261. English translations are in Gumerlock, "Chromatius of Aquileia on John 21:22 and Rev. 10:11: Against a Legend about the Apostle John," in Ian Boxall and Richard Tresley, eds., *The Book of Revelation and Its Interpreters: Short Studies and an Annotated Bibliography* (New York: Roman and Littelfield, 2016), 53-63 at 61; and M.S. O'Brien, trans., *Commentary on the Apocalypse (Translated): Part 1-From Christ with Love by Beatus of Liebana* (Amazon Digital Services, 2013), 3-4.

12 CCSL 107:193-94.

saw the end-time worldwide proclamation of the gospel in one of the four horsemen of the Apocalypse.[13] In the *Testimonies*, Gregory the Great expanded on the church's teaching of the future resurrection by discussing the nature of the beatitude which the resurrection will bring to God's people. The author of *On the Two Witnesses* saw in Revelation's visions a future coming of Enoch and Elijah along with 144,000 end-time converts from Judaism, which the author seems to have believed was imminent.

In earlier centuries, writers like Irenaeus, Justin Martyr, Hippolytus, and Commodian used the Book of Revelation to speak mainly about a coming Antichrist or a future kingdom of the saints. On the contrary, the sixth century commentators sought to show that the Book of Revelation was not exclusively about eschatology or the end of the world, but about Jesus Christ himself and about his body, the church. Hence, according to Oecumenius, Apringius, and the author of *On the Seven Seals*, the Revelation *of* Jesus Christ (cf. Rev 1:1) was a revelation *about* the earthly life and ministry of Jesus Christ and about the now enthroned Christ and his present work of redeeming humankind. According to Caesarius and Primasius, the Book of Revelation was just as much about the life of the church and her struggles as she sojourns on earth between the time of the Incarnation and the Second Coming, as it was about the Second Coming and the end times. Cassiodorus made a point of explicitly saying that numbers in the Book of Revelation could not be used to predict the date of the end of the world.

Several exegetes of the Book of Revelation in the sixth century wrote commentaries in order to affirm the canonicity of the Book of Revelation. This was especially true in the East, where there was some hesitation in the previous centuries to receive the Apocalypse as a divinely inspired book. Thus, Oecumenius often showed how the Book of Revelation was in harmonious agreement with other books of Scripture such as Daniel, Isaiah, the Gospels, and the Epistles of Saint Paul. The same is true of the *Scholia on the Apocalypse*. According to Tzamalikos, the compiler of the scholia sought to bolster the canonicity of the Apocalypse by

13 In the rider on the white horse in Rev 6:2. See Douglas W. Lumsden, *And Then the End Will Come: Early Latin Christian Interpretations of the Opening of the Seven Seals* (New York: Garland, 2001), 35.

demonstrating "that Revelation speaks exactly the same truths that the rest of the canon does."[14] As Scripture, therefore, Primasius, Caesarius, Gregory the Great, and the author of the *Encomium* used the passages in the Book of the Revelation, recognized as divinely inspired Scripture, to encourage Christian morality and faithfulness in times of tribulation.

Earlier in the West the two most popular Latin commentaries on Revelation were those of Victorinus and Tyconius, but both were tainted with what was considered false teaching, the former with chiliast beliefs, the latter with Donatist tenets. Therefore, one motivation for writing on the Book of Revelation in the sixth century was to provide commentaries that were "catholic." Primasius says as much in his prologue, that he took what was rude in Tyconius's commentary and tempered it "with catholic moderation."[15] The author of the pseudo-Athanasian "Synopsis on the Apocalypse of John" made a point of teaching that the *Son of Man* in Rev 1:13 was the same person as the *Word of God* in Rev 19:13, which seems to be directed against Nestorian Christology of two persons.

For Cassiodorus and Paterius, explanation of the Book of Revelation was simply part of their systematic exposition of the entire New Testament. Interestingly, however, all the authors of the four major commentaries on the Book of Revelation in the sixth century seem to have written only one biblical commentary, the one on the Book of Revelation. This begs the question: Of all of the books of Scripture to comment upon, why did they choose the Apocalypse? The answer could lie in the fact that it contains profound mysteries and obscurities greater than those found in most of the other books of Scripture. These mysteries presented for expositors a challenge to unlock and unveil them. Primasius explained that one of the purposes of his commentary was to provide an explanation of a book "overshadowed by many mysteries" for those less skilled.[16] The author of the pseudo-Isidore *Prologue to the Apocalypse* said that he was writing to make clear the many obscurities which the Book of

14 Tzamalikos, *Ancient Commentary*, 61.

15 Primasius, *Commentary on the Apocalypse*, Prologue. CCSL 92:1.

16 Primasius, *Commentary on the Apocalypse*, Prologue. CCSL 92:1: *sic librum apocalypsis beati Iohannis multis mysteriis opacatum...licet exiguis susceperim uiribus exponendum.*

Revelation contained.[17] Oecumenius considered the Book of Revelation the "most mystical" of all the divine Scriptures.[18] Thus he, along with others in late antiquity, seems to have found in such profundity a motivation "to seek out its elusive meaning."[19]

17 Pseudo-Isidore, *Prologue to the Apocalypse*. CCSL 107:193.

18 Oecumenius, *Commentary on the Apocalypse*, 1. FC 112:19.

19 Thomas Coffman Schmidt, "The Last Book: Revelation, Commentaries, and the Making of the New Testament" Dissertation (Yale University, 2020), 203.

Appendix 3

Pseudo-Athanasius "Synopsis of the Apocalypse of John"

Introduction

This "Synopsis of the Apocalypse of John," written by an anonymous Greek writer of the sixth or seventh century, is part of a larger work entitled *Synopsis of Sacred Scripture* (*Synopsis Scripturae Sacrae*), attributed incorrectly to Athanasius.[1] The *Synopsis*, contained in Vol 28 of Jacque-Paul Migne's *Patrologia Graeca* (PG 28:283-438) in Greek with a parallel Latin translation, provides summaries of the various books of the Bible. The "Synopsis of the Apocalypse of John" is in columns 427-432. The translation below is based on the Latin.

The "Synopsis" begins by discussing the title of the book, its author, where and when it was written, and the original recipients of the Book of Revelation. The book received the name "Apocalypse" because of the "revelation" which John, the evangelist and theologian, saw on the Lord's day when he resided on the island called Patmos. John then sent the book to the seven churches listed in Rev 1:11.

The "Synopsis" then states in summary form the contents of the Book of Revelation, moving sequentially from Chapters 1-22. Sometimes the author writes only one sentence about a specific vision or series of visions. For example, on the letters to the churches in Rev 2-3, the author simply informs the reader that John was ordered "to write to each of the angels of the aforementioned churches, according to their actions." The visions of

1 On dating of the text to the sixth or seventh century, see Thomas Coffman [T. C.] Schmidt, "The Last Book: Revelation, Commentaries, and the Making of the New Testament," Dissertation (Yale University, 2020), 57.

Rev 5-7 are summarized as follows: "He also saw seven seals to be opened and when each one was opened, a certain vision appeared." Similarly, the seven trumpet soundings of Rev 8-11 are summarized in two sentences. The visions in Rev 16 & 18 seem to be passed over entirely. The 144,000 of Rev 7 are not mentioned, although the virgins of Rev 14 are described as singing and following the Lamb. The number of the beast is 666, but the author gave no interpretations of that number. There is also no interpretation given for the thousand years of Rev 20.

Although the term "Antichrist" does not appear in the Book of Revelation, in the "Synopsis" he is referred to four times and is identified as the "false prophet" of Rev 19:20. He is portrayed as one who will come in the future out of the woman on the beast (Rev 17). He will eventually be cast into the lake of fire and will remain there forever, suggesting that the author was *not* an advocate of *apokatastasis*, a final restoration of all creatures to fellowship with God.

The author often quotes directly from the Book of Revelation, and these quotations I have rendered in italics. The "Synopsis" ends on a Christological note, which emphasizes that the Lord Jesus Christ who spoke to John is the divine *Logos* (cf. Rev 19:13) who became perfect man and thus is sometimes called "Son of Man" in the Scripture including in the Book of Revelation (cf. Rev 1:13). A phrase at the end of the "Synopsis," which reads "who in the last days became man for us," is reminiscent of similar statements in the creed of the Council of Chalcedon (451) and anathemas of the Three Chapters at the Second Council of Constantinople (533).[2]

Translation

This book is called by this name ["Apocalypse"] because John himself, the evangelist and theologian, saw this "Revelation" *on the island called Patmos on the Lord's day* (Rev 1:9-10), and was commanded to *write* it

2 John F. Clarkson, John H. Edwards, William J. Kelly, and John J. Welch, trans., *The Church Teaches: Documents of the Church in English Translation* (Rockford, IL: Tan, 1973), 172, 175.

down and *send it to the seven churches,* namely, these: *Ephesus, Smyrna, Pergamum, Thyatira, Sardis, Philadelphia, and Laodicea* (Rev 1:11). Truly the things which he saw in this vision are many and various. And then he also saw the destruction of the Antichrist with the devil. Moreover, he is ordered to first write to each of the angels of the aforementioned churches in accordance with their actions.[3] And so he saw many and wonderful visions, such as *seven golden lampstands, and in the midst of them one like the Son of Man* (Rev 1:12-13). And he received the interpretation: that these *lampstands are the seven churches* (Rev 1:20), and that the one who was in the midst of them is the Lord.[4]

Next, he saw an *open door in heaven* (Rev 4:1), and the Lord *sitting on the throne* (Rev 4:2), and *twenty-four elders sitting* (Rev 4:4) upon thrones and worshipping the Lord.[5]

He also saw seven seals to be opened, and when each one was opened, a certain vision appeared.[6] Then he saw seven angels holding seven trumpets and each one of them sounding forth a sign.[7] And when he heard the seventh one sound, the angel said: *The kingdom of the world has become that of the Lord* (Rev 11:15).

And he saw the ark of the covenant in heaven.[8] Then he saw a woman about to give birth and a fiery dragon who was pursuing her. Indeed, the woman was saved in the wilderness, and the dragon was thrown into fire.[9]

Afterward he saw a beast *having ten horns and seven heads* (Rev 13:1), and its diadem was full of blasphemies. But its name was not revealed, but its *number* was: indeed, *six hundred sixty-six* (Rev 13:18).

3 Cf. Rev 2-3.

4 Cf. Rev 1:13-18.

5 Cf. Rev 4:10-11.

6 Cf. Rev 5-7.

7 Cf. Rev 8-11.

8 Cf. Rev 11:19.

9 Cf. Rev 12.

And he heard virgins singing and following the Lamb.[10] He also saw an *angel flying through the midst of heaven* (Rev 14:6), and another one after that,[11] and afterward another.[12]

Then he also saw a *white cloud and sitting on it one like the Son of Man, having a golden crown on his head, and in his hand a sharp sickle* (Rev 14:14).

Then he saw *seven angels having the last seven plagues* (Rev 15:1) and *golden vials full of the wrath of God* (Rev 15:7).

After these things he was *carried away by the Spirit into the wilderness*, and he *saw a woman sitting upon a scarlet beast having seven heads* (Rev 17:3). And it was indicated to him that from her the Antichrist would come.[13]

Also, he *saw heaven opened* (Rev 19:11) and a white horseman, and *his name* was the *Word of God* (Rev 19:13). Then he *saw the beast and the kings of the earth* wanting *to make war with him who was sitting upon the* white *horse* (Rev 19:19). *And the beast was seized and with him the false prophet* (Rev 19:20), who is the Antichrist; and he saw them cast into the lake of fire.

After these things he *saw an angel coming down from heaven* (Rev 20:1), and casting Satan, along with those who had his mark, *into the abyss, and closing it over hm so that* after this *he should no longer deceive the nations until a thousand years had been completed* (Rev 20:3). Then he saw martyrs reigning in glory with Christ.[14] Next, he saw that Satan was to be loosed after the thousand years,[15] and was to be *thrown into the lake of fire* with the Antichrist *forever and ever* (Rev 20:10).

10 Cf. Rev 14:3-4.

11 Cf. Rev 14:8.

12 Cf. Rev 14:9.

13 Cf. Rev 17:7-17.

14 Cf. Rev 20:4.

15 Cf. Rev 20:7.

After these things he *saw a new heaven, a new earth* (Rev 21:1), and a new Jerusalem,[16] and a *river of living water* (Rev 22:1), and the servants of God seeing *his face,* and having *his name on their foreheads* (Rev 22:4). When John had seen these things he fell down, wanting to worship the angel, who had shown all these things to him.[17] But the angel forbade him, saying: *Do not worship me, but worship God. For, I am your fellow servant* (Rev 22:9).

Moreover, when he saw these things, he heard from our Lord Jesus Christ,[18] that he is the one who is,[19] and this same one is the Word of God,[20] who in the last days became man for us[21]: the man I speak of was made perfect and was called the Son of Man.

16 Cf. Rev 21:2-27.

17 Cf. Rev 22:8.

18 Cf. Rev 22:10-20.

19 Cf. Rev 22:13; 1:8.

20 Cf. Rev 19:13.

21 Cf. 1 Pet 1:20; Creed of the Council of Chalcedon.

Bibliography

Abbreviations

ACW — *Ancient Christian Writers. The Works of the Fathers in Translation*. Edited by J. Quasten, J.C. Plumpe, W.J. Burhart, J. Dillon, and D.D. McManus. New York: Newman, 1946-present.

ANF — *Ante-Nicene Fathers of the Church*. Edited by Alexander Roberts and James Donaldson. 10 vols. Buffalo: Christian Literature, 1885-96.

CCSL — *Corpus scriptorum, series latina*. Turnhout: Brepols, 1953-present.

CSEL — *Corpus scriptorum ecclesiasticorum latinorum*. Vienna: Hoelder-Pichler, Tempsky, 1866-present.

FC — *Fathers of the Church*. New York: Cima, 1947-49; New York: Fathers of the Church, 1949-60; Washington, D.C.: The Catholic University of America Press, 1960-present.

NPNF — *A Select Library of the Nicene and Post-Nicene Fathers of the Christian Church*. Edited by Philip Schaff. 2 series of 14 vols. New York: Christian Literature, 1887-94.

PG — *Patrologiae cursus completus, series graeca*. Edited by Jacques-Paul Migne, 161 vols. Paris: Petit-Montrouge, 1857-1866.

PL — *Patrologiae cursus completus, series latina*. Edited by Jacques-Paul Migne. 221 vols. Paris: Petit-Montrouge, 1844-64.

SC — *Sources chrétiennes*. Paris: Cerf, 1941-present

Primary Sources

Abelard, Peter. *Yes and No*. Priscilla Throop, trans. *Yes and No. The Complete English Translation of Peter Abelard's Sic et Non*, 2nd ed. Charlotte, VT: MedievalMS, 2008.

Alexander of Bremen. *Exposition on the Apocalypse*. Alois Wachtel, ed., *Alexander Minorita. Expositio in Apocalypsim*. Weimar: Böhlau, 1955.

Ammonius of Alexandria. *Fragments on Daniel*. PG 85.

Andrew of Caesarea. *Commentary on the Apocalypse*. FC 123.

Anonymous. *Cambridge Gloss on the Apocalypse*. CCSL 108G.

______. *Handbook on the Apocalypse of the Apostle John*. CCSL 107. English: Gumerlock, *Early Latin Apocalypse Commentaries*.

______. *On the Mysteries of the Apocalypse of John*. CCSL 107. English: Gumerlock, *Early Latin Commentaries on the Apocalypse*.

______. *Preface to the Apocalypse*. In Donatien de Bruyne, *Préfaces de la Bible Latine*. Namur: Auguste Godenne, 1920, 261. English: Gumerlock, "Chromatius of Aquileia," 59-61.

______. *Scholia on the Apocalypse*. Panayiotis Tzamalikos, *An Ancient Commentary on the Book of Revelation. A critical edition of the Scholia in Apocalypsin*. New York: Cambridge University Press, 2013.

Apringius of Beja. *Tractate on the Apocalypse*. In William Weinrich, trans., *Latin Commentaries on Revelation*. Downers Grove, IL: InterVarsity, 2011.

Arator. *On the Acts of the Apostles*. CSEL 72.

Beatus of Liebana. *Tractate on the Apocalypse*. CCSL 107 B & C. English: M. S. O'Brien, trans., *Commentary on the Apocalypse (Translated): Part 1-From Christ with Love by Beatus of Liebana*. Amazon Digital Services, 2013; *Part 2-Four Horses and the Lamb*. Amazon Digital Services, 2016.

Caesarius of Arles. *Exposition on the Apocalypse*. CCSL 105. English: Weinrich, *Latin Commentaries on Revelation*.

Cassiodorus. *Brief Explanations on the Apocalypse*. CCSL 107.

Chromatius of Aquileia. *Sermon XXI on Saint John the Evangelist and Apostle*. CCSL 9A:96-99; English: Gumerlock, "Chromatius of Aquileia," 59-61; ACW 75:73-75.

Cyprian of Carthage. *To Fortunatus*. ANF 5.

_____. *To Quirinus*. ANF 5.

Didymus of Alexandria. *Commentary on Zechariah*. SC 83 & 84.

Epiphanius of Salamis. *Panarion*. PG 41; Philip R. Amidon, trans., *The Panarion of St. Epiphanius, Bishop of Salamis: Selected Passages*. New York: Oxford University Press, 1990.

Eusebius of Caesarea. *Eclogues on Daniel*. PG 22.

Fortunatius of Aquileia. *Commentary on the Gospels*. CSEL, Extra Seriem

Gregory of Nyssa. *Against Eunomius*. PG 45.

Hippolytus. *Commentary on Daniel*. ANF 5; T. C. Schmidt, trans. *Hippolytus of Rome: Commentary on Daniel and 'Chronicon'*. Piscataway, NJ: Gorgias, 2017.

_____. *On the Apocalypse*. Fragments in Pierre Prigent, "Hippolyte, commentateur de l'Apocalypse," *Theologische Zeitschrift* 28 (1972):391-412; Prigent and R. Stehly, "Les fragments du De Apocalypsi d'Hippolyte," *Theologische Zeitschrift* 29 (1973):313-333; Adolf Harnack, *Die Gwynnschen Caius-und Hippolytus-Fragmente*. Texte und Untersuchunger 6:3 (Leipzig, 1890), 121-133; H. Achelis, *Die griechischen christlichen Schriftsteller* 1:2 (Leipzig, 1897), 239-247; John Gwynn, "Hippolytus and his 'Heads against Caius,'" *Hermathena* 14 (1888):397-418.

_____. *Treatise on Christ and the Antichrist*. ANF 5.

Jerome. *Against Jovinian.* NPNF, 2nd series, 6.

_____. *Commentary on the Apocalypse.* CSEL 49; CCSL 5; English: ANF 6 (under the name of Victorinus).

_____. *Letters.* CSEL 54; PL 22; NPNF, 2nd series, 6.

Methodius of Olympus. *Symposium.* ACW 27.

Oecumenius. *Commentary on the Apocalypse.* In William Weinrich, trans., *Greek Commentaries on Revelation.* Downers Grove, IL: InterVarsity, 2011; FC 112.

Origen. *Commentary on the Gospel of John.* ANF 10.

_____. *On First Principles.* ANF 4.

_____. *On Matthew.* PG 13. English: Ronald E. Heine, trans. *The Commentary of Origen on the Gospel of St Matthew,* 2 vols. New York: Oxford University Press, 2018.

Paul of Bush. *Commentary on the Apocalypse of St. John.* Shawqi Najib Talia, "Bulus al-Busi's Arabic Commentary on the Apocalypse of St. John. An English Translation and a Commentary." Dissertation. Washington, D.C.: The Catholic University of America Press, 1987.

Primasius of Hadrumetum. *Commentary on the Apocalypse.* CCSL 92.

Pseudo-Athanasius. *Apocalypse of Pseudo-Athanasius.* In Francisco Javier Martinez, "Eastern Christian Apocalyptic in the Early Muslim Period: Pseudo-Methodius and Pseudo-Athanasius" Ph.D. dissertation. Washington, D.C.: The Catholic University of America, 1985.

Pseudo-Athanasius. "Synopsis of the Apocalypse of John." PG 28:427-432.

Pseudo-Cyril of Alexandria. *Encomium on Revelation 7-12.* MS: Pierpont Morgan, Copt. 591. Digital images at https://archive.org/details/PhantoouLibrary. Italian translation by Tito Orlandi in *Omelie copte.* Corona Patrum, Vol. 7. Turin: Società Editrice Internazionale, 1981, 121-144.

Pseudo-Isidore. *Prologue to the Apocalypse*. CCSL 107:193-94.

Pseudo-Jerome. *Epistle to Paula and Eustochius*. PL 30:127-28.

Theodulf of Orleans. *Exposition on the Apocalypse of John*. CCSL 107; English: Gumerlock, *Carolingian Commentaries on the Apocalypse by Theodulf and Smaragdus*.

Tyconius. *Book of Rules*. William S. Babcock, trans., *Tyconius: The Book of Rules*. Atlanta: Scholars Press, 1989.

______. *Exposition of the Apocalypse*. CCSL 107A; FC 134.

Victorinus of Pettau. *Commentary on the Apocalypse*. CSEL 49; CCSL 5; English: Weinrich, *Latin Commentaries on Revelation*.

Secondary Sources

Allen, Pauline and C. T. R. Hayward. *Severus of Antioch*. New York: Routledge, 2004.

Amirav, Hagit, Emmanouela Grypeou, and Guy Stroumsa, eds. *Apocalypticism and Eschatology in Late Antiquity: Encounters in the Abrahamic Religions, 6th-8th Centuries*. Louvain: Peeters, 2017.

Askeland, Christian. "The Sahidic Apocalypse in Early Islamic Egypt." In Marcus Sigismund, Martin Karrer, and Ulrich Schmid, eds. *Studien zum Text der Apokalypse*. Berlin: De Gruyter, 2015, 271-87.

Atiya, Aziz S., ed. *Coptic Encyclopedia*. New York: Macmillan, 1991.

Bagnall, Roger S., ed. *Egypt in the Byzantine World 300-700*. New York: Cambridge University Press, 2009.

Boxall, Ian and Richard Tresley, eds. *The Book of Revelation and Its Interpreters. Short Studies and an Annotated Bibliography*. Boulder, CO: Rowan and Littlefield, 2016.

Brock, Sebastian and Brian Fitzgerald, trans., *Two Early Lives of Severos, Patriarch of Antioch*. Translated Texts for Historians 59. Liverpool, UK: Liverpool University Press, 2013.

Bruyne, Donatien de. *Préfaces de la Bible Latine*. Namur: Auguste Godenne, 1920.

Budge, E. A. Wallis, ed. *Coptic Apocrypha in the Dialect of Upper Egypt*. London: Oxford University Press, 1913.

______. *Coptic Biblical Texts in the Dialect of Upper Egypt*. London: Oxford University Press, 1912.

Clarkson, John F., John H. Edwards, William J. Kelly, John J. Welch, trans. *The Church Teaches: Documents of the Church in English Translation*. Rockford, IL: Tan, 1973.

Constantinou, Eugenia Scarvelis. "Andrew of Caesarea and the Apocalypse in the Ancient

Church of the East: Studies and Translation." Thesis. Quebec: Université Laval, 2008.

Courreau, Joël. "L'Exégèse allégorique de Saint Césaire d'Arles," *Bulletin de littérature ecclésiastique* 4 (1977):181-206.

Cowley, Roger W. *The Traditional Interpretation of the Apocalypse of St John in the Ethiopian Orthodox Church*. New York: Cambridge University Press, 1983.

Culpepper, Alan R. *John, the Son of Zebedee: The Life of a Legend*. Edinburgh: T & T Clark, 2000.

Daley, Brian E. *The Hope of the Early Church: A Handbook of Patristic Eschatology*. New York: Cambridge University Press, 1991.

______. *On the Dormition of Mary: Early Patristic Homilies*. Crestwood, NY: St Vladimir's Seminary Press, 1998.

Daly, Robert J., ed. *Apocalyptic Thought in Early Christianity*. Grand Rapids, MI: Baker, 2009.

Davis, Stephen J. *Coptic Christology in Practice. Incarnation and Divine Participation in Late Antique and Medieval Egypt.* Oxford: Oxford University Press, 2008.

______. *The Early Coptic Papacy: The Egyptian Church and Its Leadership in Late Antiquity.* New York: The American University in Cairo Press, 2004.

DeMar, Gary and Francis X. Gumerlock. *The Early Church and the End of the World.* Powder Springs, GA: American Vision, 2006.

Depuydt, Leo. *Catalogue of Coptic Manuscripts in the Pierpont Morgan Library.* Louvain: Peeters, 1993.

Draguet, René. *Julien d'Halicarnasse et sa controverse avec Sévère d'Antioche sur l'incorruptibité du corps du Christ.* Leuven: Smeesters, 1924.

Dulaey, Martine. *Victorin de Poetovio, premier exegete latin,* 2 vols. Paris: Institut d'Études Augustiniennes, 1993.

Frend, W. H. C. *The Rise of the Monophysite Movement: Chapters in the History of the Church in the Fifth and Sixth Centuries.* Cambridge, UK: Cambridge University Press, 1972.

Gabra, Gawdat. *Coptic Civilization: Two Thousand Years of Christianity in Egypt.* New York: The American University in Cairo Press, 2014.

Gabriele, Matthew and James T. Palmer, eds. *Apocalypse and Reform from Late Antiquity to the Middle Ages.* New York: Routledge, 2019.

Gryson, Roger. *Commentaria minora in Apocalypsin Johannis.* CCSL 107. Turnhout: Brepols, 2003.

______. "Les commentaires patristiques latins de l'Apocalypse," *Revue théologique de Louvain* 28 (1997):305-337.

Gumerlock, Francis X. *Carolingian Commentaries on the Apocalypse by Theodulf and Smaragdus.* Kalamazoo, MI: Medieval Institute Publications, 2019.

______. "Chromatius of Aquileia on John 21:22 and Rev. 10:11 Against a Legend about the Apostle John." In Boxall and Tresley, *The Book of Revelation and Its Interpreters*, 53-63.

______. *The Day and the Hour: Christianity's Perennial Fascination with Predicting the End of the World*. Powder Springs, GA: American Vision, 2000.

______. *Early Latin Commentaries on the Apocalypse*. Kalamazoo, MI: Medieval Institute Publications, 2016.

______. "Exegesis of the Apocalypse in the Tenth Century." In McCallister, *The Cambridge Companion to Apocalyptic Literature*, 137-155.

______. "Patristic Commentaries on Revelation: An Update," *Kerux* 27:3 (Dec 2012):37-43.

______. *Revelation and the First Century*. Powder Springs, GA: American Vision, 2013.

______. *The Seven Seals of the Apocalypse: Medieval Texts in Translation*. Kalamazoo, MI: Medieval Institute Publications, 2009.

Gumerlock, Francis X., trans. With Introduction and Notes by David C. Robinson. *Tyconius. Exposition of the Apocalypse*. FC 134. Washington, D.C.: The Catholic University of America Press, 2017.

Hannah, Darrell D. *Michael and the Christ: Michael Traditions and Angel Christology in Early Christianity*. Tübingen: Mohr Siebeck, 1999.

Hardy, Edward R., ed. *Christology of the Later Fathers*. Philadelphia: Westminster, 1954.

Hefele, Charles Joseph. *A History of the Councils of the Church*. 5 vols. Edinburgh: T & T Clark, 1895.

Hinson, Edward. *The Book of Revelation: Unlocking the Future*. Chattanooga, TN: AMG, 2002.

Hoover, Jesse A. *The Donatist Church in an Apocalyptic Age*. Oxford, UK: Oxford University Press, 2018.

Horner, George William. *The Coptic Version of the New Testament in the Southern Dialect, Otherwise Called Sahidic and Thebaic.* Oxford: Clarendon, 1911-1924.

James, Montague Rhodes. *The Apocryphal New Testament.* Oxford, UK: Clarendon, 1926.

Kelly, Douglas F. *Systematic Theology,* 2 vols. Ross-shire, Scotland: Christian Focus Publications, Ltd., 2014.

Lamareaux, John C. "The Provenance of Ecumenius' Commentary on the Apocalypse." *Vigiliae Christianae* 52 (1998):88-108.

Larson, Stan. "The Earliest Syriac Commentary on the Apocalypse: Transcription, Translation,and Importance of Brit. Lib. MS. Add. 17,127." Thesis. Birmingham, UK: University of Birmingham, 1984.

Lumsden, Douglas W. *And Then the End Will Come: Early Latin Christian Interpretations of the Opening of the Seven Seals.* New York: Garland, 2001.

MacCoull, Leslie S. B. "Pierpont Morgan MS. Copt. 591: The Apocalypse Commentary of Pseudo-Cyril of Alexandria," *Studia Patristica* 20 (1989):33-39.

MacKay, Thomas W. "Early Christian Millenarianist Interpretation of the Two Witnesses in John's Apocalypse 11:3-13." In John M. Lundquist and Stephen D. Ricks, eds. *By Study and Also By Faith,* 2 vols. Salt Lake City: Deseret, 1990, 1:222-231.

Matter, E. Ann. "The Apocalypse in Early Medieval Exegesis." In Emmerson and McGinn, *Apocalypse in the Middle Ages,* 38-50.

______. "Latin Reception of the Apocalypse in the Early Middle Ages." In McAllister, *The Cambridge Companion to Apocalyptic Literature,* 120-136.

______. "The Pseudo-Alcuinian 'De Septem Sigillis': An Early Latin Apocalypse Exegesis," *Traditio* 36 (1980):111-137.

McCallister, Colin, ed. *The Cambridge Companion to Apocalyptic Literature*. New York: Cambridge University Press, 2020.

McGuckin, John Anthony. *St. Cyril of Alexandria. On the Unity of Christ*. Popular Patristic Series 13. Crestwood, NY: St Vladimir's Seminary Press, 1995.

Meyendorff, John. *Imperial Unity and Christian Divisions: The Church 450-680* A.D. Crestwood, NY: St Vladimir's Seminary Press, 1989.

Moss, Yonatan. *Incorruptible Bodies: Christology, Society, and Authority in Late Antiquity*. Oakland: University of California Press, 2016.

Orlandi, Tito. "The History of Coptic Literature." In B.A. Pearson and J. Goehring, eds. *The Roots of Egyptian Christianity*. Philadelphia: Augsburg-Fortress, 1986, 51-81.

Palmer, James T. *The Apocalypse in the Early Middle Ages*. New York: Cambridge University Press, 2014.

______. "To Be Found Prepared: Eschatology and Reform Rhetoric ca. 570-ca.640." In Gabriele and Palmer, *Apocalypse and Reform from Late Antiquity to the Middle Ages*, 31-49.

Parry, Ken. "Providence, Resurrection, and Restoration in Byzantine Thought, Eighth to Ninth Centuries." *Studia Patristica* 97 (2017):295-304.

Poole, Kevin. "The Western Apocalypse Commentary Tradition of the Early Middle Ages," in Ryan, *Companion to the Premodern Apocalypse*, 103-143.

Riches, Aaron. *Ecce Homo: On the Divine Unity of Christ*. Grand Rapids, MI: Eerdmans, 2016.

Ryan, Michael A., ed. *A Companion to the Premodern Apocalypse*. Leiden: Brill, 2016.

Samuel, V. C. *The Council of Chalcedon Re-examined*. Kent, UK: British Orthodox Press, 2001.

Schmidt, T. C. "The Last Book: Revelation, Commentaries, and the Making of the New Testament." Dissertation. Yale University, 2020.

Sheridan, Mark. "The Encomium in the Coptic Literature of the Late Sixth Century." In Paola Buzi and Alberto Complani, eds. *Christianity in Egypt: Literary Production and Intellectual Trends. Studies in Honor of Tito Orlandi.* Rome: Institutum Patristicum Augustinianum, 2011, 443-64.

Shoemaker, Stephen J. *Ancient Traditions of the Virgin Mary's Dormition and Assumption.* Oxford: Oxford University Press, 2002.

Simonetti, Manlio. "John Philoponus." In Angelo Di Berardino, ed. *Encyclopedia of Ancient Christianity,* 3 vols. Downers Grove, IL: InterVarsity, 2014, 2:449.

Steinhauser, Kenneth B. *The Apocalypse Commentary of Tyconius: A History of Its Reception and Influence.* New York: Peter Lang, 1987.

_____. "Bemerkungen zum pseudo-hieronymischen *Commemoratorium in Apocalypsin,*" *Freiburger Zeitschrift für Philosphie und Theologie* 26 (1979):220-242.

Torrance, Iain R. *Christology after Chalcedon: Severus of Antioch and Sergius the Monophysite.* Norwich: Canterbury Press, 1988.

Trigg, Joseph Wilson. *Origen: The Bible and Philosophy in the Third Century.* Atlanta: John Knox, 1983.

Tzamalikos, Panayiotis. *An Ancient Commentary on the Book of Revelation: A critical edition of the Scholia in Apocalypsin.* New York: Cambridge University Press, 2013.

_____. *Origen: Philosophy of History and Eschatology.* Boston: Brill, 2007.

Villiers, Pieter G. R. de. "Numerical Symbolism in Oecumenius's Commentary on the Apocalypse." In Konrad Huber, Rainer Klotz,a nd Christoph Winterer, eds. *Tot Sacramenta Quot Verba.* Münster: Aschendorff, 2014, 135-52.

Weinrich, William C. *Greek Commentaries on Revelation.* Ancient Christian Texts. Downers Grove, IL: InterVarsity, 2011.

______. *Latin Commentaries on Revelation.* Ancient Christian Texts. Downers Grove, IL: InterVarsity, 2011.

Wessel, Susan. *Cyril of Alexandria and the Nestorian Controversy: The Making of a Saint and of a Heretic.* Oxford: Oxford University Press, 2004.

Wieser, Veronika. "The Chronicle of Hydatius: A Historical Guidebook to the Last Days of the Western Roman Empire." In Gabriele and Palmer, *Apocalypse and Reform from Late Antiquity to the Middle Ages*, 11-30.

Wigram, W. A. *The Separation of the Monophysites.* London: Faith Press, 1923.

Youseff, Youhanna Nessim. "The Commentary on the Apocalypse Councils and Eschatology." *Bulletin de la société d'archéologie copte* 49 (2010): 109-142.

About the Authors

Francis X. "Frank" Gumerlock (Ph.D. historical theology, Saint Louis University, 2004) teaches Latin in Colorado. He is the author of nine books, many of which are translations of early and medieval Latin texts on the Book of Revelation and the theology of grace, including *Carolingian Commentaries on the Apocalypse by Theodulf and Smaragdus* (2019), *Tyconius. Exposition of the Apocalypse* (2017), and *Gottschalk and a Medieval Predestination Controversy: Texts Translated from the Latin* (2010). His website containing links to his books and articles is francis-gumerlock.com.

Francesca M. Lecchi, MD, is a General Surgery resident at the University of Milan, Italy. She studied Latin and ancient Greek during high school in Milan. As an exchange student in Colorado, she studied Latin under Dr. Gumerlock and worked with him on the translation of the pseudo-Cyril *Commentary on the Apocalypse*.

Tito Orlandi, PhD, is professor emeritus at the Università di Roma La Sapienza where he taught from 1976 to 2010. From 2010 to 2016 he served as Director of the Centro Linceo Interdisciplinare Beniamino Segre, and from 2016-2020 as President of the Unione Accademica Nazionale. He is the author of numerous books and articles including an Italian translation of the pseudo-Cyril *Commentary on the Apocalypse* in his 1981 book *Omelie copte*. In 2018 he was the recipient of the Roberto Busa Prize of the Alliance of Digital Humanities Organizations in recognition of outstanding lifetime achievements in the application of information and communications technologies to humanities research.